"Natasha Crain's *Faithfully Different* offers a bril̶̶̶̶̶̶̶̶̶̶̶̶̶̶̶̶ tural moment—loaded with insight, yet perfectly practical—in prose that is fresh and crystal clear. Crain strikes a healthy balance between her native kindness and gentleness and her sharp biblical thinking, helping you discover, finally, how all the crazy cultural pieces fit together *and* what to do about it.

"Crain's work is not only an accessible primer for Christians who find themselves overwhelmed by the confusing array of challenges facing their convictions: from deconversions, to relativistic postmodernism, to critical race theory. She also sounds a sobering wake-up call to the multitudes who call themselves Christians yet who naively embrace secular ideologies and worldly ethics.

"In my opinion, Crain's latest work is a masterful achievement, her best yet. If you read just one book to help you understand the present-day secular assaults on Christianity—and the biblical answers to them—make it *Faithfully Different*."

Gregory Koukl, President, Stand to Reason (str.org); author of
Tactics: A Game Plan for Discussing Your Christian Convictions

"This book is *faithfully different*! Clearly written, relevant, and winsome, it is a fair-minded defense of the Christian worldview. Read it, and you will find it to be of great benefit in understanding how you can withstand the cultural pressures that are swirling around you. A great book to help Christians, but also a wonderful gift to those who are on the margins, dealing with doubts and wondering how Christianity compares with the secular answers of our culture. Read it. Share it. And live it!"

Dr. Erwin W. Lutzer, Pastor Emeritus, Moody Church,
Chicago; author of *We Will Not Be Silenced*

"In her earlier books, Natasha Crain has shown that she possesses a rare gift for unpacking complex ideas and making them clear and accessible. In *Faithfully Different*, she focuses on the struggles Christians face as society grows ever more secular. Those who follow Jesus are now a minority in Western culture, increasingly cast as extremists and treated as obstacles to social progress. Crain offers a reliable guide to navigating these new challenges."

Nancy Pearcey, author of *Total Truth* and *Finding Truth*

"If ever there was a time to reaffirm biblical morality, revitalize our notions of biblical justice, and recommit to speaking the truth of the gospel, now is that time. Natasha Crain's new book, *Faithfully Different*, is the right book written at the right moment. It will help you understand the challenges we face as a community of believers and equip you with the skills necessary to rise to these challenges. It's a *must-read* book for a time such as ours. Get a copy for yourself and every Christian you care about."

J. Warner Wallace, *Dateline*-featured cold-case detective;
author of *Person of Interest* and *Cold-Case Christianity*

"Are you being deceived? How would you know? The inherent problem with being deceived is that you don't know you're being deceived. Natasha Crain brilliantly exposes how our secular culture often deceives us about God, Jesus, the Bible, social justice, sex, love, and morality. She then points us back to truth so we can live faithfully different lives to achieve our most important mission—knowing God through Jesus Christ and building His kingdom. Read this now!"

Frank Turek, President, CrossExamined.org; coauthor
of *I Don't Have Enough Faith to Be an Atheist*

"At Summit Ministries, we train tens of thousands of young adults every year in worldview and apologetics. I can tell you this: Natasha Crain gets it. She doesn't shy away from a biblical response to tough questions. Just as important, she has her finger on the pulse of the culture. She knows its language and how to speak truth into it. *Faithfully Different* makes a powerful and very readable case that if Christians will learn to think Christianly—that is, with a Christian worldview—they can have a powerful impact in our confusing times. A bracing and timely challenge for the church."

Jeff Myers, PhD, President, Summit Ministries

"Until recently, Christian ideals in America have gone largely unchallenged. But this is rapidly changing, which has left many Christians feeling opposed, silenced, and marginalized. How can we stand for biblical truth in a culture that views that truth to be bigoted, hateful, or harmful? *Faithfully Different* will give you the tools, resources, and inspiration to live out your Christian values in an increasingly secularized culture. This is the book every Christian needs in this cultural moment."

Alisa Childers, author of *Another Gospel: A Lifelong Christian Seeks Truth in Response to Progressive Christianity*; host of *The Alisa Childers Podcast*

"*Faithfully Different* is a timely wake-up call for Christians who want to live out their faith in our secular culture. This book is well researched, full of interesting stories, and grounded deeply in Scripture. I highly recommend it for Christians who want to know what it means practically to follow Jesus today."

Sean McDowell, PhD, professor of apologetics,
Biola University; author or coauthor of nearly 20 books, including
Chasing Love: Sex, Love, and Relationships in a Confused Culture

"As a pastor, one of the biggest issues I see facing Christians today is that they don't know how much secularism has impacted their worldview and crippled their ability to think biblically about things. *Faithfully Different* not only successfully identifies and explains the relevant worldview issues but does so in a way everyone can understand. I highly recommend this book for anyone who wants to understand and defend the Christian worldview."

Mike Winger, President, BibleThinker Inc.

"Natasha Crain is absolutely correct. Christian, the world you knew just five years ago has dramatically changed, and not just among unbelievers. An aggressive secularism is sweeping into our churches that is anything but neutral. In the last two years alone, I've lost evangelical friends who not only promote ideas at odds with a biblical worldview, but who make agreement with those ideas an acid test for continued relationship. How can Christians live obediently and confidently in a world hell-bent on our total surrender? Natasha provides a refreshing answer that transcends arguing at a fever pitch: True Christians must be faithfully different. And that starts with understanding the secular worldviews that put fellow believers at risk in the first place. I thank God for this book. I now have a roadmap for living (and thriving!) as a minority."

Scott Klusendorf, President, Life Training Institute; author of
The Case for Life: Equipping Christians to Engage the Culture

"Secularism's growing influence and power is like a raging river, breaching banks and flooding everything in its path. Wading slightly into it risks getting swept in and dragged along with others who have been less careful and those who have jumped in for the ride. In *Faithfully Different*, Natasha Crain discusses the elements in secularism that seduce us away from our lover Jesus. She also takes readers by the hand and helps them recalibrate their thinking to one that is grounded in the truth of the biblical worldview. This book is well written, refreshingly insightful, and is truly an enjoyable read!"

Michael Licona, PhD, Associate Professor of
Theology, Houston Baptist University

"I can't express my excitement enough for the impact this book will have on people's lives. I am not an alarmist, but I don't know if there has been another time when there has been more confusion about beliefs and truth, even amongst Christians. Many Christians don't know what they believe, so we see them accepting counterbiblical beliefs as normal. Natasha writes practical insights and shows why we must pay attention to the way so many are drifting from historical Christian truths. This is so incredibly critical, as what we believe impacts everything— our decisions, our values, our ethics—everything! I am so thankful for a practical guide to help us see clarity in the midst of so much fog and unclarity, why it matters, and what we can then do about it."

Dan Kimball, author of *How (Not) to Read the Bible*; on staff
at Vintage Faith Church; professor at Western Seminary

FAITHFULLY
DIFFERENT

NATASHA CRAIN

HARVEST HOUSE PUBLISHERS
EUGENE, OREGON

Published in association with the literary agency of Mark Sweeney & Associates, Naples, Florida.

Cover Photo © Pixxsa / Shutterstock

Cover design by Faceout Studio, Molly von Borstel

Interior design by KUHN Design Group

For bulk, special sales, or ministry purchases, please call 1-800-547-8979. Email: Customerservice@hhpbooks.com

FAITHFULLY DIFFERENT is a trademark of the Hawkins Children's LLC. Harvest House Publishers, Inc., is the exclusive licensee of the trademark FAITHFULLY DIFFERENT.

Faithfully Different
Copyright © 2022 by Natasha Crain
Published by Harvest House Publishers
Eugene, Oregon 97408
www.harvesthousepublishers.com

ISBN 978-0-7369-8429-4 (pbk)
ISBN 978-0-7369-8430-0 (eBook)
ISBN 978-0-7369-8646-5 (eAudio)

Library of Congress Control Number: 2021937794

Printed in the United States of America

23 24 25 26 27 28 29 30 / BP / 10 9 8 7 6 5 4 3

Contents

Foreword by John Stonestreet 9

Before You Read 13

Part 1: The New Normal

1. Welcome to Your Place in a Worldview Minority! 17
   It's no longer "normal" to be a Christian in our culture

2. Surrounded by Secularism 35
   Don't be fooled: Secularism is anything but neutral

3. Why Secularism Is Compelling—Even for Christians 49
   It's a worldview that's ready-made for influence

Part 2: Faithfully Different *Believing*

4. Regaining a Supernatural Worldview 67
   Under the pressure of secular naturalism

5. Reestablishing What We (Should) Actually Believe 89
   Under the pressure of secular individualism

6. Reexamining Beliefs When Confronted with Doubt 111
   Under the pressure of secular deconversionism

Part 3: Faithfully Different *Thinking*

7. Reclaiming What Rightfully Belongs to the
   Biblical Worldview 133
   Under the pressure of the secular worldview buffet

8. Reaffirming Biblical Morality 153
   Under the pressure of secular virtue signaling

9. Reinvigorating the Spirit of Discernment 171
   Under the pressure of secular indifference

Part 4: Faithfully Different *Living*

10. Revitalizing the Call to Biblical Justice 193
    Under the pressure of secular social justice

11. Recommitting to Speaking Truth 215
    Under the pressure of secular cancel culture

12. Reshaping Our Hearts for Sharing the Gospel 237
    Under the pressure of secular relativism

    A Final Encouragement: Fruit Under Pressure 257

    Notes 261

Foreword

JOHN STONESTREET

Worldview matters.

Whether or not we realize it, everyone has a worldview. We all see the world through our most basic beliefs about life and the world. To be human is to live from a worldview. This feature of humanity separates us from all the other animals. Not only do we exist, we *think* about existing. We wonder why we are here, and what it all means. We imagine how the world could be different, and work to change it. We ask big questions like, Does life have purpose? Is there such a thing as right and wrong? Who decides?

We may not have thought much about our worldview, but it's there. Everyone we meet has a worldview too. This is why our disagreements can be so sharp. A worldview makes a big difference in how we think, how we make decisions, and how we relate with others.

It's common today to hear silly slogans like, "It doesn't matter what you believe, as long you believe in something." But, *what* we believe matters. Our ideas about life and the world have real consequences. After all, we live from our worldview. Our worldview will either help us see the world clearly or will keep us from seeing the world clearly. Our worldview will either help us live well or lead us astray.

Christians should have a Christian worldview, of course, but many don't. It's quite possible to have a sincere, private faith and to think and live like a pagan (or an atheist). In fact, many do. Many others struggle to truly make sense of life, which is a real shame. After all, if Christianity is indeed the true account of the world, it's more than big enough for life's toughest questions and the most controversial issues of our culture.

Christians not intentional about what is true will still have a world-view, but it will do more harm for them than good. People will often, in fact, catch a worldview like they catch a cold. Too many Christians have been infected in their hearts and minds by the culture around them. Theirs is more of a *whirled* view made up of random and wrong beliefs collected from the culture around them instead of from Christ. Which is why it's important to know that…

Culture matters too.

All humans are, in many important ways, shaped by cultures. Our fashions, tastes, beliefs, and so many other things about us reflect the social environments into which we are born and live. In fact, a culture is most powerful in shaping us by what it makes seem *normal*.

If you've ever traveled to another country, you've likely experienced the feeling of, seemingly, being in a *different world*. You're not, of course. You're in a different culture, a place imagined and built differently by a different group of people. This is what humans do. We build worlds within the world.

In recent decades, the Western world (which includes the United States) has shifted in dramatic ways. Things once *unthinkable* are now *unquestionable*. Beliefs and behaviors once unimaginable now seem so, well, *normal*. Christians who aren't discerning will quickly find them-selves embracing things that are wrong.

That's why this book, *Faithfully Different*, is so important and, if you read it carefully, will be so helpful. Natasha is a clear thinker and a capti-vating writer, with this knack for explaining things most essential, such as worldview and culture. Not only does she help her readers understand what they need to *know*, she helps them *act* in ways faithful to truth.

As parents of four kids, my wife and I are big fans of Natasha's pre-vious books. As someone who has spent the last two decades studying worldviews and culture, trying to convince Christians to take both seri-ously, I'm a big fan of this one too.

Faithfully Different covers an incredible amount of crucial ground without cutting any corners. It's one of those rare books that is both faithful to biblical truth and honest about our cultural situation, a work of sound cultural analysis from a solid and distinctly Christian worldview. It's just so very *helpful*.

Because of this, *Faithfully Different* is a real gift to God's people. Indeed, If we are to follow Christ in this cultural moment, we'll need to know what it means to be faithful to biblical truth while being honest about our cultural situation.

So jump in, and bring others along with you. You'll be glad you did.

John Stonestreet, president of
the Colson Center and coauthor of
A Practical Guide to Culture

Before You Read

I've always hated reading book introductions.

There's nothing worse than having a brand new book in your hand but feeling like you have to cross a 5,000-word hurdle to get to the good stuff. So, I'm sparing you that often-tedious step. But a brief and critically important note is in order about the intended audience for this book (don't skip this!).

Faithfully Different is an "in-house" discussion for those who view the Bible as the inspired and authoritative Word of God. **For purposes of this book, I'm referring to the worldview that is consistent with such a belief as a *biblical worldview*.** That's not to say that every Christian who views the Bible in this way will agree on every question about what the Bible says; there will always be interpretive differences in some areas. But there are many people who identify as Christians today while having a fundamentally different view of the very *nature* of the Bible. Though they may even use words like *inspired* or *authoritative* to describe how they see Scripture, they mean something so different that their entire worldview will be different. With that in mind, let me elaborate in order to make the intended audience even more clear.

This book is for those who

1. view the Bible as God's Word to man, rather than as a collection of writings that merely reflect man's best

understanding of God at the time when they were
produced;

2. understand the inspiration of the Bible to mean that God
Himself worked through humans to accurately convey
eternal truths, not that biblical writers were in a more
poetic sense "inspired" to write about God; and

3. consider the Bible in its entirety to be the only sufficient
and authoritative source for salvation, faith, and godliness,
rather than one of many collections of spiritual writings
that can equally point people to God (2 Timothy 3:15-17;
John 17:17).

If you've picked up this book but don't share this view of the Bible,
I certainly welcome you to read on! But I would expect you to disagree
with large parts of what I say because our beliefs about the nature of
the Bible differ so greatly.

If you seek to believe, think, and live according to a biblical worldview (as I've defined it here), I pray this book will give you the wisdom
and encouragement to stand firm in your convictions no matter what
secular pressures and cultural hostilities come your way.

PART 1

THE NEW NORMAL

CHAPTER 1

Welcome to Your Place in a Worldview Minority!

It's no longer "normal" to be a Christian in our culture

In the summer of 2020, I wrote an article on my website titled "5 Ways Christians Are Getting Swept into a Secular Worldview in This Cultural Moment."[1] I addressed several areas in which Christians need to be more discerning as we respond to emotionally charged cultural issues. More specifically, I pointed out that many Christians were inadvertently reacting to the social unrest of that summer in ways that were more consistent with a *secular* worldview than with a *biblical* one.

Apparently I wasn't the only one who noticed that our collective discernment was breaking under the weight of secular pressure: The article went viral and was liked and shared on social media more than 277,000 times. I received emails for weeks from readers who said they appreciated me putting into words what they had felt for a while but hadn't been able to put their finger on—Christians are often living more as an *extension* of the secular world today than as a distinct light *to* it.

For many believers, it was the cultural firestorm of that summer that so quickly brought to light the challenges of biblical discernment in a secular society (for the moment, we'll define secular as irreligious, but we'll explore the meaning more deeply in chapter 2). The subject area of social justice, however, is just one of many areas in which such challenges arise. To get a feel for the other places where Christians are seeing secular pressures on faith, I asked on my author Facebook page one day, "What are some ways you're seeing Christians being influenced by the secular world around us—in what we believe, how we think, or how we live out our faith?"[2] More than 150 people responded with insightful and wide-ranging observations. Here are a few examples of what they had to say:

> Everything has become very self-centered. "You be you" instead of be who God made you to be. "You got this" instead of God is in control. "Live your best life" instead of live to give glory to God. "You're so strong" instead of God is strong in our weakness.

> I see Christians get mad when other Christians point out or expose false doctrines and teachers. Today it's believed we're supposed to accept all views—even of the Bible—and if we don't, we're supposedly breaking the commandment to love one another.

> The idea of universalism, or that many roads lead up to the same summit, is causing many to loosely handle sin and other core Christian doctrines.

> I see many Christians who feel no guilt for habitually continuing in their sin, and their lives look no different than the lives of nonbelievers around them.

> I see an unhealthy and unbiblical level of mixing political views with theological views and Christian identity—on both sides of the aisle.

> I have several friends who have adopted the world's viewpoint of sexual morality. I've been shocked by how many are comfortable with couples living together outside of

marriage or even believing we have to accept the homosexual lifestyle under the guise of being loving.

I see a lot of Christians feeling like they have to choose between the Bible and science, and science is presented as being the logical, educated choice.[3]

I bet you can relate to having noticed several of these things yourself and could add examples of your own. But can you also relate to this one (emphasis mine)?

> *In my own life* it manifests itself as forgetting God's promises, prayerlessness, gracelessness, impatience, cynicism, bitterness, and failing to know or understand how I'm supposed to respond in the tough or unexpected moments.

I loved this person's humility in being the one person who applied the question to *themself.* It's easy to take note of what we see happening around us, but if we're honest, most of us can also see that our own faith has been impacted in various ways by shifting cultural pressures. *This isn't a challenge unique to all those "other" Christians—it's a challenge for all of us.*

With that in mind, I took this commenter's lead and started a separate Facebook post to ask how people have seen our secular culture impact their *own* spiritual lives. Responses like these poured in:

> I find it more challenging to witness to others and to speak up and defend my own faith and the faith of my brothers and sisters in Christ. I now fear not just rejection or ridicule but retaliation.

> I think sometimes I get affected by atheists questioning miracles (especially the resurrection). Our culture places so much emphasis on believing that the only things that are "real" are things you can prove scientifically. Sometimes I can start to doubt if God is real because I can't see and touch Him.

I let the secular culture that glorifies personal autonomy isolate me and others.

I'm lowering my standards for what media I consume. I just tell myself it's too hard to find something to watch that meets my moral standards, which is an excuse to enjoy things I probably shouldn't.

I don't get as excited during the worship of my Savior as I do during a sports event.

I share all these comments because they exemplify the diversity of ways in which secular culture is influencing Christians. At first glance, some of these observations may seem to have little in common. For example, our level of passion for worship relative to our level of passion for sports appears to be a very different kind of problem than our ability to believe in miracles. But there's an underlying thread of secular influence that connects these superficially unrelated comments. Because secularism is ultimately a *worldview*—a way of seeing all of reality—it follows that its influence will reach from the seemingly mundane (our view of sports) to some of the most fundamental questions of our faith (the existence of God and the possibility of miracles). This is likely why so many people who emailed me in response to that viral article said they hadn't been able to put their finger on what they had been seeing. They had noticed the *effects* of secular influence in widely scattered examples over time, but they hadn't necessarily seen how those effects were produced by the same deeper trend: the bleeding of secularism into the worldview of Christians everywhere.

Now, in one sense, the problem of Christians believing, thinking, and living too much like the surrounding culture isn't a modern phenomenon; it's as old as the New Testament. Paul, for example, warned the early church to not be "conformed to this world" (Romans 12:2 ESV) and urged the Colossians to not be taken captive by "hollow and deceptive philosophy, which depends on human tradition" (Colossians 2:8). Peter warned of those who were distorting Scripture "to their own destruction" (2 Peter 3:16) and exhorted believers to abstain from worldly passions so others could see their good deeds and glorify God (1 Peter 2:11-12). John reminded early Christians of the need to discern between the Spirit of truth and the spirit of falsehood (1 John 4:6) and to not love the things of this world (1 John 2:15-17). These are just a few of many examples found throughout the New Testament. Christians have *always* faced the challenge of remaining distinct from the world.

In another sense, however, something new *has* happened—and something new *is* happening. If you've been feeling that our culture is rapidly changing in some unique ways, you're right. And if you've been feeling that Christians are getting swept into secular ways of believing, thinking, and living today, you're right again. The purpose of this book is to help us as Christians move beyond these general senses and put our finger more precisely on what the "something" is that's happening right now so we can gain clarity on how to faithfully respond as individuals in the body of Christ. More specifically, the thesis of this book can be laid out as follows:

- If you have a biblical worldview, you're now in a *worldview minority*.

- The dominant worldview of the culture around us—a strident secularism—is fundamentally at odds with the biblical worldview.

- This opposing and often hostile secularism is putting extensive pressure on (1) what Christians *believe*, (2) the ways our beliefs inform how we *think*, and (3) how we *live out our faith*.

- We must each regain clarity on what it means to be faithfully different from today's world for (1) the health of our own relationship with the Lord and (2) our ability to effectively be salt and light to others (Matthew 5:13-16).

If you love the Lord, it's inevitable to feel the gravity of where we are as a culture and where we seem to be headed. Indeed, many books addressing the intersection of faith and culture are, frankly, pretty depressing. But the last thing I want is for *this* book to leave you feeling like you're living under a dark cloud. We do have to confront the grim reality of where we are, but ultimately this is a book designed to help us as Christians see our current cultural context as a God-honoring *opportunity* to be faithfully different. No, that's not a switcheroo, as in telling kids, "Spinach isn't bad; it's just an 'opportunity' to eat healthy food." It's *truly* an opportunity, as we'll see in the coming chapters. In many ways, there's a great pruning happening in the church today, and it will undoubtedly result in new fruit for the glory of God.

We'll start this journey by looking at what it means that we're now in a worldview minority. In chapter 2, we'll take a closer look at the secularism that surrounds us: What, exactly, is secularism, and why does it matter so much? In chapter 3, we'll look at what makes secularism so influential in the lives of Christians. In the remainder of the book, we'll identify nine major types of secular pressures today, work to understand how they're impacting Christians, and seek to clarify what it should look like to both resist those pressures and more deliberately live out the distinctiveness of our biblical worldview.

Are Christians Really a Minority?

I realize that many people find numbers to be tedious, so I hate to dive into them right away. If that's how you feel, rest assured I'm not going to provide an exhaustive analysis of studies on religious trends in America. But we do need to have a bit of a family meeting—a numerical "State of the Christian Union," if you will—as a starting point for our remaining discussions. Why? In the rest of this book, we'll see that our status as a worldview minority has far-reaching implications for the ways in which secular pressures influence us, so we need to start by establishing that we are, in fact, now a worldview minority.

Let's begin with the big picture from the most recent data. The Pew Research Center is perhaps the most widely known and cited organization for providing information on religious trends in America. Of particular interest for our current purpose are Pew's Religious Landscape

Studies, conducted in 2007 and 2014. These studies were national surveys involving more than 35,000 people who were asked dozens of questions regarding their religious identities, beliefs, and practices. Although the most recent Religious Landscape Study is now a few years old, the Pew Research Center has since collected five additional years of relevant data from political polls that ask about people's present religious affiliation (if any). Together, the data from political polls and the two Religious Landscape Studies provide important insights on religious trends in America from 2009 to 2019.[4]

So what does the data tell us? According to the 2019 data, 65 percent of Americans identify themselves as Christians. Stop right there! Doesn't that mean this whole idea of Christians being in a "worldview minority" is patently false? It's not lost on me that many non-Christians would look at this claim with some incredulity and annoyance. *Christians are a minority? Are you kidding me? Christians are everywhere! Here we go again with the Christian persecution complex!* But this is why we need a more nuanced understanding of the data—what we're claiming and what we're not.

It's crucial to recognize that the results of this type of research are based on how a person *self-identifies*. Among, say, five people who identify as a "Christian," you could have

1. someone who says they're a Christian simply because they were raised in a Christian home (even though they no longer have an active faith in Jesus);

2. someone who generally agrees with Christian values but rejects core doctrinal tenets of Christianity, such as the resurrection;

3. someone who rejects the authority of the Bible but considers themself a "Jesus follower";

4. someone who considers themself a Christian but also holds various beliefs that are in significant conflict with a biblical worldview (such as reincarnation); and

5. someone who holds to the tenets of the historic Christian faith and is an active follower of Jesus.

It's easy to see that these hypothetical people could view the world quite differently despite the fact they all identify as Christians. *Self-identifications tell us little about how people actually function in culture and in their personal lives because they tell us nothing about what people believe.* That's significant because our beliefs inform our thinking, and our thinking informs how we live. What we specifically need to know, then, is how many Americans share a *biblical worldview*—not just how many Americans call themselves Christians. For this, we need to look at additional research.

Christians with a Biblical Worldview

Quantifying the number of Americans who hold a biblical worldview is far more difficult than quantifying the number who self-identify as Christians. On the one hand, it's easy to omit people from the count who explicitly state they don't believe the Bible is the inspired and authoritative Word of God or who explicitly reject the individual doctrinal beliefs that would correspond with such statements. On the other hand, it's tricky to categorize people who hold to a mixture of beliefs—some of which are biblical and some of which are not. For example, researchers have found that many Americans say they believe in the "God of the Bible" yet also believe in reincarnation. Do such people hold to a biblical worldview? Probably not, because a person who believes we have many lives to live is likely to have a very different view of reality than someone who is committed to a consistently biblical worldview (even if they say they believe in the "God of the Bible"). Other unbiblical beliefs might affect a person's overall worldview much less. Researchers have the task of determining what set of questions will best identify those who have what we might call a "functioning" biblical worldview and who at least endeavor to live accordingly.

With these complexities in mind, let's briefly look at four research studies that provide some answers. They use different approaches to arrive at their conclusions but collectively paint a similar picture.

Pew Research Center's Religious Typology Study

In 2018, the Pew Research Center undertook a new and different kind of analysis on American religious beliefs, categorizing people into one of seven segments based on beliefs and behavior rather than simple self-identification. Although the research wasn't conducted in a way that allows us to quantify the percent of people committed specifically to a biblical worldview, we can infer a *maximum* percent, as follows.

Researchers found that just 39 percent of Americans are "highly religious"—seriously committed to *any* faith. The other two groups ("somewhat religious" and "nonreligious") are characterized by beliefs that aren't consistent with a biblical worldview (for example, New Age spirituality). This implies that those with a biblical worldview are primarily a subset of the highly religious group. How big is that subset of the 39 percent? The research doesn't allow us to pinpoint a number, but we can *exclude* about 11 of the 39 percent—the "Diversely Devout" segment—who say they believe in the "God of the Bible" but also hold to a mix of clearly unbiblical beliefs. We're left knowing that those with a biblical worldview make up something less than the 29 percent of Americans who remain.

Twenty-nine percent is already a far cry from the 65 percent who self-identify as Christians, and, again, that's a *maximum* number. The actual number appears to be much lower, as the following other studies have shown.

American Culture and Faith Institute's Worldview Measurement Project

In 2017, the American Culture and Faith Institute (ACFI) conducted research to specifically quantify those who have a biblical worldview. Based on an analysis of people's answers to 40 questions about spiritual beliefs and behavior, ACFI found that just 10 percent of all Americans have a biblical worldview. Millennials were less likely than other adults to have a biblical view on 19 of the 20 beliefs evaluated, with only 4 percent having a biblical worldview overall.[5]

Arizona Christian University's American Worldview Inventory

The American Worldview Inventory is an annual survey based on 51 worldview-related questions drawn from eight categories of worldview application. As done in the ACFI study, researchers categorize respondents' worldviews based on a combination of belief and behavior factors. In 2020, they found that only 6 percent of all American adults have a biblical worldview. Among 18- to 29-year-olds, the number drops to 2 percent.[6] Perhaps even more shockingly, researchers found that just 21 percent of *those attending evangelical Protestant churches* have a biblical worldview—with that number dropping to only 8 percent in mainline Protestant churches. Don't let the significance of that pass you by! The biblical worldview isn't just shrinking in American culture at large, *but also within the church.*

Barna Research

Barna Research has tracked the trends in American beliefs that make up a biblical worldview since 1995. For research purposes, they consider a person to have a biblical worldview if they agree that

- absolute moral truth exists;

- the Bible is totally accurate in all of the principles it teaches;

- Satan is a real being or force, not merely symbolic;

- a person cannot earn their way into heaven by trying to be good or doing good works;

- Jesus lived a sinless life on earth; and

- God is the all-knowing, all-powerful creator of the world who still rules the universe today.

This is a pretty broad definition. In fact, when I first read it, I thought it was far *too* broad—excluding some essential and more specific

Christian beliefs like "Jesus was raised from the dead." But even using this broad definition, Barna found that only 17 percent of Christians who consider their faith important and attend church regularly hold to a biblical worldview.[7] To be clear, that's not 17 percent of all Americans or even 17 percent of all Christians. That's 17 percent of Christians who consider their faith important and attend church regularly! Once again, we see that people with a biblical worldview are hard to find today—even in churches.

So let's summarize what we can make of the available data. Estimates of the percent of Americans committed to a biblical worldview range from 6 percent (from the American Worldview Inventory) to a maximum of 29 percent (from the Pew research), with a significant generational gap noted between millennials and older adults. Keep in mind that the Pew research wasn't attempting to specifically quantify those with a biblical worldview, so the 29 percent was only an inferred maximum based on what they *did* measure. This means the more direct estimates of 6 percent from the American Worldview Inventory and 10 percent from the ACFI research are likely to be much closer to the true picture.

The big takeaway? Those with a biblical worldview are not only a minority in America, but a small minority. Furthermore, the American Worldview Inventory and Barna Research both show that those with a biblical worldview are a small minority *even among Christians.* Yes, seven of ten people may say they're a Christian, but that in no way reflects the relative rarity of the biblical worldview in America today.

But Is This Anything New?

If the picture we just drew were the same picture that had always existed in our country, there wouldn't be much to talk about in this book. Those with a biblical worldview would already be accustomed to navigating culture as a worldview minority and would already be fully aware of all that such navigation entailed. But that's not the case. The picture *has* changed, in four major ways.

First, it's estimated that the percentage of American adults holding a biblical worldview has declined by *half* over the past 25 years.[8] Most people reading this book can remember life 25 years ago. If you're old enough, think for a moment about that time in your life. It probably doesn't seem *that* far back. But the percent of people in America with a biblical worldview was twice as high then as it is now. That's a swift and sharp decline. And it's one that has every appearance of continuing, given the widening belief gap research shows between generations. Historically, there's always been somewhat of a gap in religiosity between younger and older generations, but researchers say that millennials and their predecessors differ more now than they have during the past seven decades.[9]

Second, the percentage of Americans who self-identify as Christian—regardless of whether they actually have a biblical worldview—has dropped substantially in just the last decade. Remember the Pew Research Center data showing that about 65 percent of Americans identify as Christians today? That number was 77 percent only 12 years ago, and a drop has occurred in almost every Christian denomination.[10] Even if many of those who stopped identifying as a Christian over the last decade never held a biblical worldview to begin with, it says a lot that they're now consciously choosing to distance themselves from even the Christian label. The mainstream cultural view of Christianity has become negative so quickly that those who may have loosely identified as a Christian in the past are no longer willing to do so. That's not necessarily a bad thing—it's forcing people to more consciously consider what they actually believe—but it is a trend that's contributing to the rapidly changing picture of Christianity in America.

Third, those who no longer identify as Christians are overwhelmingly now identifying as atheist, agnostic, or "nothing in particular." Meanwhile, the percentage of Americans who identify with non-Christian *religions* has remained virtually unchanged over the last decade. This is important to know because it shows we're not seeing a significant conversion of Christians to other theistic religions that might share some fundamental worldview characteristics.[11] If that were the case, the apparent differences between Christians and non-Christians in culture might be less striking. But instead, we're seeing people adopt worldviews that inherently share very little in common with biblical Christianity. And the percent of Americans holding these worldviews has grown from 17 to 26 percent in just the last decade.[12] Importantly, this growth is not unique to any particular demographic group. It's a widespread trend seen among whites, blacks, Hispanics, men, women, geographic areas, and educational attainment. A full 40 percent of millennials now identify as atheist, agnostic, or "nothing in particular."

Finally, many of those who are abandoning Christianity are now *also* abandoning Christian values—a simultaneous rejection that hasn't always been the case. To be sure, we can't with any accuracy look back at American history and claim that we were always bound together by a steadfast commitment to the core doctrines of Christianity. But we can say that for many years we were bound together by values rooted in the Judeo-Christian worldview on which America was founded. Though people have increasingly discarded the doctrinal specifics of Christianity over time, the societal result hasn't always been as obvious as it is today because people generally continued to hold values *consistent* with Christianity (for example, the importance of the family unit, the nature of marriage, and the value of human life). But in more recent years, secular society has started discarding the long hangover of Christian *values* as well. Christianity no longer looks like a contemporary cousin to the mainstream worldview. Today it's more like a distant ancestor who no longer shares recognizable traits.

Francis Schaeffer described this turning point in his book *The Great Evangelical Disaster*:

> Christianity is no longer providing the consensus for our society. And Christianity is no longer providing the consensus upon which our law is based. That is not to say that the United States ever was a "Christian nation" in the sense that all or most of our citizens were Christians, nor in the sense that the nation, its laws, and social life were ever a full and complete expression of Christian truth. There is no golden age in the past which we can idealize—whether it is early America, the Reformation, or the early church. But until recent decades something did exist which can rightly be called a Christian consensus or ethos which gave

a distinctive shape to Western society and to the United States in a definite way. Now that consensus is all but gone, and the freedoms that it brought are being destroyed before our eyes. We are at a time when humanism is coming to its natural conclusion in morals, in values, and in law. All that society has today are relativistic values based upon statistical averages, or the arbitrary decisions of those who hold legal and political power.[13]

Schaeffer wrote this in 1984. As we saw earlier in this chapter, the percentage of those with a biblical worldview has decreased by at least 50 percent since then! The increasing rejection of Christian values isn't new—Schaeffer's words could easily have been penned today—but that rejection has snowballed in the era of the internet and social media. And, as you've surely noticed, it's not a passive rejection. It's an outright hostility that views long-held Christian values as archaic at best, morally grotesque at worst.

So is our position as a worldview minority anything new today? Yes—in significant ways. The percentage of Americans holding to an explicitly biblical worldview is quickly declining, as is the percentage of Americans identifying as Christian even in name. Those who no longer identify as Christian are overwhelmingly adopting worldviews that inherently share very little in common with Christianity. And mainstream society is now rejecting the core Christian values that Americans have shared for hundreds of years.

There's no doubt about it: It's no longer normal to be a Christian with a biblical worldview in America.

What I'm Not Saying

There are a few concerns both Christians and non-Christians sometimes raise in response to any talk of Christianity "declining" in America. It's worth a moment, therefore, to explicitly state what I'm *not* claiming in response to all this data or in this book more generally.

First, I'm not suggesting that Jesus said following Him would *ever* be the norm in this world. The truth is quite literally the opposite. In John 15:18-25, Jesus bluntly tells us:

> If the world hates you, keep in mind that it hated me first.
> If you belonged to the world, it would love you as its own.
> As it is, you do not belong to the world, but I have cho-
> sen you out of the world. That is why the world hates you.
> Remember what I told you: "A servant is not greater than
> his master." If they persecuted me, they will persecute you
> also. If they obeyed my teaching, they will obey yours also.
> They will treat you this way because of my name, for they
> do not know the one who sent me.

It's obvious from Jesus's own words that we should never expect to live in a culture where it's standard for people to have a biblical worldview. The question we need to answer isn't, "How do we create a culture where it's more normal to be a Christian?" but rather, "How can we best be faithful to our calling in a world where it will *never* be normal to be a Christian—and in a culture where it's becoming less and less so?"

Second, I'm not suggesting that the church's survival depends on humans alone, as if we're one misstep away from Christianity being wiped off the map. Again, looking to Jesus's words, we're told that the gates of hell will not overcome His church (Matthew 16:18). The body of Christ will never die, no matter how grim things look in a given place at a given time. That doesn't mean, however, that what we do doesn't matter. If that were the case, Jesus wouldn't have instructed us to share the gospel, as in Matthew 28:19-20: "Go and make disciples of all nations, baptizing them in the name of the Father and of the Son and of the Holy Spirit, and teaching them to obey everything I have commanded you." Nor would He have preached about the importance of being salt and light in a decaying and dark world (Matthew 5:13-16). Passages like these *assume* we're to be actively engaged with the culture around us. In God's sovereignty, the outcome is assured, but we're called to be part of the process.

Third, I'm not equating being in a worldview minority with being persecuted—at least not right now. There are many places in today's world where Christians are being persecuted in ways we cannot even fathom in America. According to Open Doors USA, in just the last year,

- more than 340 million Christians were living in places where they experienced high levels of persecution;

- 4,761 Christians were killed for their faith;

- 4,488 churches and other Christian buildings were attacked; and

- 4,277 Christians were detained without trial, arrested, sentenced, or imprisoned.[14]

Being in a worldview minority in America doesn't have implications right now that are anything like these. Anti-Christian discrimination and hostility? Absolutely. We'll talk about those kinds of issues throughout this book. But it must be stated up front that these challenges pale in comparison to what our brothers and sisters in Christ are facing around the globe. We should all be in prayer for the persecuted church.

Though I'm not saying any of these three things, I *am* saying that those who hold to a biblical worldview are now a shrinking minority in a secular culture, and that fact has significant (and often unrealized) implications for what it means to be faithful today. We need to regain clarity on how to respond, both for the sake of our own relationship with the Lord and for our ability to be a witness to others.

Part of regaining clarity requires that we more fully understand the secular worldview that surrounds us. To that subject we now turn: What, exactly, is secularism, and why does it matter so much?

QUESTIONS FOR DISCUSSION OR REFLECTION

1. What are some ways you see Christians being influenced by our secular culture—in what we believe, how we think, or how we live out our faith?

2. How have you seen the pressures of secular culture impact your own spiritual life?

3. Did it surprise you to learn how few people have a biblical worldview today? Why or why not?

4. Why do you think so few Christians have a biblical worldview relative to the number of people who identify as Christian? What, if anything, do you think would lead to more self-identified Christians having a biblical worldview?

CHAPTER 2

Surrounded by Secularism

*Don't be fooled: Secularism
is anything but neutral*

There are plenty of situations in life where being in a minority is of little consequence. If your favorite animal is the anteater while the favorite animal of 80 percent of those around you is the dog, you're not going to experience any kind of life pressure from the majority group. You can have your anteaters, others can have their dogs, and everyone can easily co-exist with their varied animal preferences (maybe even with a clever bumper sticker!). But being in a worldview minority is no case of anteaters and dogs. *The secular worldview by which we're surrounded is fundamentally at odds with a biblical worldview, and that has extensive implications for our daily lives.* The task of this chapter is to demonstrate just how deep this conflict is so we'll be able to fully grasp the spiritual significance of the secular pressures we'll discuss in the rest of the book.

To do this, we need to better understand what the word *secular* means. In chapter 1, I briefly defined it as "irreligious." That's a good starting point, but more needs to be said. People use the word in many different ways and contexts, and the meaning has even shifted throughout history. Furthermore, even if everyone were working from the same definition, there would still be little shared understanding of the *significance* of the word from a worldview perspective. So we need to spend some time fleshing out this term.

Secular—as a Political Structure

In saying that secular means irreligious, notice that we're defining it by what it's *not*—religious. But what, then, does it mean to be religious, and to whom or what does the word apply?

Scholars debate how to best define *religion*, but for all intents and purposes, it's a worldview that systematically defines reality based on the existence of a god or gods. By their very nature, most religions are authoritative for their adherents because they not only *describe* reality, but also *prescribe* correct human responses. Christianity, for example, is authoritative for Christians because we believe in a God who defines right and wrong and who has revealed His will for humanity in the Bible. Similarly, Muslims believe Allah's will is revealed in the Quran, Mormons believe God's will is revealed in the Book of Mormon, Sikhs believe Waheguru's will is revealed through gurus, and so on. To be religious, therefore, is ultimately to be committed to the *authority* of one such worldview, based on the will of a god or gods. Conversely, to be irreligious—secular—is to *not* be committed to the authority of a religion and its god(s).

Perhaps the most common context for the word *secular* is in how a society runs. For most of history, there has been little or no divide between religion and the state.[1] The official religion of a given country shaped all of its society, institutions, and cultural practices. It was supported financially by public money, and there was a symbiotic relationship between religious and political leaders. In other words, these societies were committed to the *authority* of a particular religion in public life. *It wasn't until the founding of the United States that an explicitly secular country was established.* The US Constitution states, "Congress shall make no law respecting an establishment of religion, or prohibiting the free exercise thereof." This so-called Establishment Clause of the First Amendment ensures that the government will not establish a state-supported church and will not force individuals to practice a particular religion. The United States, therefore, is secular in political structure because it's not committed to the authority of a particular religion in public life. Given our world's long history of problematic church-state entanglement, Christians should be happy to live in a politically secular country with freedom of religion. Secular doesn't necessarily have a negative connotation.

That said, people often misunderstand the nature of our political structure and think it's a constitutional rationale for forcing religious people to keep their beliefs to themselves. They have a mentality of "Yes, fine, believe whatever you want, but don't try to use your religious views to influence public matters—we're a *secular* country." This sentiment, however, is not what was intended by the writers of the Constitution. The Establishment Clause says nothing about how individuals should or shouldn't *use* their religious beliefs to inform their participation in public life—only that the state cannot establish a church and that people are free to exercise the religion of their choice. Although it's become considered uncouth today to openly acknowledge that your religion is what's motivating your view on a public matter, this was never intended to be the case. Our secular society may not be committed to the authority of a particular religion, but individuals who *are* have every right to bring their views into the public square for discussion and consideration.

Many people would read that last paragraph and ask, "But why? Why even try to shape society according to your personal views when you know there are so many conflicting views out there? Why not work toward social harmony by agreeing that everyone should keep their religious beliefs to themselves?"

The key to understanding the answer to those questions is in dispelling the myth of secular neutrality.

The Myth of Secular Neutrality

Our would-be questioners are confusing the secular *structure* of our society (freedom of religion and no state church) with the nature of what we should or shouldn't do with our religious freedom *given* that structure. They're assuming that in the spirit of keeping church and state separate, there's a way to build a worldview-neutral public square—like some kind of pie crust we can all agree on as a foundation for society. As the thinking goes, people should be free to add their religious fillings in private if they're so inclined, but no one should bring a filled cherry pie into public matters—that would be religiously biased! If some prefer blueberry pie, some prefer apple pie, and others prefer pecan pie, we should simply dump the fillings and run society according to the least-common denominator—the pie crust. Then everyone can be at peace and live happily ever after, right?

No, and here's why: There's no such thing as a worldview-neutral pie crust. *By their very nature, societies must function from some idea of what is good and bad, but the definition of good and bad depends on a person's worldview.* Societies make value judgments all the time, such as, What rights should its people have? Who should be protected, how should they be protected, and from what should they be protected? When one person's rights appear to conflict with another person's rights, how should the conflict be resolved? How far should parental rights extend, and how much oversight should the government have in family life? What should be considered criminal behavior? What should be taught in public education? The list could go on and on. The answers to questions like these—questions that every modern society must address—depend on one's assumptions about the existence and nature of God, the will of God (if any), the nature of man, the value and purpose of human life, and much more. These are all worldview questions. That's not to say that everyone who shares a worldview will always agree on how to answer them (or that people with different worldviews will always *disagree*), but rather, that even the most basic questions of how to run a society are inherently connected to assumptions about the nature of reality—*assumptions that aren't universal.* And without universally held assumptions, there's no way to bake a worldview-neutral pie crust.

Perhaps you're thinking of some possible exceptions, so let's look at an example of a value people often think we should all be able to agree on regardless of worldview: the idea of human equality. To be sure, if a person at a dinner party were to casually mention they *don't* believe in human equality, there would be a horrified silence in response, and they'd be encouraged to take their truffles to the door. But as it turns out, this is morally problematic only in polite company. In some (often academic) circles, it's not a foregone conclusion that human beings are equal in value. For example, ethicist Peter Singer is well known for arguing that there are morally justifiable circumstances for killing a disabled infant. Singer says,

> When the death of a disabled infant will lead to the birth of another infant with better prospects of a happy life, the total amount of happiness will be greater if the disabled infant is killed. The loss of the happy life for the first infant is outweighed by the gain of a happier life for the second. Therefore, if killing the hemophiliac infant has no adverse effect on others, it would, according to the total view, be right to kill him.[2]

While many people recoil at Singer's blunt devaluation of the lives of disabled children, such a statement is actually consistent with his atheistic worldview. If God doesn't exist, the universe came into existence by chance, the first living cell developed from nonliving matter by chance, and all living things are the eventual product of the blind, undirected process of evolution. In such a case, there's no objective basis for saying that *any* life has inherent value greater than dust, much less equal value. Singer's criteria for determining who should or shouldn't be killed would be no less moral than anyone else's criteria in an atheistic world. Only if there's an author of life who creates and imbues us with a meaning beyond our physical parts can human life actually be inherently valuable and equally so. While human equality may initially seem like a value we can safely bake into a worldview-neutral pie crust, that's far from the case. It's *inextricably* tied to worldview assumptions.

In short, having a politically secular country doesn't imply that society should then function in some kind of worldview-neutral way. It's not even possible. Answers to basic governing questions will always presuppose certain views of reality. Note that doesn't mean they'll always presuppose the *same* views of reality. Given our country's religious heritage, many values of consensus today are still rooted in a Judeo-Christian worldview (such as the idea of human equality). But as more and more Americans have explicitly rejected Christianity, other values of consensus now presuppose a very different worldview (such as the acceptance of gender fluidity). The result is a public pie crust of values rooted in varied worldviews and shifting over time as consensus changes. And that's exactly what we would *expect* in a country that's not committed to the authority of a particular religion in public life; everyone is free to bring their differing and often conflicting worldviews to bear on public matters. What we *shouldn't* expect is to develop a worldview-neutral pie crust for public life that everyone agrees on. That's a pipe dream.

These realities of living in a politically secular country place Christians at a crossroad today for two reasons. First, the changing religious makeup of our country means that the popular consensus on societal values is now increasingly rooted in a worldview at odds with Christianity. For many years, Christians have enjoyed living in a secular country with freedom of religion while *also* living in a country with people who shared many of our values in public life. With our quickly changing religious landscape, we must now process what it means to live in a secular country where that same freedom of religion has led to a popular consensus at *odds* with our values in public life.

Second, Christians must grapple not only with the result of worldviews organically shifting over time, but also with the increasing militance many are using to proactively *push* Christian values out of public life. For many people today, Christianity isn't just one more worldview in the marketplace of ideas. It's a morally offensive weed preventing the growth of a harmonious and beautiful cultural garden, and it needs to be uprooted at all costs. To understand the significance of both factors— organic shifting and aggressive pushing—we need to now transition from understanding the word *secular* in political terms to understanding it in worldview terms.

Secular(ism)—as a Worldview

When you think of worldviews, you probably think in terms of organized religions—Judaism, Christianity, Hinduism, Islam, Mormonism, and so on. Perhaps less obvious is that atheism is a worldview as well; if a person believes there is no God, that has implications for answers to major questions about the nature of reality (Who are we? Why are we here? What happens after we die?).[3] And perhaps even less obvious is that those who don't associate with a specific religion *or* atheism (for example, those who say they're "spiritual, not religious") also have a worldview. Everyone has a worldview, whether they've consciously arrived at their answers to life's biggest questions or not. But with so many different views of reality shaping people's thought lives, how is it that we see such clear cultural trends toward the same ways of thinking?

Enter *secularism*, an umbrella term for a variety of worldviews that ultimately function in the same way—without a commitment to the authority of a religion and its god(s). Just as this meaning of *secular* can be applied to a political structure, it can also be applied to the worldview of individuals and groups of individuals. *The tie that functionally binds the worldviews of millions of people is the authority of the self rather than the authority of any given religion and its god(s).*

People can be just as committed to secularism as they are to a religion. That's because secularism isn't what you get when you simply subtract so-called religious beliefs from a person's worldview. As in the political sense of the word, there's no worldview-neutral pie crust for the individual. When you take away the authority of a religion and its god(s), you aren't left with *no* authority—you're left with the authority of the self. And the umbrella worldview of self-authority has its own assumptions, beliefs, and prescriptions for life. Let's look at how that plays out in the secular view of three major worldview subjects: God, man, and morality.

The Secular View of God

In saying that secularism is a matter of worldview authority, it's important to underscore that this doesn't necessarily imply atheism.

Only about 10 percent of Americans say they don't believe in any higher power or spiritual force.[4] That means 90 percent of people believe something or someone exists out there, whatever that might mean to a given person. The following findings from Pew Research give some insight into what those eclectic spiritual beliefs are:

- 74 percent of Americans say they talk to their God/higher power

- 56 percent believe their God/higher power is all-knowing, all-powerful, and all-loving (even if it's not the God of the Bible)

- 42 percent believe spiritual energy is located in physical things like mountains

- 41 percent believe in psychics

- 33 percent believe in reincarnation

- 29 percent believe in astrology

As you can see, there's no lack of spirituality among Americans. But, as we saw in chapter 1, the vast majority don't view the Bible or other holy books as authoritative for their lives. They might have some level of respect for various scriptures revered by religious adherents, but not in the sense of consistently submitting their own lives to those teachings. Some of the general moral principles, like loving others? Sure. But specific teachings that require significant personal commitment and are at odds with the popular consensus, like a biblical view of sexuality? Likely not.

It's important to see, therefore, that belief in a generic god or spiritual force is perfectly at home in secularism as long as that belief requires nothing other than what a person decides it requires for themself. Secularism can readily accommodate a generic god who requires nothing, but not a specific one who requires everything.

In summary, a secular view of God isn't necessarily that God doesn't exist, but rather that any God who *may* exist has not given us any kind of reliable, binding revelation. If He exists, He remains comfortably in the distance, content to leave us to the authority of ourselves.

The Secular View of Humanity

The nature of man is something philosophers, theologians, and scientists have grappled with for ages. Are we merely a collection of atoms, or something more? If more, what kind of more? If a soul exists, what is the relationship between the soul and the body?

In a secular worldview, there's no divine and authoritative revelation on the nature of man to look to, so what we can know about our human identity—at least with any epistemic confidence—is limited to what we can know from science at a given time. What do scientists say? The mainstream scientific consensus is that all life developed from a single-celled organism that lived roughly 3.5 billion years ago. According to evolutionary theory, the process of natural selection acting on random mutations to DNA has produced the wide variety of life forms we see today, including humankind. Furthermore, it's assumed that the evolutionary process is blind and purposeless—not directed toward any goal. (The exception to this is "evolutionary creationism," which is a belief that God *directed* the process of evolution.)[5] Given this picture from mainstream science, man is not the product of a purposeful creator, but rather, the product of an indifferent chance process. This also implies that man is different from other living things only in degree, not kind. We're simply a highly developed animal lucky to have come into existence after billions of years.

In case it's not obvious why this secular view of man is so different from a religious one, consider what the Bible says about the nature of man as one example (other holy books would make other claims). In a biblical worldview, humans are the purposeful product of a creator. We were *intended* to exist. Importantly, the Bible says we're made in the image of God Himself—a fact that fundamentally sets us apart from animals (Genesis 1:27). While Christian theologians debate what exactly the image of God encompasses, it's generally agreed that it refers to our moral nature and our ability to enter into a relationship with God. Beyond the creation account in Genesis, the rest of the Bible reveals that God has a moral law for humanity, that every human has transgressed that law ("sinned"), that He sent a Savior—Jesus, who is God Himself—to rescue us from the consequences of sin, that those who put their trust in Jesus's sacrifice on the cross for sin will have everlasting life with Him, and that He will eventually return to judge all of humankind. *This is a very specific account of who man is.*

The secular and biblical views of man could not possibly be more different. If we're no more than a product of blind chance, we belong to ourselves and are "the measure of all things," as the ancient Greek philosopher Protagoras famously said. We owe no one anything. We can "follow our hearts" all day long because whatever *we* want is all that matters. If, however, there's a supernatural creator who has brought us into existence and has specifically revealed our identity and purposes, we ignore that information at our own peril.

The Secular View of Morality

The secular view of God and man boils down to the idea that we're free to be who we want to be and do what we want to do because there's no higher-than-human authority who's given us specific information about or directives for our lives. It would logically follow, then, that a secular view of morality is one in which everything is relative to individual preferences and nothing is right or wrong for all people. Interestingly, however, that's actually *not* the functioning view of morality in secular culture today. Instead, our culture often believes it can and should determine what's right and wrong for *everyone* based on the shifting sands of popular consensus. And if you disagree with that consensus, there will be no pat on the back for following your own heart. You can only follow your own heart if it leads you to the same conclusions about morality as everyone else.

It doesn't take much to see that secular culture is anything but devoid of moral judgments, despite having no objective basis or authority for making them. Consider, for instance, organizations that exist explicitly to support secularism. These groups aren't merely bringing irreligious people together for some kind of worldview-neutral community that gardens together on Saturdays. They nearly always express the importance of promoting specific moral values. As one example, the collegiate Secular Student Alliance (SSA) says it "empowers secular students to proudly express their identity, build welcoming communities, promote secular values, and set a course for lifelong activism."[6] This statement assumes, of course, that there's secular agreement on what good values are and that they're worth fighting for over a lifetime. A quick look over the SSA website reveals that some of the organization's values include keeping abortion legal, advocating for further political separation of church and state, promoting diverse sexual lifestyles, and planning events to highlight the supremacy of science and reason over faith (a false dichotomy, but we'll get to that in chapter 4). Clearly, the SSA assumes that if you're irreligious, you'll agree that these are the good and important values to hold—even though there's nothing about a secular worldview that would logically necessitate or even imply moral agreement. It just comes back to whatever is right according to today's consensus.

As another example, consider the Satanic Temple. While that sounds like its own kind of religion, the Satanic Temple is actually an organization that exists to promote secularism. And like the SSA, they're far from neutral in their moral judgments. Their tagline is "Empathy. Reason. Advocacy."[7] And they state that their mission is to "encourage benevolence and empathy, reject tyrannical authority, advocate practical common sense, oppose injustice, and undertake noble pursuits." The Temple doesn't leave the definition of these things to the imagination. Their website details the values they fight for, and they closely resemble those of the SSA. Ironically, however, they state, "A unifying attribute of all Satanists is our embrace of our outsider status. Satanists adhere to the principles of individual sovereignty."[8] Aside from the shock value of their name, there's little that makes them an outsider to mainstream secular thought. As we've seen, the principle of "individual sovereignty" is ultimately what *defines* a secular worldview. The Satanic Temple might think they're unique, but they're just one of many organizations promoting the secular moral values upheld by popular consensus. The devil is in the details.

Of course, you don't have to be an organization explicitly dedicated to secularism to promote the values of popular consensus. We're constantly surrounded by the powerful influence of voices informing us of what is culturally acceptable to believe and think. We'll look at that in detail in chapter 3. Suffice it to say for now that the secular moral consensus enjoys both implicit support and proactive promotion from nearly every angle of society.

Secularism: The Inescapable Worldview

The upshot of this analysis is that those with a biblical worldview are not a minority surrounded by a neutral society leaving each to their own, though people often mistakenly think that when they equate the word secular with neutral. As we've seen in this chapter, we're surrounded by *secularism*, which is a worldview unto itself. And it's not just any worldview. It's a worldview that couldn't be at greater odds with Christianity in particular:

- The Bible says that God exists, that He created all people and things, and that He has expressed His will and purposes in Scripture; He's our ultimate authority. Secularism says there may or may not be a god, but if there is one, he's content to leave us to the authority of ourselves.

- The Bible says humankind is uniquely valuable, made for a purpose in the image of God, and accountable to God. Secularism says man is one living product of many that happened to develop through the blind, undirected process of evolution, and we answer to no one but ourselves.

- The Bible says that God is a moral lawgiver, with His character being the objective standard of goodness. Secularism says (or at least functions as though) right and wrong are determined by popular consensus.

The reason these differences create so much pressure on Christians is that we can't simply separate ourselves from secularism like we can from an individual. *Secularism has become the cultural air in which we live and breathe.* It's literally inescapable. An apt analogy for this tethered relationship is playing a board game.

Imagine sitting down to play a game that some of the players believe was designed to be played in a specific way and for which instructions were given. Those players dutifully begin to read the instructions to understand the rules of the game and plan to play accordingly. Meanwhile, other players believe the game wasn't designed with any purpose in mind and that the so-called instructions are just some interesting ideas people had for how to play. They decide to make up their own rules as they go along and play the game however they want. When they begin playing in ways that don't align with the instructions, the instruction-following players say, "Hey! That's not how you're *supposed* to play!" and point to the instructions. The others just laugh, not believing there are any external constraints on how to use the game. Soon, more and more people join in, all agreeing that game play is a free-for-all. Over time, the instruction-following players are far outnumbered, with hardly anyone caring what the instructions say. The rule-followers are dismissed as annoying bystanders.

In an actual board game, this wouldn't be a big deal. If you're an instruction-follower, you can just get up and leave. But what if you *had* to play the game? What if it were an integral part of your everyday life you couldn't simply sit out, and you had to find ways to play along with people who wanted to make up their own rules? That's essentially the position Christians are in right now, where the game is life in our culture. Every day is a push and pull of competing worldviews in politics, media, entertainment, education, and much more. As secularism becomes the prevailing worldview that Christians encounter at every turn, more and more of us are mixing these mainstream secular ideas with biblical views. We take some ideas from the "instruction" book (the Bible) and some from what secular players come up with on their own. The resulting worldview is often more secular than biblical—a hybrid that's no longer faithful to the Bible, whether we realize it or not.

What makes secularism so compelling that we would allow that to happen (either intentionally or not)? That's our subject for chapter 3.

QUESTIONS FOR DISCUSSION OR REFLECTION

1. In your own words, how would you describe the difference in meaning between secular in a political sense and secular in a worldview sense?

2. Given the discussion in this chapter, why do you think a celebrity could thank God for something without much notice, but if they were to talk about their love for *Jesus* or declare their view that the Bible is the Word of God, they would likely be subject to hostile criticism?

3. Why do you think the functioning view of morality in secular culture is *not* one in which literally "everything goes," but rather, is one in which good and bad are defined by popular consensus and applied to everyone?

4. Has secularism felt like an inescapable worldview in your own life—one that constantly surrounds you? If so, what are the ways in which you most encounter it? If not, why do you think that is?

CHAPTER 3

Why Secularism Is Compelling— Even for Christians

*It's a worldview that's
ready-made for influence*

My family loves camping, but it's not always easy to find campgrounds that are a reasonable distance for a quick getaway from where we live in Southern California. When I was talking about this dilemma with a couple of friends one day, they mentioned a promising campground I hadn't heard of. There was just one catch: It was a membership-based campground, and the only way you could stay as a nonmember is if you agreed to listen to their sales presentation for an hour during your visit. One hour didn't sound like that big of a deal, so we looked into it, booked a campsite for the weekend, and packed our stuff.

After we arrived, my husband and I were taken to a tiny sales room with a wobbly round table and three chairs. The walls were covered with grainy photographs of uninspiring "sister" campgrounds where members had the questionable privilege of staying. Bob, the salesman, began his presentation by giving us a verbal quiz on our preferred camping features so he could assess what was important to us before making his pitch. He started down the long list of features with an optimistic tone, but he sounded utterly defeated by the time he got to the end—there was *nothing* on the list we could say was important to us. When we go camping, we prefer quiet campgrounds in high mountains, no organized camper activities, few fellow campers, and feeling as close to nature as possible. Bob's list included things like karaoke nights, basketball courts, an on-site minimart, a kids' club for planned camping activities, and a hot tub.

Nothing could possibly sound worse to our family of nature-seeking introverts.

We thought Bob would see that what he was offering didn't line up with what we wanted and would let us go. But he was undeterred. He turned to me ever so seriously and asked, "Natasha, do you like margaritas?" He confidently proceeded to pull out pictures (possibly from about 20 years ago) of a sister campground somewhere in Mexico where we could camp *and* have margaritas with fellow campers, should we join their club.

Bob *really* didn't understand what we wanted out of camping.

That brings us to the focus of this chapter. There's a reason secularism is so influential and Bob was not. Understanding that reason, with a little background from the field of marketing, can give us valuable insight into the nature of secularism's impact in our everyday lives. Now, I realize that sounds a bit strange—what does marketing have to do with secular influence?—but let me explain.

The Nature of Influence

My professional background is in marketing. I have an MBA in marketing and statistics and was a marketing executive and adjunct market research professor before I became an author. People have all kinds of different ideas in mind when they think of marketing, but at its core, marketing is simply the discipline of how to effectively get a given message to a given audience in order to *influence* them in some way. Humans have an innate sense of how to influence one another, but marketers take their understanding of influence several steps further.

They analyze the art and science of influence through studies in human psychology and other relevant disciplines. As you might imagine, those research findings are extensive, but for our current purpose, here's what you need to know. Influence is overwhelmingly the product of two key factors: the *relevance* and the *prominence* of a given message.

Relevance is about how well a message meets a person's *felt needs*. Our salesman friend Bob was very smart to start his presentation by going through a list of campground features in order to figure out what we most felt the need for in camping. That way, he could optimize the relevance of the rest of his presentation by speaking directly to those needs. Unfortunately for Bob, we didn't feel the need for any of what he had to offer. No matter how much he would try to influence us to become members so we could share margaritas with other campers in Mexico, it wasn't going to work.

Prominence is about how ubiquitous a message is. The most relevant message in the world can go unnoticed if it's heard or seen only once in passing. The more a person is exposed to a given message, the more influential it has the potential to be. Because Bob's presentation didn't hit on our felt needs—it wasn't *relevant* to us—there's probably no amount of prominence that could have made it more influential. Hearing about campground karaoke offerings every day for a month, for example, would only lead to intense annoyance.

However, you can probably think of certain products you didn't initially feel the need for but eventually bought because you had heard so much about them. For example, I had heard about the iPhone for years before I became convinced that I needed one. I had seen ads in all kinds of places, had noted people using them everywhere I went, and had been exposed to them in a number of beautiful Apple stores. The iPhone had become *prominent*, which led me to become a cultural sheep and buy one too. In cases like this, prominence itself can shape a person's felt needs.

The key takeaway is this: People are most influenced when (1) a message directly speaks to strongly felt needs, and (2) that message is prominent in their life. Whereas Bob didn't have either of these criteria going for his presentation, secularism has both.

The (Felt) Relevance of Secularism

If the messages of secular culture were irrelevant to people—not hitting on any felt needs—they wouldn't be very influential. But a major reason they *are* so influential is that they speak to the things that we as humans, by our very nature, want to hear most. The apostle Paul gives us insight into those basic desires in Ephesians 2:1-3:

> As for you, you were dead in your transgressions and sins, in which you used to live when you followed the ways of this world and of the ruler of the kingdom of the air, the spirit who is now at work in those who are disobedient. All of us also lived among them at one time, gratifying the cravings of our flesh and following its desires and thoughts. Like the rest, we were by nature deserving of wrath.

In this passage, we learn that humans are, by nature, in a state of disobedience to God and deserving of wrath. In other words, we want to go our own way rather than God's way. You might say we want to resort to the authority of the *self* rather than the authority of our *Creator* (see also Romans 6:6; 7:5; 1 John 1:8; 2 Peter 1:4). Sound familiar? That's precisely the distinction between the secular and Christian worldviews that we discussed in chapter 2.

A major reason secularism is so influential is that it appeals directly to the desires of our fallen nature—it reinforces the desired authority of the self.

People feel the need to be autonomous, and secular culture is ready and willing to tell us what we want to hear. While these messages can take on endless forms, we can broadly summarize the nature of most of them in just four statements: Feelings are the ultimate guide, happiness is the ultimate goal, judging is the ultimate sin, and God is the ultimate guess. Understanding how these core messages speak to people's felt needs of self-authority is a major key to understanding why secularism is so influential.

Feelings Are the Ultimate Guide

As I briefly referenced in the previous chapter, the message that we should follow our hearts is in some way, shape, or form continually trumpeted throughout popular culture. If you search online for "follow your heart" quotes, for example, you'll find endless social media images with messages like these:

- "Follow your heart, it knows the way" (unattributed).

- "I don't have to prove anything to anyone, I only have to follow my heart and concentrate on what I want to say to the world. I run my world" (attributed to singer Beyoncé).

- "Follow your heart, because if you always trust your mind, you will always act on logic, and logic doesn't always lead to happiness" (unattributed).

- "You do have to follow your heart, otherwise you're living a false life" (attributed to actor Eric Mabius).

- "Follow your heart, it's always right" (unattributed).

- "Break the rules, stand apart, ignore your head, and follow your heart" (attributed to singer Paula Abdul).

What do all these types of messages assume? That you should be led by how you feel because feelings are the most reliable guide to what you should do in life. This is the ultimate appeal to self-authority because only *you* know how you feel, so only *you* can guide yourself if feelings do indeed take priority. In essence, you are your own self-sufficient expert on reality.

Of course, it doesn't take much to show how hard it is to live consistently within such a view. If I feel that I should kill someone, should I still follow my heart to do so? It would be *consistent* with a worldview built on self-authority to say that I should—no one can tell me what I should feel or do—but few people would be willing to say that. As we saw in chapter 2, the supposed freedom of secular morality is limited by the bounds of popular consensus. At least for now, that consensus excludes murder from the list of acceptable human behaviors (unless we're talking about the killing of *preborn* humans—in today's culture, that's another subject).

Happiness Is the Ultimate Goal

Whether explicitly stated or not, in secular messages, happiness is typically the assumed goal of life. This makes perfect sense for a worldview rooted in self-authority because happiness is subjective—it's based on our old friend, feelings. One person may feel happiest living on the streets as a drug user, another person may feel happiest dedicating their life to saving baby iguanas, and yet another person may feel happiest continually pursuing new sexual partners. If the ultimate goal is happiness, and happiness is based on (subjective) feelings, then only the individual can determine what their life should look like. *In this view, the only measure of life success is whether a person has been in touch with their feelings enough to know and pursue what would make them happiest.*

This single-minded focus on happiness as a goal is on display in many forms of secular culture, but one prime exhibit is in self-help books—especially those targeted at women. Consider Glennon Doyle's best-selling book *Untamed* as one example.[1] Doyle made headlines in 2016 when she left her husband and the father of her three kids for a lesbian relationship. At the time, she was known as a "Christian mom blogger." In *Untamed*, Doyle documents (and glorifies) how she unlearned everything she had been taught about family, sex, love, God, and Christianity in order to find happiness. Her core message to women is this: Break free from whatever constraints you've been conditioned to think you have and embrace your inner wild side. If you do, you'll be *happy*.[2]

Doyle's memoir debuted at number one on *The New York Times* nonfiction best-seller list in 2020 and stayed there for seven weeks. The reviews from secular media were glowing. *People* magazine made it a book of the week, raving, "Doyle might just be the patron saint of female empowerment...Here she inspires other women to listen to their intuition and break free of what cages them...Her memoir has a message as clear as a 'go' signal: Find and honor your truest self."[3]

Kirkus Reviews called her book "an in-depth look at a courageous woman eager to share the wealth of her experiences by embracing vulnerability and reclaiming her inner strength and resiliency…[an] inspiring chronicle of female empowerment and the rewards of self-awareness and renewal." Celebrities such as Adele, Debra Messing, Reese Witherspoon, Kristen Bell, and Sara Bareilles offered gushing endorsements, with Bareilles calling it a "gospel of truth."[4]

Did you note the theme of the comments here? Happiness involves "courageously" leaving behind any external expectations, boundaries, and goals in order to be true solely to yourself. *That* is what's strong, inspiring, self-aware, and worthy of the greatest praise in secular culture. And it's a message that deeply resonates with what our fallen nature wants to hear: Your happiness is of utmost importance, and only *you* can decide what will make you happy—you're the boss.

Judging Is the Ultimate Sin

So far, we've seen how secular culture says we should navigate through life (by feelings) and where we should navigate to (happiness). But how should we relate to one another along the way? That's where our third message comes in.

If anything at all is classified as sin in secular culture, it's the act of "judging" others. Go ahead and follow your heart and pursue your own happiness, but don't stop along the way to claim that someone else is following *their* heart or pursuing *their* happiness wrongly. If you want to come alongside another person to love and help them on their journey, that entails affirming (1) their chosen path and (2) the nature of what happiness means to them. Questioning the path *or* the nature of their chosen happiness is off limits. That's "judgmental," and it's equated with hate.

There are numerous examples of this view in culture, but let's consider a particularly striking one from the world of homeless services. You might assume that a key objective for organizations serving the homeless is to help those who struggle with addictions to get clean so they can prepare to obtain a job and become financially stable. But many secular homeless services have instead adopted what's known as a "harm-reduction" philosophy. According to Harm Reduction International:

> Harm reduction refers to policies, [programs] and practices that aim to [minimize] negative health, social and legal impacts associated with drug use, drug policies and drug laws. Harm reduction is grounded in justice and human rights—it focuses on positive change and on working with people without judgement…Harm reduction practitioners accept people who use drugs as they are and are committed to meeting them "where they are" in their lives without judgement.[5]

What does this nonjudgmental philosophy look like in practice? As one example, Seattle's Downtown Emergency Service Center (DESC) is passing out heroin pipes and providing taxpayer-funded "booty-bumping" kits to addicts (booty-bumping is the rectal administration of drugs). DESC promotes their offerings with flyers around the downtown area that excitedly announce with three exclamation points, "New at the Nav!!!" and highlight how the kits are a "good choice if your veins are hard to hit," provide "less risk of infection and abscesses," and don't "leave tracks."[6] From the harm-reduction perspective, this kind of approach is where "love meets the streets," as one organization puts it.[7]

While many readers would shake their heads at how the facilitation of rectal drug use is in any way loving, it's perfectly consistent with the secular view that love means affirming whatever journey a person wants to be on. *The more we hear from culture that judging someone else's choices is wrong, the more we feel affirmed that any criticism we receive must be ill-conceived.* These messages continually offer validation that we're each in a cocoon of untouchable self-authority—just what we want to hear.

God Is the Ultimate Guess

So where does God fit into these core secular messages? As we saw in the previous chapter, a secular view can accommodate a generic belief in the supernatural as long as it doesn't *require* anything from a person—so God isn't necessarily out of the picture. What *is* out of the picture, however, is any claim that it can be known with *confidence* that God exists, has revealed His will to us, and has authority over our lives. If that knowledge were attainable, it would clearly contradict the secular dogma that we're accountable only to ourselves. Christians, of course, believe a confident knowledge of this nature *is* attainable given the evidence for God's existence and the reliability of the Bible. But the presupposition of secularism is that confidence in the truth of any particular religious worldview is unfounded. What results is an over-arching message of ambiguity that might best be summed up as "God is the ultimate guess."

Ironically, this works itself out in two conflicting ideas. The first is the superficially friendly idea that all roads lead to God or that all religions are equally true. This belief is right at home with the secular trifecta of following your heart, seeking happiness, and not judging others. After all, if all religions are equal in truth value, you can't go wrong! No matter what you land on, you win. Simply pick and choose from whatever beliefs you feel are helpful and make you happy. In this sense, God is a "guess" in that cosmic truth is perceived to be far beyond what we could ever understand, so religions are all equally valid attempts to explain the mysteries of reality. There's no certainty, only comfortable guesswork that ensures no one can ever be wrong. Once again, the individual maintains incontestable authority.

Interestingly, the idea that all religions are equally true competes with a second secular idea that all religions are equally *false*. For those who hold this perspective, God is a guess in the sense that there's no good reason to believe He exists, but if you want to take a blind leap of faith and live your life based on total speculation, knock yourself out (as long as you keep those beliefs to yourself). Some take this further to say that those blind leaps that religious people take are inevitably *harmful* to the rest of society, so it's in the best interest of the world to eradicate the "superstition" of religion altogether.

In short, secular messages about God are rooted in the assumption that confidence in the truth of any specific religious worldview is unfounded. This uncertainty lays the necessary groundwork for the self to take its place of authority: God is anyone's guess, so *we're* free to be in charge.

The Bible tells us that those who are in Christ have been given a new nature (Ephesians 4:22-24), that we're no longer slaves to sin (Romans 6:6), and that we're a "new creation" (2 Corinthians 5:17). But that doesn't mean we're never tempted again by our old nature. We are always at war with the flesh, pulled toward going our own way instead of God's way. *This is why secular messages are attractive not only to non-Christians but to all of humanity—we all share a nature that desires self-rule.* Put simply, secular messages are influential in large part because they speak to what we want to hear. But recall from our earlier discussion that this (felt) relevance is only half of the picture. Influence is a factor of both relevance *and* prominence. Now we'll look at the other half of the picture.

The *Prominence* of Secularism

A few minutes ago as I was writing this, I received a text from my husband, Bryan. He asked, "Should we perhaps consider getting a new mattress?" His question seemed to come out of nowhere, so I asked why this was suddenly top of mind. He replied, "I don't know. I'm wondering if my sleep can be better. We could get the one with that 'Sleep Number' system where we can each have our own settings! I always see the ads. Sleep is important." When I chided him for being overly enthusiastic about mattresses in his mid-forties, he jokingly shot back, "Well, I can't help it if I keep seeing Sleep Number ads and for the first time in my life wondered if that product was actually right for us!"

That's marketing *prominence* in action. Bryan had seen the ads over and over until he had become convinced that he needed what this mattress company had to offer. Similarly, the impact of secular messages is multiplied a thousandfold because they're everywhere we go today, like a ubiquitous ad campaign for how we should view reality. These messages aren't merely plastered around us like billboards that are easily ignored. In many cases, they're being actively pushed toward us by a complex array of social forces. *Relevance and prominence together equal influence, but influence plus social force can equal pressure—pressure to believe, think, and live like the majority.* In the upcoming chapters, we'll look in detail at specific types of secular pressures that Christians face in each of these areas. But to get us thinking about how all these messages become prominent in the first place, let's look at two of secular culture's most significant message distributors: social media and mainstream media.

For many people, the prominence of the secular worldview starts with social media. Research shows that about 80 percent of Americans use social media, up from just 21 percent in 2009.[8] And not only do most people now use social media, they use it frequently. Facebook, for example, is the most popular platform, with 69 percent of American adults using it, and about 75 percent of those users visit the site every day.[9] Across all platforms, the average daily time spent on social media is more than *two hours*.[10] And we're not just passively consuming cat memes during those hours. We're experiencing the pressure (both subtle and blatant) of continually watching how our social groups process the world—through the nature of what they share, how they comment, what they give "likes" to, and much more. This isn't specific to Christians; it's the nature of how social media impacts everyone. But for those of us who *are* in a worldview minority, social media can ironically make us feel more alone than ever when we sense just how differently we view the world than everyone else. If we're not well-grounded in our worldview, we can easily start grafting parts of other worldviews onto our own without realizing it or slip into thinking that we must be wrong just because we're different.

The impact of social media content is often multiplied by the power of "influencers"—personalities with very large followings—who can persuasively push ideas to the front of our cultural consciousness. Take, for example, Rhett McLaughlin and Link Neal, the hosts of the popular YouTube comedy channel *Good Mythical Morning*. The two made headlines in 2020 when they announced to their 17 million subscribers that they were both leaving the Christian faith. Rhett and Link each published their own deconversion videos, which walked fans through the many reasons they had become agnostic. Within hours, social media had exploded with people sharing the videos and thousands commenting on their own uncertainties and skepticism about Christianity. By the next day, there were parents everywhere in online groups talking about how their kids had watched the videos and had started to question their own faith. That's just a *single* example of the power of social media today, and it rocked the lives of many. One You-Tube video, Facebook post, Instagram post, or tweet can generate such a large cultural response that within hours everyone is talking about something that just a day before wasn't even on their radar.

Then there's mainstream media—traditional news outlets, such as television networks, newspapers, and magazines. When I started college as a journalism major in the mid-1990s, it was a given that your journalistic goal was to present news as objectively as possible. Today, it's a given that nearly every news outlet reports to at least some degree along ideological lines.[11] Those lines often reveal a strong secular worldview bias. In saying that, I'm not suggesting that mainstream media should be reporting from a Christian perspective. But as we discussed in chapter 2, it's important to remember that secularism isn't neutral, so it follows that secular media will reflect a secular worldview.

This worldview bias has implications for both the nature of stories selected and how those stories are presented. One study, for example, showed that the major broadcast networks gave three times more airtime to the pro-choice Women's March than to the pro-life March for Life, despite comparable participant numbers and location.[12] If you had been watching these networks, it would have been easy to assume that the pro-choice Women's March was far more culturally significant, even if that wasn't necessarily the case.

In another study, sociologists researched potential religious bias in the press by providing a group of journalists with would-be stories based on similar news scenarios, but differing in key details.[13] Their objective was to determine whether the journalists would write different narratives depending on the nature of the information given. One of these scenarios concerned a shooting inside a religious building. Half of the journalists were told the building was a *church*. The other half were told the building was a *mosque*. In a second scenario, journalists were told about a professor making hateful comments. Half were told the comments were *Christianophobic*, while the other half were told the comments were *homophobic*. The researchers found that news outlets agreed to run the stories equally, but the differing details determined *how* the journalists talked about what happened. In the case of the homophobic professor, the press highlighted hate speech and whether the professor should be fired; in the case of the anti-Christian professor, the press highlighted the right to free speech. Similarly, in the case of the mosque shooting, the journalists focused on hate crimes and bigotry, while in the case of the church shooting, they focused on the shooter.

Editorial decisions like these are made thousands of times every day, and the collective outcome strongly shapes what we understand to be happening, what's acceptable to talk about, what's important to talk about, and what's "normal" to think. If we were in the early 1980s, we might see that play out in more diverse ways—at the time, there were fifty independent companies that owned the majority of media in the US. But by 2011, just *six* conglomerates controlled 90 percent of media.[14] When a handful of companies control nearly all media outlets, it shouldn't surprise us to see relative uniformity of thought.

Of course it's not just media (whether social or mainstream) that makes the secular worldview so prominent in our lives. If you were to shut yourself off from every mainstream media outlet and never use social media, you would still encounter a prominent secularism in personal relationships, academia, entertainment, professional relationships, businesses you patronize, organizations you belong to, and even possibly in your church (see chapter 5). Secularism is everywhere we go today. We can't escape it, but we can better equip ourselves to live with biblical clarity given the reality of it.

Regaining Biblical Clarity

What we've seen in these first three chapters is that we're in a worldview minority, that the secular worldview of the majority is at fundamental odds with the biblical worldview, and that, despite those stark differences, the nature of secularism still lends itself to influencing Christians. To be clear, my intent is not to say, "Poor us…I can't believe our fragile eyes and ears are being so exposed to non-Christian ways of thinking. Can you believe what the world is doing to us?" That's a victim mentality, and that's not a mindset we want to have. Rather, the goal of these initial chapters is to factually describe the way things *are* as a preface for considering how Christians should *respond*.

It's time now to drill down from the 10,000-foot level of understanding our general situation to looking at nine specific types of pressure we're encountering. I've divided these pressures into categories of believing, thinking, and living because I think that's a helpful way of remembering that a biblical worldview should shape every aspect of our lives. We need clarity of belief to shape clarity of thought, and clarity of both belief *and* thought to provide clarity for living. When we regain biblical clarity in all three areas, our faithful differences will transform us into the salt and light we're called to be.

QUESTIONS FOR DISCUSSION OR REFLECTION

1. In what areas of your life do you feel the pull toward the "authority of the self"?

2. What are some examples you can think of where a person's focus on striving toward what makes them feel happiest could actually lead to despair?

3. How would you describe why judging is considered to be the "ultimate sin" in a secular worldview?

4. What are some key ways in which you see mainstream media, academia, entertainment, or businesses making the secular worldview prominent in everyday life?

PART 2:

FAITHFULLY DIFFERENT *BELIEVING*

CHAPTER 4

Regaining a Supernatural Worldview

Under the pressure of secular naturalism

Popular comedian Ricky Gervais once wrote a piece featured in *The Wall Street Journal* titled "Why I'm an Atheist."[1] Gervais began:

> Why don't you believe in God? I get that question all the time. I always try to give a sensitive, reasoned answer. This is usually awkward, time consuming and pointless. People who believe in God don't need proof of his existence, and they certainly don't want evidence to the contrary…I still give my logical answer because I feel that not being honest would be patronizing and impolite. It is ironic therefore that "I don't believe in God because there is absolutely no scientific evidence for his existence and from what I've heard the very definition is a logical impossibility in this known universe," comes across as both patronizing and impolite.

Gervais went on to explain why he's chosen "science over God":

> Science seeks the truth. And it does not discriminate. For better or worse it finds things out. Science is humble. It

knows what it knows and it knows what it doesn't know. It bases its conclusions and beliefs on hard evidence—evidence that is constantly updated and upgraded.

He then described how he challenges religious people:

> Since the beginning of recorded history, which is defined by the invention of writing by the Sumerians around 6,000 years ago, historians have cataloged over 3700 supernatural beings, of which 2870 can be considered deities. So next time someone tells me they believe in God, I'll say "Oh which one? Zeus? Hades? Jupiter? Mars? Odin? Thor? Krishna? Vishnu? Ra?..." If they say "Just God. I only believe in the one God," I'll point out that they are nearly as atheistic as me. I don't believe in 2870 gods, and they don't believe in 2869.

While I'm pulling these quotes from a single article, they read like a summary of the most common talking points atheists raise about religion today: There's no evidence for God's existence, people who believe in God do so in spite of the lack of evidence, science and religion are mutually exclusive, and belief in God is just plain silly (which anyone should be able to see, given all the ancient gods people no longer worship). Some atheists extend this a step further to say that not only is belief in God silly, it's *harmful*, and such belief should be eradicated from society.

In chapter 2, we saw that only about 10 percent of Americans say they don't believe in any kind of higher power or spiritual force. While that's a small minority, it's often a very vocal one. Many, like Gervais, are actively engaged in promoting an atheistic worldview or critiquing a theistic one by publishing articles, creating and sharing social media content, advocating for political causes related to greater separation of church and state, and much more. Of course, there's nothing wrong with that. In a free, secular country, everyone has the right to engage in these ways. But it does mean that as we begin this section on faithfully different believing, we need to start with the most foundational belief we have—that God exists. That's no longer a belief our culture takes for granted, and it's one that's increasingly being challenged and mocked in the public eye.

To understand why these atheistic challenges have resulted in significant worldview pressure for many Christians, we have to first understand the nature of naturalism and how it has slowly made its way to becoming a default functioning worldview today.

Naturalism: The Modern Default

An atheist once commented on my blog, "I know there was no resurrection because I know from science that dead people stay dead."

I'll never forget that comment because of how, well, stupid it made me feel. At the time, I was a relatively new blogger writing about Christian parenting. I had started receiving a steady stream of comments like this from skeptics who wanted to challenge pretty much everything I wrote. But despite being a lifelong Christian, I didn't really know how to respond. With this comment in particular, I felt stupid not because I thought it was right, but because I didn't know how to put my finger on what about it was *wrong*. The best I could come up with at the time was something to the effect of, "Well, Jesus is God, so He can do anything!" From a Christian perspective, that's true of course, but it's a statement that dances around a much more fundamental point: This commenter was presupposing a *naturalistic worldview*.

Generally speaking, *naturalism* is the belief that the natural world is all that exists. The term is sometimes further nuanced in certain contexts. For example, *methodological naturalism* is the belief that only natural laws and forces operate in the universe. Something or someone could theoretically exist outside of our natural world, but even if it does, it's irrelevant because we can't detect it.

For our purposes, however, we'll consider naturalism to be the basic idea that "the universe is all that is or ever was or ever will be," as astronomer Carl Sagan famously said in his *Cosmos* series. A naturalistic *worldview*, then, is a worldview based on this belief. When my commenter said he knew from science that dead people stay dead, he was speaking from the assumptions of his naturalistic worldview: All that exists is the natural world, and according to the laws of our natural world, dead people do not come back to life in a resurrected body. End of story.

From about AD 1500 until today, a major shift has been occurring in Western society. This shift has increasingly made naturalism the default functioning worldview. Philosopher Charles Taylor insightfully probes the depth of this shift and what it means for us today in his landmark book *A Secular Age*.[2] He sets up his nearly 900-page work with the question, "Why was it virtually impossible not to believe in God in, say, 1500 in our Western society, while in 2000 many of us find this not only easy, but even inescapable?" Taylor traces the answer to that question through the last five centuries to identify what makes something believable or unbelievable and how the conditions of belief have fundamentally changed. At the risk of oversimplifying this massive work, I want to highlight some key points that are particularly relevant to our current topic.

In late medieval times, every aspect of the social order was permeated by belief in the transcendent (that which exists beyond nature). People lived in what Taylor calls an "enchanted" world, in which a continuous relationship between the transcendent and immanent was assumed (immanent meaning the natural world). That's not to say that no one was an atheist, but that the transcendent was so taken for granted by the social order that atheism was almost inconceivable; it was far more difficult to *not* believe than *to* believe, given the social reinforcement of belief at every turn. Over the next few hundred years, however, significant societal shifts took place that culminated in the reverse: a modern social order that often makes it harder *to* believe than *not*.

Beginning in the periods of the Scientific Revolution (mid-1500s to late-1600s) and the Enlightenment (1700s), there came a new emphasis on science and human reason. Prominent thinkers began challenging ideas that had been held for centuries regarding topics like the nature of man, sources of authority, the role of government, and the structure of society. They also began to apply this emphasis to religion: What can we know about God strictly through reason and the senses? For many of the day, the result of this query was deism—belief in a God who set the world in motion and whose existence can be inferred from nature, but who hasn't otherwise revealed Himself. For many others, the result was full-blown atheism. In *both* cases, however, man came to be seen as a self-sufficient island of reason, able to discover the nature of the world and morality without any need for external revelation.

With religion no longer viewed as necessary for creating a moral social order, the road was paved for countries to become politically secular. And that secularization had profound significance for those living in such societies. *One's belief in God, or in the Christian God more specifically, would no longer be continually reinforced by social structures built on those worldview assumptions.* Christianity became just one of many worldview options considered plausible. Whereas atheism may have felt inconceivable in medieval times, it was now a live option.

Fast-forward to today. Taylor calls our present age "haunted." Everyone longs for meaning, but we encounter so many options that we often lack confidence in our own beliefs. We're haunted by the realization that any belief is contestable today, and it leaves us with a sense of unease. That sense of unease grows when we perceive that more and more people are finding our own beliefs to be implausible—and that's exactly what's happening today for Christians. As more and more people abandon Christianity and theism in general, naturalism increasingly becomes the default worldview we encounter in society. And it's not just atheists who have a naturalistic worldview.[3] In a functional sense, the many people who believe in a nonspecific God often live their day-to-day lives *as though* this world is all there is. The fact that we're increasingly surrounded by even a functional naturalism creates a certain sense of cognitive pressure: Why are so many other people convinced that God doesn't exist or that He's not in any way active if He does? Am I really so sure He's there? And when those who hold to a strict naturalism are vocal in *proactively* challenging our beliefs, the pressure can become even greater. Any unease we might already have felt in this "haunted" age is magnified to a level that's hard to ignore.

Pressing On Our Unease

This brings us full circle to the Ricky Gervaises of today. While comments like those from his *Wall Street Journal* article may seem like an off-the-cuff rant about religion, they're actually deeply rooted in the history at which we just looked. Gervais assumes naturalism and sees religion as a premodern way of life—from before we "learned" evidence-based ways of thinking in the Scientific Revolution and Enlightenment. When people see religion as the primitive ancestor of a modern naturalism, don't expect to see dispassionate comparisons of worldviews. Religion, from this perspective, is not just a worldview that's *different* from naturalism, it's a worldview that's *intellectually inferior* to it. Religion represents all that we should have grown out of as a society after the developments of the last 500 years.

The intellectual mockery that results from this view of history takes a variety of forms. We're going to look at five of the most common ones so we can see how the same underlying idea manifests itself in multiple ways. Once we better understand what this looks like in popular culture, we'll talk about how to think critically about these claims.

Religion Is Anti-Reason, Anti-Science, and Anti-Evidence

> The greatest conflict of the 21st century...will be between modern civilization and anti-modernists; between those who believe in the primacy of the individual and those who believe that human beings owe their allegiance and identity to a higher authority...between those who believe in science, reason, and logic and those who believe that truth is revealed through Scripture and religious dogma.[4]
>
> —Robert B. Reich, former Harvard University professor and former Secretary of Labor

Those with a naturalistic worldview often see religion and science as competing epistemologies—ways of obtaining knowledge about the world. You *either* learn about reality from reason, science, and evidence *or* from faith-based revelation, but not both. Setting aside for now the question of whether this is an accurate characterization (it's not), there's a reason this alleged dichotomy is typically stated with an air of condescension: We all know that the field of science has been extremely successful in giving us knowledge about the world. The implication, therefore, is that religious people are willing to reject what anyone can see *works* and instead choose an inferior alternative based on religious faith (which is assumed to mean blind belief that's not based on evidence). The three buzzwords of naturalism—*reason, science,* and *evidence*—travel together as the supposed obvious choice of modern people intelligent enough to abandon pre-Enlightenment worldviews. As we'll see, this is the underlying assumption on which the remaining four claims are based.

Religion Is an Emotional Crutch

> People find great comfort in these belief systems. I've often said it gives them a scaffolding for their structure of the world, their ethics, and their morals. They can use religion as some sort of mechanism to help them get by, something that they can climb on to ease the confusion of the unknown.[5]
>
> Joe Rogan, host of *The Joe Rogan Experience* podcast

Whereas the previous claim addressed the supposed *what* of religious worldviews (religion is anti-reason, anti-science, and anti-evidence), this one addresses the supposed *why.* The assumption here is that there's no intellectually valid reason for a person to have a religious worldview given our modern knowledge, but there's a good emotional *explanation* for why people do anyway. It helps them deal with the cold, hard reality that there's nothing more to life than this existence. Religious people are portrayed as much more fragile than naturalists, who are able to courageously live without the comfort of supernatural fairy tales. This may be mockery in its most subtle yet patronizing form: You're just not *capable* of handling the truth.

Religion Is Childish

> For me the Jewish religion like all other religions is an
> incarnation of the most childish superstitions.[6]

—Albert Einstein, Nobel Prize-winning physicist

Childish beliefs are those that are abandoned when we become capable of evidence-based thinking. The idea that religion is childish is therefore closely connected with the idea that religion is anti-evidence; it's assumed that there's no evidence for a supernatural being, and because there's not, people who continue to believe in one are childish in their thinking. In 2019, best-selling atheist author Richard Dawkins wrote a book titled *Outgrowing God* that played on this idea. Targeted at a younger audience than his earlier book, *The God Delusion* (which sold more than three million copies), Dawkins wants teens to know that the intellectually mature thing to do is leave God behind with the rest of their childhood fantasies.

Religion Is the Result of Brainwashing

> The fundamental problem with religion is that believers…
> are so sure they're "correct" on anything and everything they
> believe. This is, of course, a sure sign of insanity…Like the
> hundreds of millions of other nonreligious people out
> there, it's hard for me to fathom how religious people got
> brainwashed into being this way—this ignorant.[7]

—Zoltan Istvan, 2016 candidate for
president of the United States

Istvan certainly sounds like *he's* very sure he's correct about what he believes, despite identifying such certainty with insanity. But leaving the irony aside, the core idea here is that religious people are the victims of someone or something that has controlled their thinking to the extent that they're convinced of an obvious falsehood. If that weren't the case, they would've been able to use their ability to reason and follow evidence to its clear conclusion that naturalism is true. Again, note the implied connection to evidence. Evidence is assumed to be so strong and obvious for naturalism (and so lacking for theism) that there *must* be some crazy explanation as to why religious people continue to believe. In this case, that crazy reason is external mind control.

Religion Is Harmful

> Religion, it stops people from thinking because they think all the answers are in that one book; it impedes progress; it justifies crazy people. Flying planes into buildings was a faith-based initiative.[8]
>
> —Bill Maher, host of the HBO political talk show *Real Time with Bill Maher*

This one adds insult to injury. Not only are you personally lacking any rational thought (you've stopped thinking), but you're also hurting society. *Everyone* is the victim of your foolishness. Without religion, we would all be making much better societal progress. Some atheists place all religious views in this category, while others distinguish between religions. Maher, for example, has made it clear that he views radical Islam as a threat in its own category.[9]

Hopefully you weren't overly crushed to hear how unreasonable, unscientific, emotional, crutch-like, childish, and harmful it supposedly is to have a religious worldview. But if you were, rest assured that by doing some critical thinking (yes, Christians *are* capable of that!), we will see that these sentiments are completely unfounded.

Building a Case for the Existence of God

One of the reasons Christians are vulnerable to the pressures of naturalistic assumptions is that our own beliefs about God are often based on little more than feelings. Oftentimes, if you ask Christians why they believe in God, you'll hear answers like "I just know He's there," or "I can feel His presence." Our personal experiences with God are important, of course, but if experiences are *all* we have to go on, it can be really easy to question their basis in reality during difficult times. God isn't answering your prayer in the way you hoped? You haven't had a powerful impression of God's presence for a while? God isn't lifting a burden you're desperate to ease? In times like these, it can *feel* like He's not there. And in these dark times, the words of those who challenge and mock our worldview can shake us even further.

An important starting point for regaining confidence in a supernatural worldview is understanding the objective evidence for God's existence in the natural world (objective evidence is evidence that's independent of our personal experience). Theologians call this God's *general revelation* (as opposed to His *special revelation* through Scripture). Christians sometimes think that looking at the evidence for God in nature somehow downplays or ignores the importance of the Bible, but the Bible itself speaks to the validity of such knowledge. Psalm 19:1-2, for example, says, "The heavens declare the glory of God; the skies proclaim the work of his hands. Day after day they pour forth speech; night after night they reveal knowledge." In addition, the apostle Paul said there is no excuse for not believing in God because He has so clearly revealed himself in *nature*:

> The wrath of God is being revealed from heaven against all the godlessness and wickedness of people, who suppress the truth by their wickedness, since what may be known about God is plain to them, because God has made it plain to them. For since the creation of the world God's invisible qualities—his eternal power and divine nature—have been clearly seen, being understood from what has been made, so that people are without excuse (Romans 1:18-20; see also Romans 2:14-15).

In the following section, we'll look at some of the key evidences for God's existence that are manifest in the natural world. With that foundation, we'll then consider the claims that theism is anti-science and anti-reason.

Understanding Evidence

Within the subject of understanding evidence, we're going to look at three topics: (1) why people respond differently to evidence, (2) three arguments for the existence of God, and (3) the most reasonable explanation for the evidence.

WHY PEOPLE RESPOND DIFFERENTLY TO EVIDENCE

If you ask an atheist how much evidence there is for God's existence, they'll almost certainly say, "None." If you ask a Christian who's familiar with the subject the same question, they'll probably say, "A lot!" How is it that people can draw such vastly different conclusions? Is it even worth studying this stuff if people are going to disagree anyway? To answer these questions, we need to understand the nature of *any* evidence that doesn't literally speak for itself:[10]

1. *Evidence is a body of facts that require human interpretation.* Evidence itself says *nothing*—it must be interpreted. Humans can look at the same evidence and come to different conclusions due to varied assumptions, available information, life experiences, and motivations.

2. *Because evidence requires human interpretation, there will* always *be multiple possible explanations for it.* The relevant question is not how many possible explanations we can come up with, but rather, which one is the most *likely* explanation given the evidence.

3. *If we rule out certain possible explanations before considering the evidence, we won't ever conclude that the evidence points to those explanations.* For example, many people assume God doesn't exist, and they will only consider naturalistic explanations for evidence in the natural world. But if we rule out God as a possible explanation before even looking at the data, *of course* we'll conclude there's no evidence pointing to Him as the best explanation.

4. *The best explanation for a body of evidence is often debatable and rarely certain.* It's often easy to rule out the most *unlikely* explanations for things. But when studying the natural world, possible explanations for what we see are complex, and it's not always obvious what is more or less likely. Thoughtful people can come to different conclusions.

THREE ARGUMENTS FOR THE EXISTENCE OF GOD

While it's not possible to cover in one chapter the abundance of evidence for God's existence, there are three major arguments based on evidence in the natural world that are especially important for Christians to understand. Note that these arguments don't necessarily point to the God of the Bible—other evidence for the inspiration and reliability of the Bible is needed to make that connection. But they do strongly point to a supernatural creator, designer, and moral lawgiver who is *consistent* with the God of the Bible.

The first major argument is called the *cosmological argument*. That sounds academic, but the argument itself is easy to understand. It can be stated as follows:

1. The universe began to exist (this is the mainstream scientific consensus);

2. everything that begins to exist has a cause (nothing pops into existence on its own);

3. therefore, the universe must have had a cause.

Perhaps that conclusion sounds anticlimactic—why is it so consequential to make a case that the universe had a cause? Well, the cause couldn't have been just anything. In order to create space, time, and matter, the cause would have to be spaceless, timeless, immaterial, and uncaused itself—not to mention enormously powerful. This, of course, is consistent with the Christian understanding of God. Put simply, the cosmological argument says that the best explanation for the fact that the universe began to exist is that something or someone beyond nature *caused* it to exist.

A second argument is called the *design argument*. This argument makes the case that the complexity and specificity we find in nature is best explained by the existence of an intelligent agent (a "designer") rather than by chance processes. For example, our bodies are made up of trillions of cells containing DNA rich with the information needed to direct our functioning. The sheer volume of information in human DNA is astonishing, but it's not just the volume that's incredible. The information works amazingly like a computer code or language, and *all* known codes and languages were created by an intelligent agent—not by chance.

Another example of the design argument comes from the so-called fine-tuning of the earth and universe. It "just so happens" that our universal home is structured in exactly the ways necessary for life to exist and flourish. The constants of nature (such as the force of gravity) have extremely precise values; if they were just slightly different, life as we know it couldn't exist. As one example of dozens, if the gravitational force were too weak, it wouldn't be able to hold stars together, and stars (of the kind like our sun) are a necessary source of energy for living things. If the gravitational force were too strong, stars would burn out too quickly to support ongoing life.

Consider another example: At the solar system level, Earth orbits the sun within a narrow range of distance where liquid water—a necessity for life—can exist. If we were slightly closer to the sun, the necessary water would evaporate. If we were slightly farther from the sun, that water would turn to ice.

Astrophysicist Hugh Ross has cataloged more than 150 parameters of a planet, its planetary companions, its moon, its star, and its galaxy that must have values falling within narrowly defined ranges for physical life to exist.[11] He's estimated that there is less than 1 chance in 10^{282} that even *one* life-supporting body would occur in the universe.[12] For these reasons, even many atheist scientists concede that the universe *appears* to be finely tuned; they just conclude it's a lucky accident that things all worked together for us to exist (and if things hadn't worked out, we wouldn't be here to know it). The design argument concludes, however, that the best explanation for the extraordinarily unlikely fine-tuning we see is that it's the product of intelligence.

That brings us to the third argument: the *moral argument*. This argument states that (1) objective moral standards—a "moral law"—exists outside of personal opinion, and (2) the best explanation for the existence of that moral law is the existence of a moral lawgiver. We all have a moral intuition that tells us certain things are wrong regardless of one's personal opinion (for example, rape or torture). If there are things that are indeed right or wrong for all people, those moral laws are just as much facts about reality as statements like "Humans breathe air." But where would a universal moral law come from if there's no higher-than-human moral authority? If the universe is all that exists, there can be no objective moral law that applies to all people because there's no moral lawgiver. Our views on morality would simply be a matter of personal opinion. *In such a world, rape and torture are as morally acceptable as they are unacceptable because there's no objective moral standard by which to judge them.* Most people realize that's a tough pill to swallow because our deepest intuition tells us this isn't the case.

The Most Reasonable Explanation for the Evidence

If you're new to the subject of the evidence for God's existence, I realize that all this can be a lot of information to take in. But don't feel like you need to remember all the details right now. Here's the bottom line: Those who hold to a naturalistic worldview claim there's no evidence that anything outside of nature exists. Many, as we saw, condescendingly mock those who hold to a theistic worldview because it supposedly belongs to the medieval era, before we learned evidence-based thinking. *But evidence and a theistic worldview are not mutually exclusive.*

Yes, throughout the Scientific Revolution, the Enlightenment, and beyond, there was an increased focus on gaining knowledge about the natural world through evidence, science, and reason. But that doesn't imply those things were necessarily a *replacement* for theism! As we just saw, evidence and theism go hand in hand. We looked at the evidence in nature and asked, What's the best explanation for what we observe? Is it more reasonable to conclude that the universe popped into existence without cause, that it then just happened to be finely tuned to support life despite the extraordinary improbability, that complex life then developed entirely by chance over time from nonliving matter, and that the moral laws we intuitively think are an objective reality are nothing more than an illusion…or that these things are best explained by the existence of a supernatural intelligence—a creator, designer, and moral lawgiver?

As I said earlier, people will answer that question in different ways depending on a variety of factors. But what should be clear to everyone, regardless of worldview, is that the existence of a supernatural intelligence is an extremely reasonable explanation for the *evidence* we just looked at in nature. Theists, of course, would say it's clearly the *best* explanation if you haven't ruled it out beforehand.

Understanding the Nature of Science

The subject of the relationship between science and religion is a broad one involving many more facets than we can address here.[13] What I want to highlight about this relationship, however, is why the oft-repeated claim that a theistic worldview is inherently anti-science is unfounded.

Science, by definition, is the study of the structure and behavior of the natural world through observation and experimentation. It tells us how nature *works*. But just because we know how nature works doesn't mean there didn't need to be an intelligent being to make it work in the first place. In fact, the feasibility of doing science at all depends on assumptions that are more consistent with theism than naturalism. As I explain in *Talking with Your Kids about God*:

> The universe is both understandable and logical— something mathematician and philosopher John Lennox calls the "rational intelligibility of the universe." These characteristics allow us to do science in the first place. If the universe was just a hodgepodge of chaotic events ungoverned

by structured laws, science would be a hopeless task. But *why* is the world intelligible rather than chaotic? If the universe is truly the product of unguided evolutionary forces, as atheists claim, there's no reason to expect that an elegant ordering of nature would have happened on its own. But if the universe is the product of intelligence, as Christians and other theists claim, we would *expect* it to be orderly—a reflection of its rational designer.[14]

Furthermore, it's important to note that the idea that a person gets knowledge from science *or* revelation rests on a significant mischaracterization of both. First, the notion that our only valid knowledge of reality comes from science is self-refuting; that statement *itself* can't be determined by science (it's philosophical in nature). In addition, there are several types of knowledge outside of science that we accept in everyday life, such as sense experience and reason itself. A person may claim that our only valid knowledge comes from science, but no one lives that way. Second, Christians don't claim that the Bible tells us *everything* about the world and that we don't need other sources of information. We recognize that science reveals the detailed workings of the world God created and believe that the intricate design evident in nature points back to its Designer. To suggest that people must choose between science and revelation is simply a false dichotomy.

Understanding the Nature of Reason

In the one-two-three punch of naturalism—evidence, science, and reason—that brings us to reason. Simply put, reason is the process of thinking. *Everyone* reasons. Sometimes people do it well, and sometimes people do it poorly. The act of reasoning well isn't owned by all the individuals holding any one worldview, despite the way atheists sometimes make it sound. That said, at a broader level, it's important to understand the connection between evidence and good reason.

Generally speaking, it's *reasonable* to base our beliefs on good evidence and *unreasonable* to hold beliefs without evidence or in the face of contrary evidence. On this we should agree with atheists! But here's where we disagree: Atheists believe there's *no* evidence for a god's existence, so it's unreasonable to believe in one. Christians and other theists believe there *is* evidence for a god's existence, and theistic belief is therefore reasonable. What a person considers reasonable, therefore, depends to a great degree on their evaluation of the evidence. That means it's relatively meaningless to debate with someone over what's "reasonable"—the real discussion should take place at the level of *evidence*.

On a final (important!) note regarding reason, all of this assumes that humans have the ability to reason in a reliable way. But naturalists believe our mental processes are the product of purposeless, unguided evolution. In that case, there's no reason to trust our reasoning! Our thoughts are just the result of various physical laws acting upon us. As atheist philosopher Thomas Nagel admits, "Evolutionary naturalism provides an account of our capacities that undermines their reliability, and in doing so undermines itself."[15] It's hard to miss the irony that atheists consider good reason to be synonymous with a naturalistic worldview, yet in a naturalistic worldview, there's no basis for assuming our reasoning is even reliable.

The Existence of God Is Amazing News

Despite the mockery so common today, there's absolutely no reason for Christians to feel intellectually inferior for believing in God. As we've seen, there is strong evidence pointing to the existence of a supernatural creator, designer, and moral lawgiver—an extremely important starting point for making the case for the truth of Christianity more specifically.

While that should give us confidence under the pressure of secular naturalism, there's something else that's important to fully grasp about the strength of this case: It's *really* good news.

Consider the implications that flow from naturalism:

- Human life is essentially an accident with no objective purpose or meaning.

- We're chemical specks in a vast, indifferent universe with no more inherent value than rocks.

- There's little reason to believe we have free will—the thoughts that arise in our minds are just the result of physical laws acting upon us.

- No one should live in any particular way because it makes no objective moral difference.

- No one has a responsibility to anyone else because we're just a collection of molecules without moral obligations.

- There's no such thing as objective moral evil, so we can't condemn even the worst actions of society as objectively wrong.

That's bleak.

No one should *want* these implications to be true.

Not wanting something to be true doesn't determine whether it *is* true, of course, but when what's true converges with what's desirable, that's a beautiful thing. If there's a supernatural creator, designer, and moral lawgiver, human life is a purposeful creation with objective meaning and value given to it by that creator. *We matter.* Our (free) choices matter. How we live matters. *Everything* matters because we're not just an accident of space and time. We should be elated to know we're not just collections of molecules moving about meaninglessly in the universe!

What an incredible difference this makes for our outlook on life. Knowing that our lives matter and that this world is not all there is should give us a profound sense of peace. For example, when hard times come, which is inevitable, we can rest in knowing that there's more to the picture of life than the difficulties staring us in the face. When we question our self-worth, we can rest in knowing that we were *worth* creating. When we feel we've lost our purpose, we can rest in knowing there's a purpose to be found. It's easy to forget how much our outlook depends on the existence of God, but when we remember, His existence should clearly be amazing news for all people.

Now, establishing that there's good reason to believe a supernatural being exists who's *consistent* with what the Bible teaches is an important first step toward confidence in a biblical worldview. But in order for us to know the specifics of who this being is, who we are, and how we relate to one another, additional revelation is needed—and additional revelation was given.

Now it's time to look at the Bible.

FOR FURTHER READING

On the Relationship between Science and Religion

- Melissa Cain Travis, *Science and the Mind of the Maker: What the Conversation Between Faith and Science Reveals About God* (Eugene, OR: Harvest House, 2018).

- John Lennox, *Can Science Explain Everything?* (Surrey, England: The Good Book Company, 2019).

- J.P. Moreland, *Scientism and Secularism: Learning to Respond to a Dangerous Ideology* (Wheaton, IL: Crossway, 2018).

On the Evidence for God's Existence

- Natasha Crain, *Talking with Your Kids about God: 30 Conversations Every Christian Parent Must Have* (Grand Rapids, MI: Baker Books, 2017).

- Lee Strobel, *The Case for a Creator: A Journalist Investigates Scientific Evidence That Points Toward God* (Grand Rapids, MI: Zondervan, 2014).

- J. Warner Wallace, *God's Crime Scene: A Cold-Case Detective Examines the Evidence for a Divinely Created Universe* (Colorado Springs, CO: David C. Cook, 2015).

QUESTIONS FOR DISCUSSION OR REFLECTION

1. What do you think are the most compelling reasons for believing that God exists?

2. What, if anything, sometimes makes you question God's existence?

3. Based on the discussion in this chapter, how would you explain to someone why Christianity is not (1) anti-reason, (2) anti-science, and (3) anti-evidence?

4. Do you agree that the implications of naturalism (stated at the end of this chapter) are bleak? Why or why not?

CHAPTER 5

Reestablishing What We (Should) Actually Believe

*Under the pressure of
secular individualism*

In a culture where feelings are the ultimate guide, happiness is the ultimate goal, judging is the ultimate sin, and God is the ultimate guess, *should* is a dirty word.

Should implies an obligation of some sort. To suggest that a person has any external directives—moral or otherwise—is offensive in secular culture because it runs contrary to the deeply held and assumed authority of the self. *Should* suggests that feelings are *not* all that matter, that something external can legitimately stand in the way of a person's subjective happiness goal, that judgment can have an objective basis, and that the objective basis may come from an authoritative God. To say this is offensive is not an exaggerated projection onto the secular worldview. If you do a Google search of the phrase "*should* is a dirty word," you'll turn up more than 250,000 articles, podcasts, and videos talking about why it's important to be true to yourself. One blogger says, for example:

> I've been trying to think of a context in which that word [should] has a kind, benign or even neutral connotation. I

can't come up with a single one. Even saying the word, a single syllable with a hard ending, creates a tightness in my throat and upper chest, as if to reinforce its judgment and sternness. Yet, in our culture, we use this word a great deal, often without thinking about how obscenely insane it is and how painfully it often lands.[1]

This blog is rather appropriately titled *À La Carte Spirit: Bringing Awareness to the Menu of Life*. In a restaurant context, to order à la carte means to order items individually rather than as part of a set meal. This writer is applying the same idea to the spiritual context of picking and choosing individual beliefs from the menu of life's possibilities. Given her assumption that this is a valid way to determine truth, she finds it "insane" and "painful" for others to implicitly question her belief selections. (She also seems to miss the irony that she's telling everyone what they *should not* do—which is just another *should* claim.)

You might be surprised to know that researchers have actually quantified the number of people who mix beliefs from otherwise incompatible worldviews. The 2021 American Worldview Inventory found that *88 percent* of all Americans embrace an "impure, unrecognizable worldview that blends ideas from these multiple perspectives"—a worldview that Director of Research George Barna refers to as "syncretism." Barna explains:

> Syncretism is a cut-and-paste approach to making sense of life. Rather than developing an internally consistent and philosophically coherent perspective, Americans embrace points of view or actions that feel comfortable or most convenient. Those beliefs and behaviors are often inconsistent, or even contradictory, but few Americans seemed troubled by that.[2]

Given our culture's emphasis on individualism, it really shouldn't shock us that so few people have a consistent and coherent worldview. When your authority is yourself and you're picking beliefs here, there, and everywhere along the feelings-based path to personal happiness, you may well end up with worldview pieces that don't logically fit together. Few people stop to consider whether their beliefs are coherent because, as Barna implies, most simply don't care. After all, to suggest that anyone's beliefs *should* collectively make sense is just one more application of that dirty *should* word.

For Christians who seek to have a biblical worldview, however, an à la carte belief system of this nature is not an option. If the Bible is God's authoritative Word for all time, then what it teaches is not a menu from which to choose; it's truth on which to feast. We must come to the table ready and willing to learn what God says, accept His Word as truth, and apply that truth to our lives.

But it's not always easy.

It takes far more intentionality than we often recognize to establish and maintain the specific beliefs we *should* (yes, *should*) have in a culture that constantly tells us the individual reigns supreme. When we don't fully grasp what the Bible teaches in the first place or we aren't vigilant in protecting those beliefs, we can easily allow unbiblical ideas to creep into the biblical worldview we think we have.

As I wrote in the "Before You Read" preface, this book is primarily for those who accept the Bible as the inspired and authoritative Word of God, so the purpose of this chapter is not to make a case for why we should view the Bible in that way (though I've provided recommended resources at the end of the chapter in case you would like a better foundation in this area). Rather, we're going to look at the pressures we face as we *seek* to maintain a coherent biblical worldview in the midst of an individualistic, à la carte belief culture.

À La Carte Beliefs from a Biblical Menu

You might recall from chapter 1 that only about 17 percent of Christians who consider their faith important and attend church regularly have beliefs consistent with a biblical worldview. What we didn't look at is what the research shows the other 83 percent believe. Researchers found that

- 61 percent agree with ideas rooted in New Spirituality (for example, agreeing that "meaning and purpose come from becoming one with all that is");

- 54 percent resonate with postmodernist views (for example, agreeing that "no one can know for certain what meaning and purpose there is to life");

- 36 percent accept ideas associated with Marxism (for example, agreeing that "the government, rather than individuals, should control as much of the resources as necessary to ensure that everyone gets their fair share"); and

- 29 percent believe ideas based on secularism (for example, agreeing that "meaning and purpose comes from working hard to earn as much as possible so you can make the most of life").[3]

To be sure, some of the people in this group would say they don't accept the Bible as the Word of God, and therefore have no problem combining ideas from varying worldviews. But many others are simply unaware of how various popular but unbiblical ideas have crept into the content of their theological beliefs.

While we don't have the space in this chapter to address all these ideas individually, we'll encounter and discuss many aspects of them throughout the rest of the book. What I do want to focus on here, however, is a type of pressure to mix worldviews that's perhaps less obvious to many readers than the examples above yet is becoming increasingly pervasive: the pressure that comes from Christians who *don't* believe the Bible is the inspired and authoritative Word of God and who often chastise or belittle those who do.

For many who identify as *progressive* Christians, the Bible is its own menu of beliefs. Generally speaking, progressive Christians believe that the Bible reflects *man's* understanding of God in the time it was written, and therefore it's not *God's* final say for all time. In other words, the Bible is seen as a valuable spiritual tool—maybe even a beautiful one—but it's not authoritative in the sense that it always accurately describes who God is, what He's done, or what He wants from us. As one progressive Christian church stated on Facebook, "The Bible isn't the Word of God...the Bible is a product of community, a library of texts, multi-vocal, a human response to God, [and] living and dynamic."[4] Of course, those who view the Bible as God's authoritative Word for all time would agree that in some sense, it is all of the things this church lists. The difference for progressive Christians is that the Bible is those things *and nothing more.*

How, then, do progressive Christians choose what they believe to be accurate and applicable truth for all time and what they don't? That depends on the individual. And that's precisely why progressive Christianity is so hard to define in terms of actual beliefs. When people place themselves in a position of deciding what *they* believe to be accurate or applicable from the Bible, they'll inevitably end up with beliefs that vary from one person to the next, even under the same collective label of "progressive Christianity."

That said, there are many common beliefs among progressive Christians, both in what they reject and what they accept. The biblical teachings that are most often on the chopping block are those that secular culture tends to have problems with—for example, hell, the atonement, sexuality, and gender roles/identity. Hell is seen as an unconscionably immoral idea that could never be compatible with a God of love. The atonement (Jesus's sacrifice on the cross for sin) is seen as a view that developed out of ancient beliefs that blood was needed to appease the gods. Biblical sexuality is seen as repressive to our very nature. And the idea that God made humans male and female, with equal value but sometimes different roles, is considered sexist, patriarchal, and (again) repressive. These aren't the only beliefs progressive Christians commonly reject, but they're some of the most significant ones.

On the flip side, progressive Christians overwhelmingly accept and champion love and social justice. Progressive Christian messages can sound a lot like they're consistent with a biblical worldview when they center on those two ideas—God is love, we need to love others, we need to help the hurting, we need to be a voice for the marginalized, we need to care for the poor, and so on. There's an important reason, however, why progressive Christian messages of this nature only *sound* like they're consistent with a biblical worldview but often aren't: Progressive Christians typically *define* love and justice differently than the Bible does.

I'm devoting a whole chapter (chapter 10) to a discussion about justice, so for now I want to focus specifically on the significance of how the biblical and progressive definitions of love differ. As you might expect by now, it comes back to a question of authority: Who gets to define what love means? For Christians with a biblical worldview, the answer is that God does, and we look to the Bible to see what *He* has said.

A key passage for our understanding of love is Matthew 22:36-40. A Pharisee asked Jesus, "Teacher, which is the greatest commandment in the Law?" Jesus replied,

> "Love the Lord your God with all your heart and with all your soul and with all your mind." This is the first and greatest commandment. And the second is like it: "Love your neighbor as yourself." All the Law and the Prophets hang on these two commandments.

Note that Jesus said loving God is the *greatest* commandment. This implies that any other commandments should be obeyed within that context. *What it means to love others, therefore, depends on what it means to first love God.* If we take the Bible to be His Word, we can know what it means to love God because He has revealed who He is, what He has done, and how we are to respond in relationship and obedience. To love others, therefore, means to want what God wants for them based on what He has revealed in the Bible.

Love often means something quite different to progressive Christians because they aren't looking to the Bible as their final, authoritative source for knowing God and His will. And, as we discussed in chapter 2, if you're not looking to revelation for your ultimate authority, you're looking to yourself. In this case, that means the *individual* becomes the authority on what it means to love others. While that theoretically could result in love meaning just about anything, the dominant conclusion among progressive Christians is that love means affirming whatever journey a person wants to be on, such that they don't feel judged.

In practice, that can take many forms, depending on the subject. In the context of sexuality, for example, progressive Lutheran pastor Nadia Bolz-Weber says, "Whatever sexual flourishing looks like for you, that's what I would love to see happen in your life" (which, for Bolz-Weber, includes things like pornography, as long as your behavior isn't "compulsive").[5] Whereas Christians with a biblical worldview should understand love to be the act of wanting for others what *God* wants for them, progressive Christians tend to understand love as the act of wanting for others what *they* want for themselves.

Does the progressive Christian idea of love sound familiar? It should. It's no different from the secular idea of love that we discussed in chapter 3 (feelings are the ultimate guide, happiness is the ultimate goal, and judging is the ultimate sin, so love equals affirmation). Driven by a secularized understanding of love, progressive Christians typically center their faith on a correspondingly secularized notion of social justice—justice that is primarily aimed at liberating people from perceived or real earthly oppression so they can be free to be *whomever they want*. As we'll see in chapter 10, this isn't consistent with the biblical concept of justice. But when you start with a secularized definition of love, it's not surprising that you end up with a secularized definition of justice as well.

Therein lies the oxymoron of progressive Christianity. Because progressive Christians ultimately have the same source of authority as secular culture—the self—the way they see the world often dovetails with the way those who consider themselves *irreligious* see the world. Progressive Christians may have an added appreciation or love for Jesus relative to their secular counterparts who dismiss Him entirely, but that doesn't necessarily play out in significant worldview differences. When the self is in charge, Jesus can start looking an awful lot like what modern culture thinks He *should* look like.

As we can see from this brief overview, there's a substantial gulf between the beliefs of progressive Christians and Christians with a biblical worldview. *The very gospel it teaches is different.*[6] Rather than the gospel being about the depth of human sinfulness, our need for a Savior, and the good news that Jesus's sacrifice on the cross has provided the way for reconciliation with a holy God, it's primarily about secularized versions of love and justice. To be clear, this isn't a caricature. In describing what he says most progressive Christians believe, John Pavlovitz (a leading progressive Christian author) says very directly, "We [progressive Christians] believe that social justice is the heart of the Gospel."[7] Though justice is an important biblical theme rooted in God's very nature and it's something Christians *should* be concerned about, it's not the gospel itself. Biblical justice is something quite different than the secularized justice popularly conceived of today.

Ironically, the pressure to view the Bible as progressive Christians do is just another type of secular pressure. It's one that's more amenable to incorporating certain biblical teachings into one's views, but it's still the pressure to revert to the authority of the self.

Back to Basics: What Should Christians Believe?

With so many people forming their worldview from hand-picked beliefs, how can Christians ensure their beliefs truly are biblical and not a product of a similar individualism? I'll answer that in two parts. First, we'll consider what it looks like to establish the beliefs we *should* have. Then we'll look at how to be vigilant in guarding those truths against the pressure of unbiblical ideas seeping in over time.

Perhaps the most important starting point for us is recognizing that what we believe does indeed matter. Christianity is not some kind of behavioral system wherein our beliefs are incidental to the nature of our actions. There are atheists, Buddhists, Mormons, Sikhs, Christians, and others who live in ways that can appear similar on the outside. But the Bible is clear that what a person *believes about Jesus* has eternal significance:

- "God so loved the world that he gave his one and only Son, that whoever *believes* in him shall not perish but have eternal life" (John 3:16; emphasis added).

- "If you declare with your mouth, 'Jesus is Lord,' and believe in your heart that God raised him from the dead, you will be saved" (Romans 10:9).

- "I am the way and the truth and the life. No one comes to the Father except through me" (John 14:6).

From a biblical perspective, what you believe about Jesus determines where you will spend eternity. That doesn't mean, of course, that the way in which a Christian lives their life doesn't matter. The Bible says that "faith by itself, if it is not accompanied by action, is dead" (James 2:17). A genuine faith in Jesus will result in a life lived for His glory, in obedience to His commands. Belief produces action—they go hand in hand.

It's not possible to outline here all the beliefs Christians with a biblical worldview should have, but among the most foundational truths of our faith are who Jesus is, what He has done, and what that means for us today. (We'll talk more specifically about gospel basics in chapter 12.)

Who Jesus Is

Saying that belief in Jesus matters in an eternal way doesn't mean that *any* belief about Jesus leads to salvation. Romans 10:9 (quoted above) is very specific about this: We must declare Jesus as *Lord* and believe he was *raised from the dead*. And it's clear from the New Testament context that "Lord" wasn't simply a title of respect—the earliest Christians equated Jesus with God Himself. In their book *Putting Jesus in His Place*, Robert M. Bowman Jr. and J. Ed Komoszewski encapsulate the early Christian view of Jesus's divine identity in the memorable acronym H-A-N-D-S.[8] They demonstrate that the New Testament repeatedly claims that Jesus shares the *H*onors, *A*ttributes, *N*ames, *D*eeds, and judgment *S*eat of God. The significance of this cannot be overstated. First-century Jews were strict monotheists (believing in only one God) yet spoke of Jesus sharing in God's *unique identity* in these ways. In other words, for all intents and purposes, they equated Him with God.

But is that how Jesus saw Himself? Absolutely. In John 8:58, Jesus said, "Very truly I tell you…before Abraham was born, I am!" This isn't a grammatical oddity. The wording "I am" echoes the name God revealed for Himself in Exodus 3:14. Though that seems like a cryptic reference to us today, Jesus's critics immediately understood He was claiming to be God and picked up stones to kill Him for blasphemy. Jesus also accepted the disciples' worship (Matthew 28:17), applied the attributes of God to Himself (for example, pre-existence in John 17:5), applied names and titles of God to Himself (for example, the bridegroom in Mark 2:19; see Isaiah 54:5; 62:5), and acted with God's authority in His miracle-working. These are just a *few* examples of Jesus's many claims to deity.

While it's popular today to say that Jesus was a good moral teacher or a good example of how we should live, these statements are meaningless if we don't acknowledge that *Jesus is God* and make Him Lord of our lives. If He was only a good teacher without any higher-than-human authority, what He taught matters no more than what any other person in history taught and was just one more *opinion*.

What Jesus Has Done

Jesus did many things while on earth, but no understanding of Him is complete without acknowledging the nature and significance of what He accomplished on the cross: atonement for our sins. People who theologically downplay the seriousness of sin often downplay or outright reject the atonement (if sin's not a big problem, why would we need a big solution?). But the need for atonement was *so* important that God established a sacrificial system hundreds of years before Jesus came. That system taught people that sin is real, sin is serious, and sin separates us from God, leading to death. In His mercy, God allowed animals to die in place of sinful humans for hundreds of years. But the entire system was there to point forward to Jesus's death on the cross as the final, perfect sacrifice in our place. Those who accept that substitutionary sacrifice as payment for their sin are reconciled to God and will inherit eternal life (John 3:16).

Good Friday, of course, isn't the end of the story. As all four Gospels report, three days later, Jesus rose bodily from the dead. This is no small detail. According to the apostle Paul in 1 Corinthians 15:14, "If Christ has not been raised, our preaching is useless and so is your faith." *If Jesus wasn't raised from the dead, there's no point in following Him.* Many progressive Christian churches teach that the resurrection was only metaphorical in nature—that Jesus didn't *literally* come back to life. But there's no doubt the Bible teaches that the resurrection event on which the truth of Christianity hangs was bodily in nature—not some kind of fuzzy symbolism.

The Gospel writers reported that the risen Jesus ate food, was touched, showed His bodily wounds, accepted an invitation to visit a home, and had conversations! He personally emphasized the bodily nature of His resurrection when He told the disciples, "Look at my hands and my feet. It is I myself! Touch me and see; a ghost does not have flesh and bones, as you see I have" (Luke 24:39). It's specifically a *bodily* resurrection that is central to the truth of Christianity.

Christians should also know that there is significant historical evidence to support the biblical claims of Jesus's resurrection. Though a discussion of that evidence is outside the scope of this book, I've provided recommended resources for further reading at the end of this chapter.

What That Means for Us

Given that Jesus is God, that He died to save us from sin, and that He was raised from the dead, what exactly does that mean for our earthly lives? Many, many books have been written on the various facets of Christian living—including this one!—but what I most want to point out in this brief section is that our answer shouldn't be whatever happens to make sense to us. That's exactly how people end up believing popular but unbiblical ideas like we should never judge, God helps those who help themselves, God cares most about our happiness, or

God won't give us more than we can handle. In order for us to live in light of who Jesus is and what He has done, *we need to be lifelong students of the Bible.*

I realize that sounds pretty obvious, but according to Lifeway Research, about 40 percent of Protestant churchgoers read the Bible only once per week or less.[9] Yet Lifeway also found that Bible reading is one of the behavioral characteristics that are most predictive of spiritual maturity. The reason for that relationship should be obvious. God's Word tells us who He is, what He has done throughout history, what He requires of us, how we are to relate to Him, how we are to relate to others, what the early Christian church faced, and much more. When we defer to our own understanding more than we seek answers in what God has already said, we descend into an individualism that's hardly different than what we find in secular culture. We may mean well, but the result is the same.

The Push and Pull of Unbiblical Ideas

Even after we've established ourselves in essential beliefs based on what the Bible teaches, we constantly face a push and pull from culture that can put pressure on our convictions—both as people proactively challenge us (the push), and as we find popular ideas compelling because they speak to our natural desires (the pull). Though there are numerous ways in which this can happen, the following five principles are especially pertinent for guarding a biblical worldview in today's secular culture.

Principle 1: The nicest sounding *beliefs are not necessarily the* right *beliefs.*

The progressive Christian and secular focus on love and affirmation can often make their beliefs sound "nicer" than a more theologically accurate and comprehensive set of biblical beliefs. Statements like, "Love is all that matters," or "You're perfect the way you are" are more readily received by people than anything along the lines of "We're all sinners deserving of God's wrath," or "We all need a Savior because we're *not* perfect as we are." The difficulty is that those who proclaim the first set of statements are seen by society as loving, whereas those who proclaim the other statements are seen as hateful. Most of us feel a natural desire to be liked by others, so if we're not careful, we can start to gauge the truth of biblical beliefs by the world's *response* to those beliefs.

That's why we would do well to remember Jesus's own words here: "If the world hates you, keep in mind that it hated me first. If you belonged to the world, it would love you as its own. As it is, you do not belong to the world, but I have chosen you out of the world. That is why the world hates you" (John 15:18-19). That's not a license to lob truth bombs without grace, of course. If people hate us, we need to be sure they hate us for the right reasons—because of the truth we share, not because of the way in which we share it.

Principle 2: Truth is narrow and that's okay.

Chances are that if someone called you narrow-minded, you'd take it as an insult. Culture has convinced us that "open-mindedness" is a virtue in and of itself. But being narrow-minded may not be a bad thing, depending on the context. If narrow-minded means that you hold certain beliefs to be true regardless of anyone's personal opinion (and, therefore, other beliefs to be false), take it as a compliment. Your thinking is grounded in a biblical worldview. Despite the common secular distaste for this so-called narrow-mindedness, the Bible teaches that objective truth exists. And truth, by definition, *is* narrow—it excludes infinite falsities. Don't be tempted to think that you need to be more flexible with the essentials of your faith just because people today think objective truth is narrow. That, too, is a narrow belief.

Principle 3: Godly humility doesn't require indecision about our beliefs.

A popular sentiment today is that questions are more important than answers. The idea is that we're all on our own spiritual journey, and the goal isn't to arrive at any kind of end point, but rather, to just keep searching. This appeals to secular culture because (1) if we never arrive at objective answers, no one can ever be told their conclusions are wrong (individualism at its finest!), and (2) it can sound more humble. One leading progressive Christian author, for example, has written, "I'm sure I am wrong about many things, although I'm not sure exactly which things I'm wrong about. I'm even sure I'm wrong about what I think I'm right about in at least some cases."[10] For those who accept the Bible as God's inspired and authoritative Word, there's no need to remain in this kind of perpetual ambiguity in order to be humble. *Godly humility is knowing one's rightful place in subordination to God.* If the Bible is God's own Word to us, we're not being arrogant by believing and proclaiming what the Creator of the universe has Himself said is true. Rather, we are humbly *submitting* to that truth.

Principle 4: Experience doesn't supersede the Bible as a source of knowledge.

Recently, I received an email from someone who was angered by my claim that objective truth exists. This person told me that the "most important answers will never be found in a book," and that the only place we can find answers is in our "heart and soul" (which, of course, is its own objective truth claim).

I can't count the number of times I've heard or seen similar ideas over the last few years in response to content I've shared on social media. Experience is seen as a "get out of biblical jail free" card; if a person has an experience that leads them to believe something in conflict with what the Bible says, they prioritize their experience as a superior source of knowledge. But experiences are subjective and can be contradictory between people. For example, Mormons may say they've experienced that Mormonism is true, Muslims may say they've experienced that Islam is true, and Christians may say they've experienced that Christianity is true. These religions make mutually exclusive claims about reality, so they can't logically be true at the same time. *That means many very convincing experiences still lead to false conclusions.* Given that God has revealed what's true in the Bible, our experiences, if Spirit-led, will not contradict His Word. We must test our experiences against the Bible, not change our beliefs to fit our experiences.

Principle 5: The cure for cultural disagreement will never be to compromise biblical beliefs.

It can be tiring to constantly see our beliefs conflict with secular culture—and not only with secular culture, but even with other believers. However, a biblical response to disagreement fatigue is *never* to compromise our beliefs in pursuit of unity (whether it's with nonbelievers or believers). Paul warned against this in his instructions to Timothy in 2 Timothy 4:2-4:

> Preach the word; be prepared in season and out of season; correct, rebuke and encourage—with great patience and careful instruction. For the time will come when people will not put up with sound doctrine. Instead, to suit their own desires, they will gather around them a great number of teachers to say what their itching ears want to hear. They will turn their ears away from the truth and turn aside to myths.

Ironically, well-meaning Christians sometimes want to agree to disagree on much more than Jesus ever would have. But the Bible in no way suggests that we should sacrifice truth to achieve polite agreement. Unity without truth isn't even unity—it's pure individualism.

God's Word Is a (Wonderfully!) Firm Foundation

When my son was little, he hated the idea that anyone could tell him what to do—so much so that he started trying to ban any authoritative-sounding phrases from our home. If I said, for example, "I'm going to have you clean your room today," he would yell, "Don't say the H-Y words!" (H-Y meaning "have you.") Or if I said, "I'm telling you this needs to be done right now," he would say, "Don't say the T-Y words!" Yes, "telling you" was an affront to his sense of independence.

At some point, my husband and I realized we needed to help him understand a crucial fact: Authority isn't necessarily a bad thing. Authority can be good *or* bad, depending on the context. If someone is trying to assert authority who doesn't have the right to do so or is using their rightful authority in a harmful way, that's bad. But if someone is in a rightful place of authority and uses it well, that's something we should be grateful for, not resentful of.

My husband and I then explained that God is the best example of good authority that we can imagine. He's our *rightful* authority because He's the one who created us. Furthermore, we can be confident in the *goodness* of His authority because it's His character that *defines* goodness. That's the kind of authority we should be excited to submit to—an authority who knows what's best for us far better than we ever could.

Many adults today find the idea of giving up the authority of the self as offensive as my son. They're effectively saying, "Don't say the G-I-I-C [God is in charge] words!" They build a foundation for their lives with dissimilar worldview pieces, believing that their approach represents freedom from the restriction of authority. But true freedom can never be built on a false sense of self-authority—that just enslaves a person to a lie.

The greatest freedom we can have is when we build our lives on the good and rightful authority of the Lord. Jesus spoke of that freedom when He told believers, "If you hold to my teaching, you are really my disciples. Then you will know the truth, and the truth will set you free" (John 8:31-32). And Jesus didn't leave the definition of freedom to our imagination. He subsequently explained, "Very truly I tell you, everyone who sins is a slave to sin. Now a slave has no permanent place in the family, but a son belongs to it forever. So if the Son sets you free, you will be free indeed" (verses 34-36). When we build our lives on truth, we are freed from the bondage of sin and welcomed into the family of God. But to know truth, Jesus says we must "hold to" His teachings (verse 31). This is a critical connection to make! Freedom *doesn't* come from placing ourselves in a position of authority to pick and choose what *we* believe to be true. Freedom comes from trusting in Jesus as our authority. When we do, it should be our joy to stand with confidence on the unshakeable foundation of His Word...and to proclaim that G-I-I-C (God is in charge)!

FOR FURTHER READING

On Progressive Christianity

- Alisa Childers, *Another Gospel: A Lifelong Christian Seeks Truth in Response to Progressive Christianity* (Carol Stream, IL: Tyndale Momentum, 2020).

- Michael J. Kruger, *The Ten Commandments of Progressive Christianity* (Minneapolis, MN: Cruciform Press, 2019).

- J. Gresham Machen, *Christianity and Liberalism* (1923; multiple editions available).

On the Biblical Worldview

- Robert M. Bowman Jr. and J. Ed Komoszewski, *Putting Jesus in His Place: The Case for the Deity of Christ* (Grand Rapids, MI: Kregel, 2007).

- Natasha Crain, *Talking with Your Kids about Jesus: 30 Conversations Every Christian Parent Must Have* (Grand Rapids, MI: Baker Books, 2020).

- Gregory Koukl, *The Story of Reality: How the World Began, How It Ends, and Everything Important that Happens in Between* (Grand Rapids, MI: Zondervan, 2017).

- John N. Oswalt, *The Bible Among the Myths: Unique Revelation or Just Ancient Literature?* (Grand Rapids, MI: Zondervan, 2009).

On the Historical Evidence for the Resurrection

INTRODUCTORY

- Gary R. Habermas and Michael R. Licona, *The Case for the Resurrection of Jesus* (Grand Rapids, MI: Kregel, 2004).

IN-DEPTH

- N.T. Wright, *The Resurrection of the Son of God (Christian Origins and the Question of God, Vol. 3)* (Philadelphia, PA: Fortress Press, 2003).

On Biblical Reliability

INTRODUCTORY

- Jonathan Morrow, *Questioning the Bible: 11 Major Challenges to the Bible's Authority* (Chicago, IL: Moody, 2014).

- J. Warner Wallace, *Cold-Case Christianity* (Colorado Springs, CO: David C. Cook, 2013).

- Peter J. Williams, *Can We Trust the Gospels?* (Wheaton, IL: Crossway, 2018).

IN-DEPTH

- Richard Bauckham, *Jesus and the Eyewitnesses: The Gospels as Eyewitness Testimony*, 2d ed. (Grand Rapids, MI: Eerdmans, 2017).

- Craig Blomberg, *The Historical Reliability of the New Testament: Countering the Challenges to Evangelical Christian Beliefs* (Nashville, TN: B&H Academic, 2016).

- K.A. Kitchen, *On the Reliability of the Old Testament* (Grand Rapids, MI: Eerdmans, 2006).

- Josh McDowell and Sean McDowell, *Evidence That Demands a Verdict: Life-Changing Truth for a Skeptical World* (Nashville, TN: Thomas Nelson, 2017).

On Apologetics and Culture

- Summit Ministries offers excellent biblical worldview conferences and resources for churches, families, schools, youth groups, and individuals. Their instructors include some of the best teachers on worldview, apologetics, culture, and Christianity. You can find out more at https://summit.org.

QUESTIONS FOR DISCUSSION OR REFLECTION

1. In your own words, why is the word *should* so often resented by those with a secular worldview?

2. How would you describe why progressive Christians and Christians with a biblical worldview often see the world so differently?

3. Why does a person's view of what love means ultimately depend on their view of the authority of God and the Bible?

4. Of the five principles given in this chapter for guarding biblical beliefs, which one(s) do you think Christians struggle with most? Which one, if any, have *you* struggled with most? What do you think would help you to resolve that struggle?

CHAPTER 6

Reexamining Beliefs When Confronted with Doubt

*Under the pressure of
secular deconversionism*

As I write this, a *New York Times* article titled "A Pastor's Son Becomes a Critic of Religion on TikTok" is going viral. The subtitle elaborates, "John Piper is one of the most influential theologians in America. His son Abraham calls evangelicalism 'a destructive, narrow-minded worldview.'" (Incidentally, note the claim of narrow-mindedness here that we discussed in the previous chapter, and how the belief that evangelicalism is "destructive" is just as narrow.)

The article tells the story of how Abraham Piper became an overnight TikTok sensation, gaining almost one million followers since posting his first video just five months prior. What got everyone's attention so quickly? Piper has posted more than 300 videos mocking the evangelical faith he grew up with but now rejects. Major publications (both Christian and secular) are talking about it, social media is buzzing over it, and podcasters are already dissecting what the church needs to do better. For at least this week, all of this seems like a big deal.

But Piper is just the latest in a string of high-profile deconversions that get everyone talking. By the time you read this book, there will certainly have been more, and the buzz around Piper will have long since subsided. In just the last couple of years, people with stories like Piper's have crossed the headlines with an almost predictable frequency. Joshua Harris, known for his book *I Kissed Dating Goodbye*, announced he was divorcing his wife and that he's no longer a Christian. Jon Steingard, singer and guitarist for the Christian band Hawk Nelson, shared on social media that he no longer believes in God and that his faith has slowly faded away. Rhett and Link, the YouTube celebrities I shared about in chapter 3, produced elaborate videos explaining why they were deconverting. Marty Sampson, songwriter for the Christian band Hillsong, shared on Instagram that he was losing his faith but now feels at peace with the world.

And then there's a homeschool mom who goes by the moniker "Janet deconverted."[1] Janet was a lifelong Christian who had been raising her kids in the Christian faith until she and her husband both deconverted. I personally became aware of her because she blogged chapter by chapter through one of my books to critique the content from her new perspective as a nonbeliever. Janet isn't a singer or author with a big platform who would become the subject of "shocking" news headlines; she's just one of many deconverts who quietly show up in statistics.

All of that said, deconversions to atheism or agnosticism are only one part of the collective secular narrative that glorifies doubt about the historic Christian faith. In other cases, people are vocal about the doubts that pushed them away from a biblical worldview and toward an ongoing process of *spiritual seeking*. The popular term for this is *deconstruction*.

Deconstruction is the process of pulling apart one's faith in order to re-examine long-held beliefs. Sometimes when people say they're deconstructing, they simply mean they're trying to take a step back and assess which of their beliefs are biblical and which aren't. Christian hip-hop artist Lecrae, for example, posted on Facebook that he's finding it "helpful to deconstruct some unhealthy views," but advised others who deconstruct to "reconstruct and build on the solid Rock of Christ."[2]

This kind of faith rebuilding process isn't typically what people have in mind when they use the word *deconstruction*, however. Deconstruction is more popularly used as a term in progressive Christian circles to indicate that a person is in the process of walking away from or has already walked away from the historic Christian faith—with no intention of going back. The term usually implies that a person has rejected the perceived "constraints" of a biblical worldview and is now open to anything *but* that. Deconstruction doesn't usually imply a deconversion to atheism, but it's certainly a deconversion of its own kind—from a worldview rooted in the authority of the Bible to a worldview rooted in the authority of the self. For that reason, I'll use the term *deconversion* in this chapter to include both atheist/agnostic-type deconversions and deconstruction-type deconversions.

In the previous chapter, we looked at the importance of establishing and maintaining the essential beliefs Christians should have, given that the Bible is the inspired and authoritative Word of God. But what if you start to have doubts that the Bible *is* inspired and authoritative? What if you start to feel that you can't make sense of some of what it teaches? What if you start wondering whether everything you believe is false?

There are a lot of ways to approach questions like these. *But if you approach them in the ways that are often glorified in public deconversion narratives, you may well find yourself struggling with or losing your faith for all the wrong reasons.*

In this chapter, we'll look at the powerful social pressure deconversion stories can place on believers and how the cumulative effect of those stories can negatively influence the way in which we handle our own doubts when they arise. Then we'll look at several ways we can process those doubts better.

The Power of Public Deconversion Stories

Biola University professor John Marriott has conducted what is perhaps the most comprehensive research to date on deconversions from Christianity to atheism in particular. Based on his personal interviews, analysis of written narratives, and prior research on the subject,

Marriott identifies and describes a typical set of steps toward deconversion in his book *The Anatomy of Deconversion*: (1) context (that is, the nature of a person's background), (2) a crisis of faith, (3) seeking to know the truth, (4) trying to retain the faith, (5) moving to agnosticism, (6) becoming an atheist, and (7) coming out as an atheist.[3] While Marriott acknowledges that not every person passes through every one of these stages, he says that each stage featured prominently in the majority of cases he studied.

Marriott's analysis is important because it dissects the long-term *private* experiences people have had that ultimately led to them walking away from Christianity—insights well beyond what collective statistics can ever provide. Those stories are nuanced, complex, and varied. They're also different in some important ways from the deconversion stories that are shared on social media and take the headlines by storm.

Public deconversion accounts are often presented in a specific way for influence—intended to not only inform people of a life change, but to also persuade others of the problems with Christianity.

They are, in a very real sense, "testimonies."

Just as Christians share their testimonies of coming to Jesus in the hope that others will want to share in a similar joy, deconverts often go public with their testimonies of rejecting the historic Christian faith in the hope that others will share in their rejection. Before the internet, a person may have quietly deconverted and gone on with their life, but today there's a whole cottage industry encouraging people to go public with their stories. There are podcasts, books, hashtags, and websites all dedicated to the cause—a growing movement and approach to publicly cultivating doubts about the biblical worldview. I'll call it *deconversionism*.

Blake Chastain, the originator of the popular #exvangelical hashtag, offered a glimpse into the breadth and nature of online deconversionism in this Facebook comment:

> #Exvangelical has flourished since 2016. Over 102M views on TikTok. Over 37K public uses on Instagram. On average 100K impressions per day on Twitter. It's wild. It's a

form of dissent, of validation, and connection (for as long as one needs). There are so many projects and aspects of the exvangelical dispersal. I'm humbled to have played a part in this public discussion of religion in America and the world.[4]

Those are remarkable numbers...and they're just for *one hashtag*! Note, too, that Chastain doesn't shy away from acknowledging the strong social nature of deconversionism ("dissent, validation, and connection")—it's not hyperbole to call this a movement.

With that said, *why* do these public stories get so many people talking? What makes them so impactful? Just as Marriott identified a seven-stage anatomy common to private deconversion experiences, I think we can similarly identify a three-stage anatomy common to public *accounts* of those experiences (including the deconstruction type): (1) the catalyst (roughly corresponding to Marriott's "crisis of faith" step); (2) the avalanche of questions (a critical, retrospective version of Marriott's "seeking to know the truth" step); and (3) the happy ending (a broader and rosier version of Marriott's "coming out as an atheist" step). Understanding the nature of these three aspects of public deconversion accounts will help us see why they're often so influential.

The Catalyst

When people speak publicly about their deconversion, they typically identify what "got the ball rolling" on the unraveling of their faith—the catalyst. These catalysts generally fall into one of three categories: intellectual, emotional, and what I'll call "moral indignation" (which straddles the intellectual and emotional).

Intellectual catalysts are doubts that arise about the facts of Christianity. Rhett (the YouTube celebrity of Rhett and Link fame), for example, said his doubts started with questions about science and evolution, and then continued to the reliability of the Bible and the evidence for the resurrection.

Emotional catalysts are doubts that arise from a more subjective response to experiences with the church or Christians. Marriott, for example, tells the story of a man who saw the church as a "social club with rules." If you didn't follow the rules, you wouldn't fit in. When the man eventually got a divorce, he felt that put him out of the "club," and he began the process of walking away from faith.[5]

Moral indignation catalysts are those rooted in a person's perception that their innate sense of morality is superior to the morality they believe is taught in the Bible or supported by the church. A good example of this comes from a story on the 2019 Evolving Faith Conference (a conference for progressive Christians):

> The catalysts of deconstruction may have been different for each speaker—racism, sexism, colonialism, LGBTQ exclusion, illness or the "problem of evil"—but their experiences mirrored one another: personal doubts and questions, hostility and even rejection from their churches once they questioned authority or otherwise came out of the closet.[6]

Nearly all of these noted catalysts of deconstruction have their roots in moral indignation. For example, a person who begins to deconstruct over concerns about LGBTQ "exclusion" is reacting with moral indignation to the Bible's teachings on homosexuality. A person who begins to deconstruct over concerns about colonialism is reacting with moral indignation to the historical actions of nations that colonized people groups in the name of Christianity.

Whether the catalyst is rooted in intellectual, emotional, or moral concerns, there's a common sentiment that runs through the public accounts of how deconversion began: "I was like you for a long time, but then I started to see what is self-evidently wrong with Christianity." Few people put it in exactly those terms, but the sentiment is often there. For those citing intellectual reasons, it's often presented as seeing how *unreasonable* believing in God or the Bible is. For those citing emotional reasons, it's often presented as seeing how *hurtful* the church or Christians are. And for those citing moral indignation reasons, it's often presented as seeing how *guilty* the historic Christian church has been for its position or role in social or historical issues.

What's often missing from public deconversion accounts, however, is information on what Marriott labels "context" (stage one in his model). Context refers to things like a person's education, profession, age, geographic location, or specific type of Christian background. Marriott found that among all the contextual factors that could possibly frame private deconversion experiences, the dominant one was the type of Christian background a person had. *More often than not, deconverts had little good to say about their time as Christians; leaving their faith felt like liberation from an oppressive system.*[7]

While Marriott's analysis was based on deconversions to atheism, the same feeling of liberation is commonly seen in deconstruction accounts. Marriott notes that a disproportionate number of deconverts with this perspective came from a "fundamentalist" background (a specific approach to faith that he characterizes as the avoidance of taboos, an embrace of anti-intellectualism, and a negative posture to those outside Christianity).[8] He also found that the vast majority had problems with Christianity *while being a Christian*—75 percent of deconverts identified with "a theological position, social issue, or lifestyle choice considered aberrant by their conservative Christian communities."[9]

This kind of *context* to the catalyst, missing from most public accounts, says a lot. In many cases, people are either deconverting from a legalistic form of Christianity (which isn't always consistent with what the Bible teaches), or they had long felt like an outsider in their church community—two circumstances that can lead to a certain kind of bitterness in how the catalyst for a deconversion experience is publicly framed. By implicitly (or explicitly) characterizing their deconversion catalyst as a realization that Christianity is *unreasonable*, *hurtful*, and/or *guilty*, the message is clear: Others should reexamine their beliefs, too, because the problems with Christianity are so obvious.

The Avalanche of Questions

The second component of many public deconversion narratives is a recounting of the many questions that ultimately led a person to reject their long-held beliefs. This "avalanche of questions" is often prefaced with comments about how either no one in the church *welcomed* their questions or how those who did couldn't give *satisfactory answers*. The implication in both cases is that Christianity can't stand up to tough questions. As an example, Marty Sampson from Hillsong wrote on Instagram:

> This is a soapbox moment so here I go…How many preachers fall? Many. No one talks about it. How many miracles happen. [sic] Not many. No one talks about it. Why is the Bible full of contradictions? No one talks about it. How can God be love yet send four billion people to a place, all 'coz they don't believe? No one talks about it.[10]

Popular ex-Christian rapper Jahaziel put his questions in a more declarative form in his deconversion announcement:

> Now, after 20 years of being vocal about the positives of Christian faith, I would like to take some time to be equally vocal about the negatives I have found, i.e., Christianity and its controlling dictatorship, its historic blood trail, its plagiarized Bible stories, characters and concepts, the many human errors of the Bible and its contradictions, the brutal nature of its God, its involvement in the slave trade, the crusades, the inquisition, the witch hunts…you get the drift.[11]

The presentation of an avalanche of questions can be particularly influential on Christians who aren't aware of the common claims of skeptics. The list can be shocking! The Bible has "plagiarized" stories? It's full of "contradictions"? No one knows who wrote the Gospels? The Bible was changed over time? If a person has never heard (much less researched) claims like these, doubts can be triggered quickly: If this is true, what *else* do I not know? Furthermore, the implication that the deconvert has already looked into the answers and *deconverted* because of what they found sends a powerful message to the uninitiated: There's a reason Christians don't want to talk about this stuff. Once you look into these things, there are no good answers.

The fact so many questions are raised adds to the impact of the message because it signals that there aren't just two or three tough issues Christians must grapple with, but an insurmountable heap. And on top of that, there are often hundreds or even thousands of social media responses from skeptics reinforcing the same ideas. When you couple all of this with the credibility people often assume celebrities have, you get a headline-making doubt propeller that can trigger faith insecurities across an ocean of believers.

The Happy Ending

Having declared the catalyst for deconversion and the avalanche of questions that were never satisfactorily answered, the narrative typically concludes with a happy ending that proclaims the joy of deconversion. For example, Joshua Harris's Instagram deconversion announcement ended, "To my Christians friends, I am grateful for your prayers. Don't take it personally if I don't immediately return calls. I can't join in your mourning. I don't view this moment negatively. I feel very much alive, and awake, and surprisingly hopeful."[12] The feelings of freedom that we saw in Marriott's analysis often show up in the happy ending of public narratives.

Those with deconstruction narratives tend to present their happy ending a bit differently. Instead of expressing a sentiment of, "I feel better than ever without God," they often say something more like, "I've recovered from the pain of my former beliefs and now want to bring hope to others who similarly see the need to find their own path to God outside of traditional Christianity." Progressive Christian pastor Colby Martin says on his website, for example, "Having experienced his fair share of pain and rejection from mainstream Christianity, Colby is awake to the flaws, tragic missteps, and misplaced earnestness that too often define the direction of the church. But God's vision for creation as revealed in Jesus still compels him."[13] In an interview with apologist Sean McDowell, Martin detailed the painful experiences his biography alludes to while emphasizing the happy ending: "I'm really glad it happened because my life now is full of so much joy and light and hope and goodness."[14]

For onlookers who have a faith background that has led them to feel that Christianity is oppressive, the happy ending reported in deconversion narratives can be extremely appealing. It appears to be the freedom they've never felt! And for those who have experienced pain from the church, deconstruction can sound like the path to spiritual healing, complete with a like-minded support group awaiting them at the end. Marriott's analysis shows that people often go through significant personal pain in the deconversion process, but that rarely shows up in public accounts. To the contrary, the happy ending of public deconversion narratives is a public assurance that there's nothing to worry about if you walk away from a biblical worldview. It serves as a powerful testimonial for secularism: *You can have the self-authority you've been wanting, and things will be better than ever.*

Now that we've seen how the nature of public deconversion accounts can powerfully trigger or reinforce doubts that Christians have, it's time to look at doubt from a biblical perspective.

Doubt Is Normal...and It's Okay

It's natural for people to see doubt as a bad thing, and perhaps that's why Christians often don't talk about it more openly—for fear of being seen negatively in their church community (something that surely needs to change). One of the reasons people tend to see doubt in a bad light is that they have a misunderstanding of the nature of *faith*; faith and doubt are seen as opposites. As Christians, we know the importance the Bible places on faith, so if we view doubt to be the *opposite* of that, we're going to think we're in big trouble when doubts arise. But faith and doubt *aren't* opposites, so we need to begin this discussion by establishing a better understanding of their relationship.

Faith, at its core, is trust. We can have faith in something or someone for good reasons or bad. If I have faith that a magical fairy will appear in my house today simply because I wish that would happen, that would be an example of blind and poorly placed faith. Unfortunately, skeptics often treat the word *faith* like it's synonymous with faith of this nature. Atheist author and ex-Christian pastor Dan Barker, for example, says, "Faith is a cop-out. It is intellectual bankruptcy. If the only way you can accept an assertion is by faith, then you are conceding that it can't be taken on its own merits."[15] Skeptics like Barker have been so vocal in portraying faith as if it's inherently blind that a lot of people—including Christians—have lost sight of the word's basic meaning.

Despite this negative association, everyone exercises faith every day. When you get into a car, you have faith that you'll get to your destination alive. When you eat an apple from your refrigerator, you have faith that it won't hurt you. When you agree to surgery, you have faith that the surgeon hasn't mispresented their expertise and will do the work to the best of their ability. But in none of these cases do you have *certainty*. You *could* get into a fatal car accident, find out that your apple was contaminated, or discover your surgeon was a con artist—even though you had good reason to trust otherwise. When you don't have absolute mathematical-type certainty about something, there is *always* room for doubt. Sometimes that room is large and sometimes it's small.

So what kind of faith does the Bible call us to have? The most direct description of faith is found in Hebrews 11:1: "Faith is the assurance of things hoped for, the conviction of things not seen" (ESV). Skeptics sometimes point to the words "hoped for" in this verse and claim that biblical faith is wishful thinking. But that ignores the other key words here—"assurance" and "conviction." Biblical hope isn't based on a fantasy. It *presupposes* that Christians have good reasons for belief, leading to assurance and conviction. Many verses in the Bible speak to the importance of good reasoning in the Christian life, despite the insistence of skeptics to the contrary (for example, Matthew 22:37; 1 Corinthians 13:11; 14:20; 1 Peter 3:15). The internal testimony of the Holy Spirit, as well as the external evidence for God's existence (see chapter 4), the reliability of the Bible (see reading recommendations in chapter 5), and the historical evidence for the resurrection (see reading recommendations at the end of this chapter) all form a robust foundation for having a confident faith.

But that doesn't mean Christians will never have doubts. In fact, the Bible itself reveals that doubt is normal in the human experience. My favorite example is from Luke 7. John the Baptist had been preaching in the wilderness of Judea about the coming of Jesus, baptizing people, and surviving on a diet of locusts and honey. To live the life he did, he was surely very convicted of the truth of his beliefs. But when he was later imprisoned for condemning the immoral actions of Herod Antipas, *he started to have doubts.* John sent two of his own disciples to ask Jesus, "Are you the one who is to come, or should we expect someone else?" (verse 20). Jesus replied, "Go back and report to John what you have seen and heard: The blind receive sight, the lame walk, those who have leprosy are cleansed, the deaf hear, the dead are raised, and the good news is proclaimed to the poor" (verse 22).

For those who struggle with doubt, Jesus's response should be balm for the soul. Notice what He didn't do: He didn't gasp, "How could you have doubts after all you've seen?" He didn't accuse John of not having faith. He didn't get angry. He didn't suggest John was unworthy of his calling. Instead, he calmly reaffirmed to the disciples that He was, indeed, the Messiah (borrowing language from Isaiah 35:5-6 and 61:1).

Then there's the event that forever earned Thomas, one of Jesus's disciples, the nickname *doubting* Thomas. Even though Thomas had witnessed Jesus's amazing life and miracles, he still questioned the other disciples' initial reports of Jesus's resurrection. He told them, "Unless I see the nail marks in his hands and put my finger where the nails were, and put my hand into his side, I will not believe" (John 20:25). One week later, Jesus appeared to the disciples again, this time when Thomas was present. He told Thomas, "Put your finger here; see my hands. Reach out your hand and put it into my side. Stop doubting and believe" (verse 27). Once again, Jesus didn't criticize the person doubting; He provided the evidence Thomas needed to believe.

Note, however, that Jesus did tell Thomas to stop doubting once He showed him the evidence. Just because doubt is a normal part of the journey doesn't mean it should be our destination! Jesus spoke several times about how doubt can hinder us spiritually (Matthew 14:31; 21:21; Luke 24:38). With that in mind, let's look at several practical ways to faithfully deal with doubts when they do arise.

Dealing with Doubts

Over the last decade of writing about worldview topics, I've heard from many people struggling to know what to do with an impending faith crisis. Based on those interactions and the analysis in this chapter, here are ten principles I believe are key to dealing with doubt.

1. Be honest with yourself about the nature of truth.

Truth doesn't depend on what we like, what our friends think, what costs us the least, or what makes the most sense to us personally. Truth is something we must commit to seeking regardless of those things. If we don't start with that acknowledgment, we can easily end up discovering the "truth" we prefer rather than the truth that exists. Having the right objective for the search is a critically important starting point.

2. Remember that truth has nothing to fear—even if the Christians you know don't welcome or can't answer your questions.

It's not surprising that deconverts often say their questions weren't welcomed or couldn't be answered. Unfortunately, many Christians have never taken the time to explore the rich evidence for their faith and don't know how to respond to challenges. That's why it's important to recognize that if those you know can't answer your questions, it just means that *those you know* can't answer your questions! For just about any question you can imagine, much has been written and discussed for hundreds of years. If you're searching for answers, be thorough. If Christianity is true, there's no need to fear what you will find by investigating.

3. Search your doubt to find its root.

Doubt can become a large ball of tangled spiritual yarn in your mind (like the "avalanche of questions" we looked at), where you don't even know how to begin unraveling all the entangled questions. That can feel overwhelming and seem like an unsolvable problem. But there's often a foundational question at the core of all those doubts.

If you can identify the *core* question, it will help narrow your spiritual searching.

Many people, for example, have a long list of "Why would God…?" questions (fill in the blank: allow evil, remain so hidden, not seem to answer more prayers, etc.). Collectively, those questions may feel too difficult to resolve. But at the root of them all is likely a nagging uncertainty over whether God even exists. In such a case, it would likely be more beneficial to study the evidence for God's existence than to dive into answers for every individual question in the ball of yarn. Once you're convicted of God's existence, you can come back to those individual questions with a fresh look that's focused on gaining understanding *given* your conviction that God exists.

4. Know the truth test for Christianity.

Regardless of what kinds of doubt you have, it's important to always be mindful of Paul's words from 1 Corinthians 15:14: "If Christ has not been raised, our preaching is useless and so is your faith." *According to the Bible itself, the resurrection is the truth test for Christianity.* Too often, I've seen people use everything *but* the resurrection as a truth test. In fact, I can't remember a single time someone has said to me, "I know this all comes down to the resurrection, but I'm struggling to see how the evidence points to Jesus being raised from the dead." Instead, people focus on things like whether they've personally seen a miracle, whether the church has responded to cultural issues in the way they think it should, whether God has answered a specific prayer in the way they had hoped, and so on. While it's understandable that questions like these can raise doubts in the first place, we need to remember that ultimately, they don't determine whether Christianity is true or not.

5. Make sure the things you're doubting are things the Bible actually teaches.

If you read or watch enough deconversion narratives, after a while, you'll notice that many of the things people say they're rejecting are the same things those with a biblical worldview reject. For example, you'll hear things like, "I could no longer believe that if I didn't spend my life reading the Bible, I would go to hell," or "I could no longer hate my LGBTQ friends," or "I could no longer support the abuse I've seen in the church." There's absolutely nothing in the Bible that suggests a person would go to hell for not reading Scripture, that we should hate anyone, or that we should support abuse in the church! If you're struggling with faith questions, be sure you're struggling with things the Bible actually teaches and not with popularized mischaracterizations.

6. Separate problems with the church or Christians from problems with Christianity.

As we saw earlier in this chapter, people who deconvert often have much to say about hurt they've experienced in churches or from individual Christians. Claims of things like legalism, hypocrisy, spiritual abuse, sexism, racism, and bigotry abound. And you know what? These things *are* a problem in some churches and with some Christians. But we have to remember that hurtful experiences don't necessarily have anything to do with the truth of Christianity. If a church or Christian is acting in a way that's contrary to what the Bible teaches, that shouldn't reflect poorly on Christianity itself. This is one of many reasons it's so important to know what the Bible says.

7. Be willing to put in the work to resolve your questions.

When someone emails me to share about their faith crisis, I immediately ask myself, *What are the best resources to recommend for these particular questions?* But I've found time after time that when I reply with recommendations for how and where to research, people will respond that they don't have time to read; they just want me to give them quick answers in an email format. Let me be blunt: If Christianity is true, there are eternal implications for what you believe. Could anything be a greater priority than resolving in your heart and mind whether your faith is well placed in Jesus? If you have questions, be willing to put in the work needed to find the answers.

8. Proactively expose yourself to faith challenges.

A young Christian college student I know posted on social media one day about a humanities class he was taking. He said that so far in the semester, he had "learned" that Jesus never claimed to be God in the synoptic Gospels (Matthew, Mark, and Luke), Christianity borrowed ideas from earlier pagan myths, and the church arbitrarily picked which books to include in the Bible according to its own biases. He noted:

> The reactions of other students are of shock and disbelief. Yesterday the professor asked a student how these facts made her feel. She said she was mad and couldn't wait to go yell at her pastor and parents. The professor egged her on. It was like watching a commander rally up his troops to tear down his enemy.

Sometimes Christians are shaken by the first challenges they encounter—whether in college or many years later—simply because they were unaware of the specific claims skeptics make. Just like this college student, they hear the claims, assume they're true (or at least true enough to be concerned), and then slide into anger or despair. *This is totally unnecessary.* Though it sounds counterintuitive, it's actually very healthy to proactively expose yourself to the claims of skeptics through the study of apologetics (making a case for and defending the truth of Christianity). When you expose yourself to more challenges along with thoughtful Christian answers, your confidence will grow, and you'll no longer be shocked when you come across new claims.

9. Explicitly identify your alternative to Christianity.

Many people struggling with their beliefs never take the next mental step and ask, "If I decide Christianity is *not* true, what will I then believe?" They assume that they'll no longer struggle with doubts about their worldview if they walk away—after all, don't all the deconversion narratives have a happy ending? But the reality is that there are unanswered questions in *any* worldview. No one has all the answers.

The question should never be "How do I get rid of all the unanswered questions I have?" but rather, "Which worldview offers the *best* explanation of reality?"

10. Pray and read the Bible.

Last but certainly not least, when you're struggling with faith, don't give up on prayer and reading the Bible. Much of what we've discussed in this and the previous chapter hinges on knowing what the Bible teaches and being able to distinguish that from what people *claim* it teaches. Ask God to illuminate His truth for you as you read Scripture, bringing clarity to your questions and the understanding He knows you need.

God Can Handle Our Doubts

Sometimes I have to remind myself that God isn't surprised by anything. The things that take me by surprise are things He knew before the foundation of the world—and the same goes for the things that can sometimes make us doubt Him or His Word. God knew precisely *what* He would reveal of Himself to humankind, *how* He would do that, what He would *not* reveal, and which unanswered questions would trouble us. In other words, God is perfect, so it's not as if He accidentally gave us too little information on the problem of evil, for example, and then regretted how much doubt that issue ended up causing humans throughout history. Given God's perfect nature, the revelation we *have* must be the revelation we *need*. We may want more, but we don't need more (see 2 Timothy 3:15-17).

This means that if Christianity is true, the solution for doubt isn't to bury it in the fear of what you might find; it's to investigate questions more deeply. Stories of people who struggle with doubt, search for answers, find answers, and subsequently deepen their faith don't make headlines the way deconversions do, but those stories happen all the time too.

Ian Harber is one of those stories. In his article "'Progressive' Christianity: Even Shallower Than the Evangelical Faith I Left," Harber wrote of how he deconstructed only to realize that the progressive vision of the world was like searching for "the kingdom without the King"—seeking blessings without submitting to God's rule and reign, progress without God's presence, justice without God's justification, the horizontal implications of the gospel for society without the vertical reconciliation of sinners with God, and conformity to our standard of morality without God's standard of holiness.[16] Once Harber saw these inconsistencies, he decided to pursue a formal theological education. It was through that *deeper understanding* of Christianity—which he didn't have before deconstruction—that he rebuilt his faith. We'll end this chapter with Harber's wise words from after his deconversion-reconversion experience:

> We need *more* theology, nuance, grace, compassion, and understanding in our churches, not less. But these things are made possible by orthodox doctrine, not in spite of it. Doubt and questions need not catalyze a pendulum swing from belief to unbelief. If worked out in healthy, thoughtful Christian community—and with an abiding connection to Christ, our true vine (John 15)—they can actually deepen faith and strengthen roots, producing a life where we bear fruit and withstand the fierce winds of a secular age.[17]

FOR FURTHER READING

On Deconversion

- John Marriott, *The Anatomy of Deconversion: Keys to a Life-long Faith in a Culture Abandoning Christianity* (Abilene, TX: Abilene University Press, 2020).

On Doubt

- Bobby Conway, *Doubting Toward Faith: The Journey to Confident Christianity* (Eugene, OR: Harvest House, 2015).

- Gary Habermas, *Dealing with Doubt* (Chicago, IL: Moody, 1990). This entire book is available for free online at http://www.garyhabermas.com/books/dealing_with_doubt/dealing_with_doubt.htm.

On Bible Difficulties

- Paul Copan, *Is God a Moral Monster?: Making Sense of the Old Testament God* (Grand Rapids, MI: Baker, 2011).

- Clay Jones, *Why Does God Allow Evil?: Compelling Answers for Life's Toughest Questions* (Eugene, OR: Harvest House, 2017).

- Dan Kimball, *How (Not) to Read the Bible: Making Sense of the Anti-women, Anti-science, Pro-violence, Pro-slavery and Other Crazy-Sounding Parts of Scripture* (Grand Rapids, MI: Zondervan, 2020).

QUESTIONS FOR DISCUSSION OR REFLECTION

1. Why do you think headline-making deconversion stories shake the faith of so many people?

2. Which type of catalyst for deconversion do you think is most common in today's culture—intellectual, emotional, or moral indignation? Why?

3. What are some questions you've struggled with in the past or currently struggle with regarding the truth of Christianity? Which one(s) do you feel you most need to prioritize seeking biblical answers to?

4. If a Christian friend of yours confided that they were struggling to still believe in Jesus because of the hurt they believe the church has caused, what are some suggestions you would share with them for dealing with those doubts (either from the "Dealing with Doubts" points in this chapter or from your own experience)?

PART 3:

FAITHFULLY DIFFERENT *THINKING*

Reclaiming What Rightfully Belongs to the Biblical Worldview

*Under the pressure of the
secular worldview buffet*

Something interesting I've learned over my years as a writer is that there are certain ways of phrasing things that seem perfectly normal to most people, but that can really trouble others. You don't know what you don't know, so as a writer, you generally learn these things *after* you make the mistake and receive comments and emails from the people you upset.

One example that especially took me by surprise was when someone chastised me for beginning a sentence with these two words: "Atheists believe…" Though I no longer have the exact comment to quote, it was something like this:

> I'm an atheist and you don't know what I believe. You don't know what my atheist friends believe. You don't know what any atheist believes! You would have to ask each person. It's not like a religion where we all believe the same thing. Just

because we lack belief in a god doesn't mean you can say *anything* about what atheists (in general) believe.

In one sense, he was right. When we say, for example, that Christians believe something, we're talking about the beliefs generally held by those who call themselves Christians. But that doesn't necessarily mean you can know what any individual Christian believes. As we saw in chapter 5, those who identify as Christians have all kinds of beliefs that aren't consistent with a biblical worldview.

But in another and more important sense, this commenter had a significant misunderstanding about the nature of worldviews. Yes, people can believe whatever they want to believe, and therefore you can never know what any individual holds to be true, but there are certain logical *implications* that flow from a person's fundamental assumptions about reality, whether they accept those implications or not. While I couldn't tell this commenter what he personally believed, I *could* tell him what's *consistent* with a naturalistic worldview.[1] If nothing exists beyond nature, that implies the natural world must be explained solely by natural forces. The universe had to come into existence by chance, the first living cell had to develop from nonliving matter by chance, and all living things must be the eventual product of some blind, undirected process (with evolutionary theory being the prevailing scientific consensus of what that process was). These three claims alone have numerous implications about the nature of reality, as we saw at the end of chapter 4.

In spite of these implications, many atheists have beliefs that aren't logically consistent with their worldview. Nearly everyone in our culture—including atheists—takes for granted the existence, definition, and positive value of things like objective morality, human equality, human rights, freedom, love, and justice. But, as we'll see in this chapter, there's no objective basis for any of them in a naturalistic worldview. And although I've started with the example of atheism, the same holds true for other secular worldviews as well. *Any worldview in which the ultimate authority is the individual will lack an objective basis for defining and defending some of our culture's most cherished values.*

A biblical worldview, on the other hand, provides an objective basis for *all* these things. As Christians, we need to better understand what rightfully belongs to the biblical worldview but is often "borrowed" by secular culture. Why does it matter? Today's culture often uses concepts that *belong* to a biblical worldview *against* those with a biblical worldview—and then pressures Christians to reject the very worldview that provides a basis for those concepts in the first place!

In the previous three chapters, we focused on what it means to be a worldview minority that *believes* differently than the dominant culture. Understanding what logically flows from those biblical beliefs—and what does *not* logically flow from secularism—is one of three subjects we'll now explore as we consider how what we *believe* should translate into how we *think*.

When Your Worldview Won't Fit in Its Box

In her book *Finding Truth: 5 Principles for Unmasking Atheism, Secularism, and Other God Substitutes*, author Nancy Pearcey develops five principles that reveal how almost every non-Christian worldview borrows from Christianity.[2] Her work builds off of Paul's important words in Romans 1:18-25:

> The wrath of God is being revealed from heaven against all the godlessness and wickedness of people, who suppress the truth by their wickedness, since what may be known about God is plain to them, because God has made it plain to them. For since the creation of the world God's invisible qualities—his eternal power and divine nature—have been clearly seen, being understood from what has been made, so that people are without excuse.
>
> For although they knew God, they neither glorified him as God nor gave thanks to him, but their thinking became futile and their foolish hearts were darkened. Although they claimed to be wise, they became fools and exchanged the glory of the immortal God for images made to look like a mortal human being and birds and animals and reptiles.

Therefore God gave them over in the sinful desires of their
hearts to sexual impurity for the degrading of their bodies
with one another. They exchanged the truth about God for
a lie, and worshiped and served created things rather than
the Creator.

According to this passage, those who reject the Creator will create an idol out of some part of the created order—a false absolute to
replace the one true God. But, as Pearcey shows, *idols always lead to a
lower view of human life*. She explains:

We can be confident that every idol-based worldview *will*
fail. Why? Precisely because it leads to reductionism. If
reductionism is like trying to stuff the entire universe into
a box, we could say that inevitably something will stick
out of the box. A box that deifies a *part* of creation will
always be too limited to explain the *whole*. Whatever does
not fit into the box will be denigrated, devalued, or dismissed as unreal.[3]

Pearcey points out that in materialism, for example, people are reduced
to products of physical forces because nothing immaterial is believed
to exist. In postmodernism, people are reduced to products of social
forces because humans are viewed as having no power to transcend
social and historical conditions. In pantheistic worldviews such as Hinduism and Buddhism, people are (literally) reduced to nothing because
the divine and the universe are believed to be one—the self doesn't even
exist. But when you try to press the fullness of human personhood into
a reductionist worldview box, something inevitably sticks out; we intuitively know we're more than that.

Pearcey gives the example of philosopher John Searle, who embraces
materialism yet admits humans cannot consistently live by its principles. Searle acknowledges that in his materialistic view, the universe is
like a vast machine in which all human action is determined, but he
concedes that we nonetheless seem to be capable of making free decisions. He says, "We can *say*, OK, I believe in determinism, but the

conviction of freedom is built into our experiences…We *can't give up* our conviction of our own freedom, even though there's no ground for it."[4] As Pearcey observes, Searle recognizes that "his worldview box is too small to account for reality as *he himself* experiences it. He 'can't give up' his conviction of freedom. He 'can't live with' his own philosophy. Searle is trapped in cognitive dissonance—what his worldview tells him contradicts what he knows from general revelation,"[5]

One of the beauties of a biblical worldview is that it doesn't require any reductionist stuffing. It accounts for and affirms the fullness of our unique human identity. Continuing with Pearcey's analogy, we're going to look at how the secular worldview box can never fully contain some of the ideas we value and take for granted most: objective morality, human equality, human rights, and freedom.

Evaluating the Sources for Some of Our Most Cherished Values

Objective Morality: Who or What Defines Good and Evil?

You'll recall from chapter 2 that the secular view of God and man boils down to the idea that we're free to be who we want to be and do what we want to do because there's no higher-than-human authority who's given us specific information about or moral directives for our lives (either because that authority doesn't exist or because any such authority who *might* exist hasn't revealed those things). While that was a helpful starting point for discussion, we're going to dig more deeply now into the logical implications of a secular worldview for morality—and why objective morality will never fit in the secular worldview box.

In a naturalistic worldview, we are nothing more than our physical parts. We're effectively just molecular machines moving about a machine-like universe. In order for there to be some kind of moral law that would apply to all these molecular machines, there would have to be a moral *lawgiver* with the moral *authority* to define morality for all. That being doesn't exist in a naturalistic worldview, so good and evil can be nothing more than subjective labels any given molecular machine places on an action (and this ignores the question of whether molecular machines are even capable of the free will necessary to make moral decisions, which we'll get to shortly).

Other secular worldviews suffer from a similar problem, even when they include a belief in a supernatural being or force (for example, the type of worldview held by those who consider themselves "spiritual but not religious"). If a supernatural being or force exists but has no moral will or has not *revealed* a moral will, an individual has no objective basis for telling other individuals what is good or evil—how would that person know better than anyone else?

A secular worldview, therefore, has no place in its box for *objective* morality—moral values and duties that apply to all people—because there's no basis for it. When you hold a worldview in which the authority is the self, you gain the perceived freedom to do what you want but lose the objective basis for telling anyone else what is morally good or evil. To a degree, this is the dream of secular culture! Remember: Feelings are the ultimate guide, happiness is the ultimate goal, judging is the ultimate sin, and God is the ultimate guess. But as we saw in chapter 2, that doesn't mean secular culture has given up on categories of good and evil in order to live consistently within its worldview box. To the contrary, our culture has its own *very* strong ideas of what's right and wrong.

Now, there wouldn't be a logical problem with that if the corresponding secular message was something like, "Hey, we recognize we have no objective basis for claiming what's good or evil because we're each our own authority. But there are a bunch of us who have the same (subjective) opinion about what people should do, so we're going to band together to try to convince others to change *their* opinions. Even so, we recognize that every moral opinion is equally valid. That means there's nothing inherently right about what we think or inherently wrong about what you think. We just hope you'll change your opinion to believe as we do! Have a nice day."

I'm guessing that's a far cry from what you're hearing today. Secular culture doesn't see the popular moral consensus as simply the number of people collectively holding the same *opinion*. Rather, they see the popular moral consensus as objective moral truth for everyone. If you don't agree with secular views of sexuality, for example, you'll be told that you're *wrong*, not that your view is simply different but equally valid. And that's where the worldview sticks out of the box; it has no basis for making such claims.

There's a lot of confusion about this topic in culture, so let's take time to apply what we just discussed to three common misunderstandings that underlie secular moral criticisms of Christianity.

MISUNDERSTANDING #1: SECULARISM DOESN'T REALLY MAKE CLAIMS OF OBJECTIVE MORALITY—IT JUST FOLLOWS A "DO NO HARM" PRINCIPLE.

Many secularists would insist they *are* fine with what anyone wants to do—as long as it doesn't hurt others. For example, an online course called "Introducing Humanism: Non-religious Approaches to Life" says, "Humanists believe everyone should have the right to hold and manifest whichever religious or non-religious beliefs they want, so long as they do no harm to others, and that should include the right to change one's beliefs."[6] Do you see the logical inconsistency here? This philosophy attempts to leave everyone to their own authority but smuggles in a moral *exception*: Do whatever you want "so long as" you do no harm to others! The idea that all that matters is you don't harm someone else is just as much an objective moral claim as any other claim in which you're telling people what they should or shouldn't do. If a secular worldview has no basis for objective morality, it has no basis for even *one* objective moral claim. It's going to stick out of the box.

Furthermore, this popular idea raises questions about what constitutes harm in the first place. Secularists often claim, for example, that Christians are "harming" certain groups when they advocate for biblical morality that conflicts with the popular moral consensus. The conversation then quickly turns from "Christians can believe whatever they want" to "Christians are *hurting* others with their views." It's easy to see that people who say as much believe that what they're saying is *objectively* true—Christians are hurting others regardless of whether they think they are or not. That's where the emotional pressure comes in. No one wants to feel like they're hurting others! But from a biblical perspective, we have to be mindful that the definition of what is good or harmful for people has an objective basis in who God is and what He wills for us. Secular culture may think Christians are *harming* people by advocating for pro-life policies, for example, but in the context of a biblical worldview—in which every human is inherently valuable and made in the image of God—Christians are actually working for an objective *good.*

MISUNDERSTANDING #2: CHRISTIANS THINK ONLY THOSE WHO BELIEVE IN GOD (OR IN THE CHRISTIAN GOD SPECIFICALLY) CAN BE MORAL.

This may be the most common misunderstanding people have today about the nature of morality in a biblical worldview. The following excerpt from a blog post perfectly captures the popular sentiment. Though the blogger wrote this from his perspective as an atheist, the same sentiment is commonly shared by others with a secular worldview:

> I have been a believing Christian and I have "de-converted" to atheism. Nowhere along the way did I say to myself "Oh, hey, now I can go out raping and killing people. What a relief that I can finally just let these base urges run rampant."…If you don't think people can live moral lives without God, aren't you really just admitting that you couldn't live a moral life without God?…If that's the case, my friend, then I'm thankful there is a religion that is capable of containing the vile and base urges of people like you. I'm thankful for the religion that is putting a stop to the immorality of all those who couldn't be moral without it. But to assume that everyone is like that is to misunderstand people and morality. I don't need God to be moral or to understand what morality is.[7]

When this blogger rhetorically said, "If you don't think people can live moral lives without God," he betrayed a significant misunderstanding. In all our preceding discussion about objective morality, note that nothing was said about who is *capable* of acting in accordance with an objective morality rooted in a biblical worldview. Christians should recognize that *anyone* can behave morally because the Bible says that the moral law is written on the human heart and our consciences bear witness to it (Romans 2:15). The question is not whether people of any worldview can behave morally (they can!), it's whether people with a secular worldview have any objective basis for *defining* morality within their own worldview box. This blogger assumes, for example, that we all know raping and killing people are bad things to do. But in his worldview, there's no objective basis for everyone agreeing on even that! He appeals to what people sense to be obviously wrong, but without the existence of a moral lawgiver, there can be no objective moral difference between giving someone a hug and killing them.

Ironically, it's *because* of our biblical worldview that we don't believe non-Christians are one step away from raping and pillaging society or that Christians would be acting on "vile and base urges" but for their religious beliefs. As we saw, the Bible tells us that everyone has a God-given moral compass. People will often choose to do what's right based on that compass, regardless of whether they acknowledge its source or not. But a biblical worldview explains why humans act on vile and base urges as well. The Bible says, "All have sinned and fall short of the glory of God" (Romans 3:23) and that "if we say we have no sin, we deceive ourselves, and the truth is not in us" (1 John 1:8 ESV). Humans are by nature in rebellion against God, so we won't always choose what we know to be right no matter what we hold as a worldview. However, as born-again Christians, we are to "put off [our] old self" (Ephesians 4:22) and yield to the Holy Spirit so we can be conformed to the likeness of Christ (Romans 8:29). We're given a new nature, but that doesn't mean we'll no longer sin.

In short, this blogger was correct in his conclusion ("I don't need God to be moral or to understand what morality is") if he meant he doesn't need to *believe* in God for those things to be true about him. The irony is that he was correct only according to the biblical worldview he attempted to challenge. In his own worldview, he had no objective basis for defining morality at all.

MISUNDERSTANDING #3: PEOPLE WHO DON'T BELIEVE IN GOD
ARE MORE MORAL WHEN THEY DO WHAT'S RIGHT BECAUSE THEY
AREN'T MOTIVATED BY SPIRITUAL REWARDS OR PUNISHMENT.

It follows from my prior point that Christians don't necessarily behave more morally than anyone else. Anyone can behave morally, and Christians are at varying places in their growth toward sanctification (the process of becoming more like Jesus). But sometimes the opposite claim is made: that nonbelievers are actually *more* moral when they do what's right because they're not motivated by a spiritual reward or punishment.

As an example, a Facebook friend of mine recently shared the following story, to the great enthusiasm of many who responded:

> A Master teaches a student that God created everything in the world to be appreciated, since everything is here to teach us a lesson. One clever student asked, "What lesson can we learn from atheists? Why did God create them?"
>
> The Master responded, "God created atheists to teach us the most important lesson of them all—the lesson of true compassion. You see, when an atheist performs an act of charity, visits someone who is sick, helps someone in need, and cares for the world, he is not doing so because of some religious teaching. He does not believe that god [sic] commanded him to perform this act. In fact, he does not believe in God at all, so his acts are based on an inner sense of morality. And look at the kindness he can bestow upon others simply because he feels it to be right.
>
> "This means," the Master continued, "that when someone reaches out to you for help, you should never say, 'I pray that God will help you.' Instead for the moment, you should become an atheist, imagine that there is no God who can help, and say 'I will help you.'"[8]

I hope that in reading this, several things have already jumped out to you based on our earlier discussion. The Master assumes that "true" compassion depends on whether someone has followed their "inner sense of morality" versus a "religious teaching." But that's a false dichotomy. In a secular worldview, as we've seen, compassion can have no objective moral value. And if there's no objective moral value to deem it something anyone *ought* to have, it doesn't matter *where* it originates from; it's just one more type of amoral behavior in an amoral universe. Also, in the atheist's worldview, that "inner sense of morality" would be nothing more than a subjective feeling. The Master is seemingly quite impressed with the atheist who does what's right, but he never acknowledges how the atheist's own worldview provides no objective basis for any of this to even matter, nor that the missing relationship with his Creator is of any significance (eternal or otherwise).

In a biblical worldview, however, the inner sense of morality has an objective basis in God Himself. The fact that God has *additionally* revealed who He is and His moral will in the "religious teachings" of Scripture doesn't make a person who's being obedient to what He said any less compassionate! In fact, it's the Bible that makes clear what it means to be compassionate in the first place. Our inner sense of morality (general revelation) goes hand in hand with the teachings of Scripture (special revelation).

Though what I'm about to say is not directly related to our point here, it's worth mentioning that the story concludes with another false dichotomy: that a person must choose between praying God will help someone and doing something themselves. But the Bible tells us to pray without ceasing (1 Thessalonians 5:17) *and* care for God's people (Matthew 25:40). There's no need to pretend you're an atheist, as the Master suggests, in order to be motivated to help others. In a biblical worldview, loving others flows out of a love for God.

When secular culture cheers on stories like this, the message to Christians is clear: "We don't need what your religion has to offer. You think you're more moral than we are, but not only is that not true, we're actually more moral than *you!*" As we've seen, however, this is based on logical inconsistencies within the secular worldview, coupled with misunderstandings of the biblical worldview. It's also based on the assumption that religions are nothing more than ethical systems. But as we saw in chapter 5, Christianity is about who Jesus is, what He has done, and how we are to respond—both in belief and behavior.

I've devoted a lot of space here to the topic of morality because it's so often a point of confusion among both Christians and secularists. But much of what we discussed here provides a foundation for our remaining points, so we'll now be able to cover those more briefly.

Human Equality: What Makes People Equal?

We touched on the subject of equality in chapter 2 when we looked at the views of ethicist Peter Singer, who argues that there are morally justifiable circumstances for killing a disabled infant. While that is reprehensible to most people, we saw why his reasoning is consistent with his naturalistic worldview. If humankind is nothing more than the product of the blind, undirected process of evolution, human life can be no more inherently valuable than its physical components. Speaking of equality within that worldview box is like comparing rocks. Rocks can be equal in size, shape, weight, or other physical characteristics, but there can be no comparison of *value* unless there are humans who *give* the rocks value.

Similarly, without a creator of life to give *us* value, there's no such thing as human equality in the sense that every human is inherently equal. For secularists who accept the naturalistic evolutionary view, a more consistent understanding would be that people are very *unequal* because we can only be compared on the basis of our physical traits. If being tall is particularly beneficial to society, for example, those who are taller would be considered more valuable in a practical sense. There would be no objective basis for claiming that shorter people have just as much value simply because they're *human*.

For secularists who believe that a supernatural being exists but hasn't revealed anything specific about him/her/itself outside of nature, there's still no objective basis for claiming that humans were created with equal value. If we know nothing specific about that supernatural being, we have no way of knowing whether he/she/it did, in fact, give every human the same value. What if those with freckles were given *more* value by this mysterious author of life? That sounds absurd, but the point is, we simply wouldn't know.

Although human equality doesn't fit in the secular worldview box, it's a buzzword often used against those who hold to a biblical view of sexuality. If you search the hashtag #humanequality on social media, for example, you'll see a stream of posts alleging that those who don't agree that gender is fluid or that marriage should be redefined are opposed to "human equality." There are three problems with such claims. First, as we've seen, it's actually a *biblical* worldview—not a secular one— that provides an objective basis for believing that all humans are truly equal. Second, these posts conflate equality and morality. Christians believe every human is equal in value and made in the image of God, but the *morality* of the choices humans make is a separate question. Third, these posts also conflate equality with rights. Again, Christians believe everyone is equal, but that doesn't imply that everyone has an inherent "right" to all the same things in society (we assume, for example, that adults and kids have different rights).

And, as it turns out, the question of human rights is yet another one that hinges on worldview. Let's look at that now.

Human Rights: Where Do They Come From?

Human rights are the rights considered to be inherent to all human beings. The United Nations' Office of the High Commissioner for Human Rights puts it this way:

> Human rights are rights we have simply because we exist as human beings—they are not granted by any state. These universal rights are inherent to us all, regardless of nationality, sex, national or ethnic origin, color, religion, language, or any other status.[9]

Most people would read this statement and agree that such rights exist and are important to protect. But—and I hope you saw this coming— the secular worldview provides neither an objective basis for claiming inherent human rights exist nor an objective basis for defining what they are.

Once again, consider the implications of secular worldviews that assume naturalistic evolution. A "right" is something to which a person is entitled, but we can't be entitled to something unless someone entitles us to it. A government can pass laws to create societal rights for its citizens, but those aren't the kind of universally held rights meant by the term "human rights." Without a higher-than-human authority to give *all* people rights, universally held rights can't exist.

Furthermore, the idea of *human* rights assumes there's something special about humans relative to other living creatures—that we have rights to things like life and liberty, even though no one presumes animals have those same rights in the same sense. *Yet, in naturalistic evolution, humans are just another animal that developed by chance over time.* People care about animal welfare, of course, yet you don't see activists working to make sure animals don't kill each other due to their inherent "right" to life. But there's no reason in such a worldview to assume humans have unique rights that other animals don't. Some secularists have tried to get around this by suggesting that it's our cognitive capabilities that make us uniquely entitled to rights, but the possession of certain cognitive capabilities doesn't change the fundamental worldview problem: There's still no one to give us those rights in the first place, and there's no reason to assume that cognitive abilities are a rights-distinguishing biological feature while something like the kangaroo pouch isn't. Using cognitive abilities as a justification for human rights also implies that humans who *lack* certain abilities are entitled to fewer rights than others.

Moreover, even *if* a secular case could be made that humans have rights because we're in some sense special, in a secular worldview, there's no objective basis for defining what those rights would be. One person could claim we have the inherent human right to eat bananas all day, while another could claim we have the inherent human right to take another person's life whenever we want. *Given that there's no objective basis for morality in secularism, it can't even be assumed that the rights we supposedly have are rights we would categorize as being good!*

In a biblical worldview, human rights logically follow from the inherent value and equality of all people. *Given* that all people are valuable and equal as image bearers of God, we can infer a right to live freely and with dignity. Human equality and human rights fit naturally together in the biblical worldview box, but neither fits in a secular one.

Freedom: What Makes It Possible?

Earlier in this chapter, we saw how philosopher John Searle acknowledged that in a materialistic worldview, there's no ground for freedom of thought to exist. If the universe is just a physical machine, our thoughts are nothing more than physical forces acting within the brain. As evolutionary biologist Jerry Coyne says:

> To assert that we can freely choose among alternatives is to claim, then, that we can somehow step outside the physical structure of our brain and change its workings. That is impossible. Like the output of a programmed computer, only one choice is ever physically possible: the one you made.[10]

This is not a small issue. The nature of reality significantly depends on whether we have some degree of free will. For example, if we don't have free will, no one can be held morally accountable for their actions—they only did what they *had* to do according to their biology. In that case, defining what's morally right or wrong is a moot point. We don't even have the *freedom* to do what's right or wrong! Neither do we have the freedom to do any number of other things people just assume to be important in life. We can't, for example, genuinely love others, act justly, or use reason if we're merely puppets of our biology.

According to the biblical worldview, God created us in His image, giving us the freedom to make meaningful choices. He wanted to be in genuine *relationship* with us and gave us the freedom to love Him… or not. The choices we make in this life matter because they're actual choices, not robotic actions prompted by biology. It's ironic, then, that so many people who deconvert from Christianity speak of how "freeing" their new worldview is (see chapter 6). While they're thinking in terms of freedom from the constraints of biblical morality and God's authority, they're failing to recognize that a worldview without God (or without a God who has revealed anything about who we are) has no basis for assuming *any* kind of freedom. Once again, we see that something humans take for granted—freedom—fits right into the biblical worldview box but sticks out of the secular one.

Reclaiming Our Worldview Pieces Is Worth the Effort

I realize that for many readers the contents of this chapter may be challenging. Yet these concepts are important because they demonstrate the inconsistencies in many people's secular worldview—inconsistencies held while those same people champion their worldview as being *superior to* a biblical one. Unfortunately, this subject is rarely discussed in churches, so thinking about these concepts is new for most people and can take some initiative and effort.

But let's put the value of doing so in a bit of historical perspective.

If you were a new Christian living in Rome around the year AD 200, you would have been required to do three years of schooling with an authorized teacher once a week, outside of the weekly church service, in order to be baptized—a minimum of 144 hours of lectures (granting a month off per year).[11] Students studied the Scriptures in-depth, and the material was heavily apologetic, instructing new believers on how Christian truth stood superior to pagan philosophy and religion. To modern ears, this sounds rather intense. Today, we would fear that such requirements would turn away too many prospective believers. After all, there are barbeques to get to and baseball games to watch. But Christians of that period were a minority surrounded by a pagan culture and faced persecution. They *had* to put in the time to deeply understand their faith if they were going to persevere through great hardships.

In the context of church history, it's eye-opening to think of how similar our situation is becoming today as a worldview minority. The difference in the approach taken by early Christians was rooted in the fact that they didn't have hundreds of years of Christianity-infused culture behind them to blind them to the need for developing a robust intellectual foundation for their faith. For them, the need was obvious.

They understood that in order for new believers to stand strong in a culture dominated by an opposing worldview, they needed more preparation than weekly worship and potlucks. *They needed to understand why Christ was literally worth being persecuted for.*

Today, we're on the other side of Christianity having proliferated, having become the dominant worldview influence in America, and having waned as the mainstream cultural view of reality. Because of that history, there's a significant hangover of Christian values that secular society simply takes for granted. As I said in chapter 1, much of the cultural conflict Christians are experiencing today is the delayed effect of culture throwing out values that have lingered on long after people discarded the corresponding Christian doctrines. But, as we saw in this chapter, there are many other values rooted in a biblical worldview that secular culture continues to cherish without realizing they're borrowing capital from a Christian legacy.

Whereas the early church needed a strong apologetic foundation to *introduce* its worldview to the dominant culture, today's church needs a strong apologetic foundation to reclaim the borrowed parts of its worldview *from* a dominant culture. In doing so, we strengthen our own convictions as we grasp how only a biblical worldview can accommodate all we intuitively know about the nature of humanity in its worldview "box"—a coherence that speaks volumes about the truth of Christianity. But we can also strengthen our case to the secular world when we're able to graciously articulate one of the greatest (and most telling) ironies of our time: *Humans gravitate to the authority of the self, yet intuitively continue to cherish values that depend on the existence and authority of God*—a God who can define morality, imbue humans with equality, entitle humans to rights, and create humans with the free will needed to make genuine choices like loving others, acting justly, and utilizing reason.

As was the case for those in the early church, it takes effort to gain this understanding. But that effort is extraordinarily valuable for loving the Lord with our minds and helping others to open *their* minds to His truth.

FOR FURTHER READING

- Nancy Pearcey, *Finding Truth: 5 Principles for Unmasking Atheism, Secularism, and Other God Substitutes* (Colorado Springs, CO: David C. Cook, 2015).

- Michael Sherrard, *Why You Matter: How Your Quest for Meaning Is Meaningless without God* (Grand Rapids, MI: Baker, 2021).

- Andy Steiger and Sheri Hiebert, *Reclaimed: How Jesus Restores Our Humanity in a Dehumanized World* (Grand Rapids, MI: Zondervan, 2020).

- Frank Turek, *Stealing from God: Why Atheists Need God to Make Their Case* (Colorado Springs, CO: NavPress, 2015).

QUESTIONS FOR DISCUSSION OR REFLECTION

1. How would you summarize why the concept of objective morality sticks out of the secular worldview "box"? And why does it fit coherently within the biblical one?

2. Based on this chapter's discussion, how would you respond if a friend said to you, "I don't need to believe in God in order to know what's right and wrong"?

3. Why do you think most people believe in human equality even though many of them hold a worldview in which there's no objective basis for it?

4. What are some ways the church could better train Christians today to be familiar with subjects like the ones presented in this chapter?

CHAPTER 8

Reaffirming Biblical Morality

*Under the pressure of
secular virtue signaling*

n April 2015, author James Bartholomew wrote an article in *The Spectator* about the concept of "easy virtue"—saying things publicly (especially on social media) to indicate to the world you are "kind, decent, and virtuous" without actually doing anything.[1] Bartholomew called this increasingly common phenomenon "virtue signaling," and the rest is history. The term was launched into the everyday vocabulary of millions of people ready to critically label anything that smacks of mere virtue signaling.

The phrase has since taken on a life of its own, with people using it in many different ways and contexts. In some cases, it's turned into a label people apply indiscriminately to any public statement they disagree with: "Oh, that person doesn't *really* care about [fill-in-the-blank issue]. They're just *virtue signaling*." But in plenty of other cases, it's an appropriate description of some highly significant cultural trends, particularly with respect to the promotion of the secular moral consensus.

To understand why, we need to first look at the multidimensional definitions of the phrase. One dictionary says virtue signaling is "the action or practice of publicly expressing opinions or sentiments intended to demonstrate one's good character or the moral correctness of one's position on a particular issue."[2] This definition makes virtue signaling a statement about the individual expressing themself.

But another dictionary extends the meaning to the intended *social effect* of virtue signaling, saying it's "the sharing of one's point of view on a social or political issue, often on social media, in order to garner praise or acknowledgment of one's righteousness from others who share that point of view, or to passively rebuke those who do not."[3] In this definition, we've moved from virtue signaling being about how a person hopes people will see them to how they hope people will *respond* to them—in praise or in feeling rebuked for not sharing the same position.

A third definition adds yet another dimension, this time related to inaction: "An effort to demonstrate one's high moral standing by expressing opinions on political and social issues that will likely be agreeable to others, often with little or no intent to act on said opinions."[4] The emphasis in this definition is on the *ineffectiveness* of what's being said; the person is merely staking out a moral position without doing anything tangible to effect change for what they supposedly care about.

As we can see, there are a lot of nuances to what people popularly call virtue signaling. I'm detailing them here for two reasons: (1) to introduce the term to those who may not be familiar with it, and (2) to clearly distinguish which aspects of virtue signaling we're going to address in this chapter and which we're not. For the purposes of this book, I'm not interested in psychoanalyzing people's motivations (only God knows the heart) or whether they're sufficiently acting beyond their words to give credibility to their statements (who's in a position to judge that?). My objective is both simpler and more important.

I want to take the moral statements people and institutions publicly make at face value and assume (1) they truly believe the position they're stating is the morally good position to have, and (2) they believe there's some kind of value in stating that position publicly (otherwise they wouldn't have bothered to say anything at all). *What we'll see is that these bare-bones aspects of virtue signaling play an important role in promoting the secular moral consensus over and against a biblical view of morality.* Christians must be able to think carefully about the morality that is quite literally being *marketed* today and how God calls us to respond to these significant moral pressures.

Virtue Signaling as Moral Marketing

In my years as a marketing executive, I came to deeply appreciate one particular model that people in the marketing field have used for more than 100 years in various shapes and forms. It's a simple funnel that describes the psychological stages people go through before committing to a behavior: Awareness, Interest, Desire, Action (AIDA). In the context of marketing, this is typically used to analyze how people get to a purchase action. With low-involvement purchases like gum, consumers don't spend much time in the funnel; they see something appealing in the grocery store check-out line and grab it. But with high-involvement purchases like cars, the funnel is an excellent tool for describing the longer-term mental processes that lead to a person taking action.

Just as we used some insights from marketing in chapter 3, we're going to use insights derived from the AIDA funnel as they relate to the psychology of marketing *morality*. For our purpose, the desired action at the end of the funnel isn't a physical buy-in (as with a car), but rather, a *moral* buy-in. Though this isn't how the AIDA funnel is normally applied, we'll see how remarkably relevant this concept is for understanding how virtue signaling functions in culture to advance notions of secular morality toward acceptance.

Virtue Signaling for Redefinition (Awareness Stage)

It should make intuitive sense that the first stage in a funnel toward any kind of buy-in is *awareness*. You can't buy into something you're not aware of. Sometimes this is a simple matter of publicity: "Our new toothpaste brand is now available!" But marketers often fight a different kind of battle at the awareness stage—that of ensuring prospective consumers have the *right* awareness of their product. If, for example, people are already aware of your toothpaste brand, but they have in

mind that it causes offensively bad breath, you'll have to work on *redefining* their awareness. The wrong kind of awareness is often worse than no awareness.

Similarly, when it comes to changing the popular moral consensus, the first step is to revise language associated with a cause to eliminate negative associations and create new positive ones.

One of the most notable examples of recent successes in redefinition includes the words *equality, diversity,* and *tolerance* in relation to LGBTQ causes. In 2004, only 31 percent of Americans favored same-sex marriage. By 2019, support had grown to more than 60 percent of Americans.[5] In less than two decades, those who held to a biblical view of marriage went from having a relatively mainstream position to being shamed in culture for being against "equality, diversity, and tolerance." Of course, those who hold to a biblical view of marriage aren't against equality, diversity, and tolerance as traditionally defined, but these words have come to mean something different now. *Equality* no longer means believing every human is of equal inherent value; it means believing that everyone's sexual choices are of equal *moral* value. *Diversity* no longer means believing in the benefit of discussing multiple viewpoints; it means elevating popular moral viewpoints and silencing others. And *tolerance* no longer means bearing with ideas other than your own; it means affirming the current moral consensus.

There's much more than rebranding that's required for a movement to eventually gain buy-in, and that's why the AIDA funnel is a funnel and not a one-step task. To be sure, there are plenty of causes that get stuck at the first *A* (awareness) with their redefinition attempts and never get further. Pedophiles, for example, have been working to redefine themselves as "minor attracted persons" (MAPs), but you don't see the giant supportive displays at your local big-box store for MAPs that you do for LGBTQ causes—their movement hasn't made it through the rest of the funnel. The redefinition efforts that become successful are those that catch on outside the circles of those with an immediate interest in the cause. They're the efforts that end up getting championed by a mainstream culture that's motivated to publicly "signal" the virtue of the new idea on behalf of those directly affected.

There's a key to driving that motivation. *In order for people to eventually care enough to change their language and publicly signal their support, they have to believe others are being harmed by the status quo and that they're contributing to a moral good by speaking up.* For example, a writer advocating for the use of the term *sex worker* instead of *prostitute* says, "Although political correctness frequently comes in for mocking, we cannot and will not achieve social equality for anyone if the language we use to describe marginalised [sic] groups actually reinforces the stigma they face."[6]

Activists clearly understand that language is a key stepping-stone toward changing public perceptions of morality and that framing the discussion in terms of steps toward "equality" for the "marginalized" to reduce "stigma" is an important success factor. It's no coincidence, therefore, that words like *equality*, *diversity*, and *tolerance* have led the way for the public shift in LGBTQ attitudes. These words imply there was a harmful status quo that wanted something *less* than equality, diversity, and tolerance for the LGBTQ community. Of course, that implication rests on some very specific definitions of those words, but that's the power of successful redefinition efforts. People eventually stop thinking about the original definitions, start taking the new ones for granted, and then condemn those who don't support what now *sounds* like an obvious moral good that everyone *should* support (like equality).

Virtue Signaling for Normalization (Interest Stage)

The next step in the AIDA funnel is *interest*. With purchasing decisions, the movement from awareness to interest happens when people conclude a product is *relevant* to their lives. You might have a positive awareness of a local gardening store from your friend who has a green thumb, but if you have no interest in gardening yourself, you exit the funnel at this stage—you're not going to make it to the purchase point. With morality, the equivalent step is *normalization*. The more pervasive ("normal") people believe an action to be, the more willing they are to deem it morally acceptable because of its perceived *relevance* to society.

The Shout Your Abortion movement is an excellent case study of this point. In 2015, a woman named Amelia Bonow had an abortion and wrote an article for the website *Salon* titled "My Abortion Made Me Happy." A friend tweeted it with the hashtag #shoutyour abortion, and it was subsequently retweeted more than 150,000 times, with women everywhere proudly sharing their own abortion stories. The Shout Your Abortion movement was born, aimed at "humanizing, normalizing and de-stigmatizing the procedure," and the hashtag is still active today.[7] There's now a book with the same name and a website that's continually updated with user-submitted stories that strive to present abortion in a positive light.

In her *Salon* article, Bonow articulated why she felt it was important to share her experience in the way she did:

> I ache for women who feel shame after having an abortion, because I think shame is a dangerous and counterproductive emotion, and I believe that shame is almost always a product of social conditioning. I'm telling you my story plainly, proudly, flippantly even, because we have all been

brainwashed to believe that the absence of negative emotions around having an abortion is the mark of an emotionally bankrupt person. It's not. I have a good heart and my abortion made me happy. It's perfectly reasonable to feel happy that you were not forced to become a mother. Your life belongs to nobody but you; don't ever let someone make you feel any other way.[8]

There's so much to say about all this that it's hard to know where to begin.

In years past, there was a lot of time and energy given to redefining a fetus as something less than human in order to make the case that abortion wasn't the equivalent of murder (an attempt to work on the awareness stage of redefining what abortion is). While people certainly still make arguments at that level, the Shout Your Abortion movement is an effort to work on the next step in the funnel: What's in the womb doesn't matter—define the fetus however you want—because abortion doesn't need defending. Abortion is *normal*, and normal is *good*.

If you're thinking right now that normal doesn't necessarily mean good, you're correct. But it's important to understand why there's so often an assumed connection between normal and good in secularism.

For the answer, we need to return to three of our secular worldview foundations: Feelings are the ultimate guide, happiness is the ultimate goal, and judging is the ultimate sin. On the one hand, secularism is all about the individual defining their own journey. On the other hand, if there's a negative prevailing societal judgment about the morality of certain choices, it can make people question the validity of their journey—whether they *want* that gut check or not. Yes, the secular ideal is to live in a self-contained judgment-free zone, but when the reality is that there's a holy God who defines morality and gives humankind an inner sense of right and wrong, there *will* be a battle fought with the conscience.

Through virtue signaling, people are fighting this inner battle in the public sphere.

The battle commonly has three steps. First, publicly proclaim that the action leads to the holy secular grail of happiness (if it makes you happy, how could it possibly be wrong?). Don't miss the significance of Bonow titling her *Salon* article "My Abortion Made Me Happy." The implication is that her psychological end justified the means. For those who believe that happiness is the ultimate goal, it makes a powerful statement to juxtapose a morally questionable action with the achievement of secularism's greatest good.

Second, proclaim the action with as many people as possible to demonstrate that there's no shame in it (if everyone's willing to tell the world they've done something of this nature, clearly there's nothing to be ashamed of). Bonow claims that shame is "a dangerous and counterproductive emotion" because it's "almost always a product of social conditioning." Ironically, she's acknowledging the power of negative social conditioning (judgment) about the morality of abortion, but is herself working to socially *recondition* people to see it in a positive light. *Given that secularism doesn't defer to an objective higher authority, the closest thing it has to a moral standard is the popular consensus.* Increasing the number of people who share a positive moral judgment of an action is therefore a proxy for transforming that action into a moral *good*.

Third, remind everyone that life is all about self-authority anyway. Sure, you've shown it's possible to justify your moral choice in steps 1 and 2, but this reminds people you never really had to anyway. As Bonow asserts, "Your life belongs to nobody but you."

Normalization is ultimately a process of publicly signaling to society that an action is so commonplace it's unnecessarily taboo. Normal is the social validation secularism needs to minimize conflict with the conscience.

Virtue Signaling for Celebration (Desire Stage)

As marketers well know, it's not enough for a person to be aware of and interested in a product. The *degree* of interest must be strong enough to drive purchase *desire*. Would-be product purchases die a quick death between the interest and desire stages for many reasons, but a key one that's relevant for our discussion here is when a person doesn't have a sufficient emotional connection to the product. Emotional appeal is the greatest tool a marketer has to convert a prospective buyer from having a general interest to having the desire to purchase.

This is true for morality as well. Redefining and normalizing are important steps, but they only get you so far—to the point of establishing the moral acceptability of a position. Mere moral acceptability, however, is a lukewarm reward for your efforts. The real victory is in societal celebration. When you can move people from interest in your cause to the desire to *celebrate* your cause, you've reached true moral buy-in.

Drag Queen Story Hour is an interesting example of how that can be achieved. This is a program that features drag queens reading books to preschool and young elementary age kids at public libraries across America (and now across several other countries as well). Most of the featured books are about characters who question their gender identity or have same-sex parents. According to the DQSH website:

> Drag Queen Story Hour (DQSH) is just what it sounds like—drag queens reading stories to children in libraries, schools, and bookstores. DQSH captures the imagination and play of the gender fluidity of childhood and gives kids glamorous, positive, and unabashedly queer role models. In spaces like this, kids are able to see people who defy rigid gender restrictions and imagine a world where people can present as they wish, where dress up is real.[9]

It would be tempting but a mistake to write off DQSH as something developed for good old-fashioned shock value. The flamboyance of drag queens paired with the simple innocence of a young audience and the staid setting of a public library is certainly attention-getting (as evidenced by the widespread media coverage of the events), but DQSH is about something far more significant than generating public conversation.

Of all the language in DQSH's description, there are two words that are particularly telling: *role models*. In other words, we're past the need to redefine or normalize the drag queen lifestyle within society. Now we're ready to celebrate them as figures to *look up to*.

The fact that these events are targeted at children is highly significant. The drag queen community could have created any number of public events to encourage the celebration of their cause, but events for *children* send a powerful message: "Society now understands that what we do is so morally *positive*, we're teaching kids!" Pictures in the press of proud parents taking photos with delighted children and drag queens emotionally reinforce the idea that the DQSH message is worth celebrating, even with three-year-olds. Note the implication: If toddlers understand the "beauty" of it all, the adults who don't must be *really* ignorant.

The virtue signaling related to these events comes from a variety of sources. First, there are the drag queens themselves, who post a steady stream of pictures from their events on social media. Second, there are the public libraries that host the events and actively promote them. There have been pockets of pushback against the events taking place in publicly funded settings, but that hasn't quieted public library support online. In fact, there are now collections of resources available for helping libraries overcome any DQSH opposition they may face.[10] Third, there are the parents who take their kids to the events and share their photos online to signal their support. Fourth, there are the glowing media reviews, often with the corresponding demonization of any local pushback (typically presented as a conflict between love and "hate").[11] And fifth, there are the churches—yes, churches—that host the events when local libraries won't. Progressive Christian churches welcome and promote the events as a way to "respect the dignity of every human being," as one church put it.[12]

Using the emotional pull associated with the perceived innocence of conducting kids' events, DQSH has successfully moved through the marketing funnel toward broad moral buy-in. Publicly funded institutions, parents, kids, the media, and even churches are now lining up to celebrate the victory.

As you can see, secular virtue signaling is a complex phenomenon that plays a variety of roles at different stages of shifting the secular moral consensus. At any given time, it can be a vehicle for redefinition, normalization, or celebration. *Christians with a biblical worldview, however, must remain clear that God's moral standards never change because they're based on His unchanging character.* Let's look at this now from a biblical perspective.

Putting Secular Morality in Biblical Perspective

In order to see how we can reaffirm biblical morality, it's helpful to frame our discussion in the same terms as the funnel we just evaluated. As such, we're going to consider the biblical perspective on (1) redefinition, (2) normalization, and (3) celebration.

Putting Redefinition in Biblical Perspective

Given our preceding discussion, I believe there are two key things Christians need to do to put redefinition attempts in a biblical perspective.

First, we need to recalibrate our view of God as our moral authority. Most committed Christians would intuitively say they *know* God is our moral authority, but research offers plenty of evidence that we don't necessarily form our moral views accordingly. The American Worldview Inventory found, for example, that only 51 percent of evangelical Christians say the Bible is the source of guidance they're most likely to rely upon when they have an important moral decision to make! Twenty-three percent say they're most likely to rely on "trusted people," and 13 percent say they just rely on themself.[13]

Why is it that so many Christians theoretically know God should be their moral authority but don't live as if He is? I believe it's because they're not theologically well-grounded in the nature of His character. They see His moral authority as a fact, but fail to grasp why His character warrants their *trust*. Then when secular culture makes an emotionally compelling case for a moral cause by redefining key concepts, they're swayed into believing they can trust their own reasoning over God's Word.

But when we take the time to fully understand the implications of God *alone* being all-good, all-powerful, all-knowing, and perfectly just, we won't feel the need to resort to ourselves as a moral authority. Instead, we will gladly submit to His perfect will. (If you would like a deeper grounding in the nature of God's character, I highly recommend A.W. Tozer's *The Knowledge of the Holy*.[14])

Second, we need to ground ourselves in what constitutes harm from a biblical perspective. As we saw in this chapter, those who advocate for new language understand that it's not just *any* new language that's effective in redefining awareness; it's language that suggests the prevailing view of an action's morality is *harming* people. Our view of what's harmful or beneficial, however, must flow from God's objective standards—not from how people *feel*. I realize that's tough. We don't want people to even *feel* harmed! But the reality is that feelings are subjective and God's truth is not. As we discussed in chapter 5, we are called to love others in the context of first loving God, and that means we should want for them what *God* wants, even when they label it "harmful."

It's worth noting here, however, that there's a difference between understanding this logically for the sake of remaining firmly rooted in a biblical worldview and the way in which we communicate with those who believe biblical morality is harmful to themselves or to others they love. Bluntly telling someone the equivalent of "It's what God says that matters, not your feelings" is a swift way to push people further away from hearing what you have to say. Conversations on these subjects must be handled with both gentleness *and* truth.

Putting Normalization in Biblical Perspective

From a literary perspective, one of my favorite lines in the Bible is Judges 21:25: "In those days Israel had no king; everyone did as they saw fit." It's the modern-day equivalent of a mic drop, but you have to know the context in order to understand why this last line of the book is so chilling.

In Judges 19–21, a Levite's concubine is raped and killed in the town of Gibeah in the territory of Benjamin. Incensed by what happened, the Levite cut her body into twelve parts and sent them throughout the land of Israel to garner support for retaliation against the townspeople. The tribe of Benjamin, however, would not turn against their own men, and a civil war began. The Benjamites were all but wiped out, and the rest of the Israelites vowed to never give their daughters in marriage to a surviving Benjamite man.

Not wanting one of their tribes to be completely erased from history, however, the Israelites decided to find an alternative way for the Benjamite line to be carried on: They killed all the male and nonvirgin female inhabitants of the town of Jabesh Gilead and gave the virgins to the Benjamites as wives. When there weren't quite enough women to go around, they made up the difference by kidnapping women from a festival in the town of Shiloh. *Now* everything was settled, and everyone went home. This story ends the book of Judges, with only the single verse I quoted earlier as a commentary on the two-chapter-long ordeal: "In those days Israel had no king; everyone did as they saw fit."

Skeptics often pull stories like this out of context to claim God is immoral—as though He wanted or commanded all of this to happen. But they fail to understand that the Bible often describes horrible events in order to paint a picture of just how *ungodly* people and societies have always been. As the author of Judges coolly implies, this is what was *normal* at that time, when everyone lived according to their own authority.

The fact that what's normal in society at a given time isn't necessarily what's morally right is the ongoing story of Scripture. It was normal, for example, for the nations surrounding Israel to worship false gods and offer child sacrifices. It was normal for the Israelites to continually turn away from God despite the repeated prophetic calls to repentance (eventually leading to exile). It was normal in the Roman Empire to worship a pantheon of gods. Normal has never implied right.

Knowing that normal can't tell us what's good should consistently point us back to Scripture as our guide. Only God has the authority to say what's right, no matter how many people try to get together and say otherwise.

Putting Celebration in Biblical Perspective

One of the most disturbing scenes I've ever seen on the news was the public celebration of abortion becoming legal in Argentina. In

January 2021, people took to the streets weeping in joy, shouting in exuberance, and hugging in relief that preborn infants could be killed by their mother's choice. I'm going to be honest with you: My initial response to this was not godly. It was one of self-righteous anger. How could they be so blind? How could they be so selfish? How could they be so happy about evil? *Do these people even think?* I had no love in my heart for the people celebrating—just a cold condescension.

Ironically, it was the rather chilly response of other Christians online that opened my eyes to the problems with my reaction. They were leaving comments all over the news coverage about how God would deal with these people when he sends them to hell. The comments weren't always phrased in exactly that way, but the sentiment was there: *These people will get what's coming to them.*

It's true that plenty of people will eventually be condemned by God to an eternity apart from Him. But is that something any of us should revel in with our emotionally detached statements about God's final judgment? While it's easy to pronounce woes of condemnation upon people, I would suggest that there are three better and more biblical responses when culture celebrates sin.

First, we have to remain humbly aware of our own sinfulness. If we find ourselves taking solace in people's eventual condemnation, we've lost sight of our own wretched state and God's heart for humankind. There is *no one* righteous—not one (Mark 10:18; Romans 3:10). While we were *all* sinners, God showed His love for us by sending Jesus to die on the cross (Romans 5:8), and God wants *all* people to be saved and to come to a knowledge of the truth (1 Timothy 2:4). Do we want something less for our fellow humans than what God wants? An awareness of our own sinfulness should lead us to have broken hearts for those who are far from God rather than to have a self-righteous attitude of superiority.

Second, we shouldn't be surprised. At all. Perhaps what I most hope readers will take from this chapter is just how consistent it is with a secular worldview that sin will be celebrated. When the authority is the self, the self will rebel against God, and the self will proclaim victory at the illusion of freedom from authority. That should be entirely unsurprising to us if we understand the nature and implications of a secular worldview. And here's why it matters: A lot of Christians are continually shocked by the morality secular culture promotes today. As an outflow of that shock, we often respond in some less-than-godly ways—with self-righteousness, indignation, condescension, sarcasm, mockery, or accusatory outrage. Responding in these ways rather than out of thoughtful and prayerful consideration can lead us to make all kinds of comments that shut down what could otherwise have been a valuable conversation.

Third, we should take every opportunity to speak out in a celebratory way about *God's* truth. While it's important to speak truth in *response* to sin, we miss huge opportunities if we stop at simply pointing out what is wrong with the world. If the only time we post on social media, for example, is to express our anger, disappointment, frustration, or sadness about the latest victory of secular morality, nonbelievers will come to know us for what we're *against*. But what about everything we're *for*? Share photos that celebrate the beauty of God's design in nature. Share content about the evidence for God's existence. Share stories about Christians serving the community. Share interesting interviews with Christians talking about how their faith has been critical for dealing with deep suffering in their lives. Share the gospel itself! There are numerous ways to share the beauty and truth of a Christian worldview. We just need to be proactive in doing so.

Remember: The Battle Has Already Been Won

There's no doubt that it can be overwhelming to be continually confronted by the virtue signaling of a secular culture. If you pay any attention to the news, there are days (every day?) when it seems all we hear or read about is how much further society is going in its embrace of secular morality. While we may wish it were otherwise, and we should grieve over what we see, we have to resist the temptation to feel like discouraged or disgruntled losers in a culture war.

I know this may sound trite, but let's take these words to heart: *The battle has already been won.* God never loses. But for those words to give us right perspective, we have to know what kind of battle has been won. Ephesians 6:12 reminds us that we face a *spiritual* battle specifically: "Our struggle is not against flesh and blood, but against the rulers, against the authorities, against the powers of this dark world and against the spiritual forces of evil in the heavenly realms." And Jesus emphasizes in John 18:36, "My kingdom is not of this world. If it were, my servants would fight to prevent my arrest by the Jewish leaders. But now my kingdom is from another place."

Saying the battle has been won, therefore, is no assurance of where things will go in any particular society, including our current one. But we *are* assured that at the end of time there will be a final victory of all that is good and true. In the meantime, we are to focus on being obedient to Jesus's command to be "the light of the world" (Matthew 5:14)—while keeping in proper perspective that plenty of darkness will continue to abound. The existence of that darkness shouldn't lead to our discouragement, but rather, to our desire to bring glory to God where light is desperately needed.

FOR FURTHER READING

- Scott Klusendorf, *The Case for Life: Equipping Christians to Engage the Culture* (Wheaton, IL: Crossway, 2009).

- Nancy Pearcey, *Love Thy Body: Answering Hard Questions about Life and Sexuality* (Grand Rapids, MI: Baker, 2019).

- A.W. Tozer, *The Knowledge of the Holy* (New York: Harper-One, 1961).

- Carl Trueman, *The Rise and Triumph of the Modern Self: Cultural Amnesia, Expressive Individualism, and the Road to Sexual Revolution* (Wheaton, IL: Crossway, 2020).

QUESTIONS FOR DISCUSSION OR REFLECTION

1. When you think of virtue signaling in the sense discussed in this chapter, what examples come to mind?

2. Why do you think the redefinition and subsequent use of the words *equality*, *diversity*, and *tolerance* has been so effective for promoting the cultural acceptance of LGBTQ causes?

3. What types of sin have become so normal that they're considered acceptable or even good in secular culture? What about within the church?

4. What are some ways Christians can best avoid developing a self-righteous attitude in response to the celebration of sin in culture?

CHAPTER 9

Reinvigorating the Spirit of Discernment

*Under the pressure of
secular indifference*

I f you're not familiar with baseball, one of the ways that players practice hitting is by using what are called batting cages. These are simple, enclosed areas with a pitching machine that repeatedly shoots baseballs to the player so they can practice hitting a lot of balls in a short period of time. The speed at which the machine throws can be adjusted, but the player typically can't change the angle at which the balls are thrown.

Batting cages can offer great practice, but when machines consistently throw balls at the same angle and speed, a player can get too used to the pattern. They might get into a rhythm where they're crushing every ball that comes their way in the cage but struggle to hit *anything* in an actual game. That's because during a game, pitching is far more variable. A human pitcher will throw a ball at different speeds, spins, and directions. When a batter is inexperienced at identifying and responding to the types of pitches that will come their way in a game, they'll often strike out. The benefits of practicing in a predictable batting cage can only get you so far. Live-pitcher batting practice is a critical part of any player's training.

In the same way, most Christians are able to quickly identify claims that obviously conflict with biblical truth, such as "God doesn't exist," "Jesus never existed," or "The Bible says we can do whatever we want." Those are like the straightforward pitches coming out of a batting-cage machine. We know what to make of them as soon as we see them— they're wrong. But biblical error is often not so obvious in everyday life. People say things all the time that are subtly inaccurate from a biblical perspective, and we don't always know what to do when those curve-balls come. Sometimes they're so cleverly presented that we don't even recognize them as errors. Other times, we know something is wrong but can't put our finger on what it is. And still other times, we recognize that truth and error have been mixed together, but we aren't sure how to untangle them.

The ability to distinguish between truth and error, or right and wrong, is called discernment. Theologian Sinclair Ferguson puts it this way: "Discernment is learning to think God's thoughts after Him, practically and spiritually; it means having a sense of how things look in God's eyes and seeing them in some measure 'uncovered and laid bare' (Heb. 4:13)."[1] The Bible speaks to the importance of discernment in many places. First Thessalonians 5:21-22 says, for example, "Test everything; hold fast what is good. Abstain from every form of evil" (ESV). Similarly, 1 John 4:1 says, "Do not believe every spirit, but test the spirits to see whether they are from God, because many false prophets have gone out into the world." And Hebrews 5:14 says, "Solid food is for the mature, who by constant use have trained themselves to distinguish good from evil." Don't miss the significance of the words "by constant use"—the polar opposites of good and evil can be so cleverly entangled that Christians need consistent *training* in the truths of God's Word to be able to distinguish them.

At first blush, it might seem like the subject of discernment would belong under the *Believing* section of this book rather than the *Thinking* section. After all, discernment relates to true and false beliefs. There's certainly overlap, but I'm classifying this as a thinking subject because I want to focus on discerning truth from error *once theologically accurate beliefs have already been established.* In other words, *assuming* we have solid biblical beliefs as a foundation, how do we think carefully about the ideas we encounter *relative* to those solid beliefs?

Discernment applies to how we should think biblically about everything in life, so the sky's the limit on what we could cover here. But because discernment is especially important when it comes to what people say about God, Jesus, and the Bible, I thought we would get the greatest benefit from narrowing down our options to one of those three subjects. And because we've already addressed popular misconceptions about God and the Bible, we're going to take the opportunity now to focus on errant ideas about who Jesus is.

You've probably noticed that there are a lot of false Jesuses running around in the public sphere (and even in churches) today. In fact, when I asked the audience of my author Facebook page for examples of inaccurate versions of Jesus they see, more than 200 people had one to share! We're going to look at six of the most common false Jesuses that Christians encounter today and do some "live-pitch training" by analyzing actual quotes promoting those false identities. My hope is that these examples will give you a better idea of how errant ideas show up in subtle ways and encourage you to closely guard the biblical truth of who Jesus is against the secular pressure to make Him anything we want. Culture may be indifferent to what the Bible actually says about Jesus, but Christians with a biblical worldview can't be.

Everyman Jesus

> Jesus napped regularly, got frustrated with religious systems, experienced anger, occasionally ignored his family's advice, and happily ran away when people wanted to control him. His humanity was part of his godliness. And so is yours.[2]
>
> —Carlos A. Rodriguez, founder and
> CEO of The Happy NPO

Our first Jesus, the Everyman Jesus, is a Jesus who is far more human than divine—He's portrayed as just like us, though He set a particularly good example for humankind with His life and teachings.

Everyman Jesus can show up in many different forms. Most of the time it's not as obvious as someone explicitly stating that Jesus wasn't God. More often, this idea shows up in an overemphasis on Jesus's humanity for the purpose of justifying some kind of human action—Jesus did x, y, and z, and therefore you should too (for example, He got "frustrated with religious systems," as Carlos Rodriguez says).

In Rodriguez's statement, the diminishment of Jesus's deity is rather subtle (which, again, is why we need discernment!). First, there's a confusion about the *relationship* between Jesus's humanity and His divinity. Jesus's humanity is not *part* of His "godliness," as Rodriguez says. The Bible affirms that Jesus is both fully human and fully God. In AD 451, the church leaders who participated in the Council of Chalcedon developed a statement on this relationship that is still considered by Protestants and Catholics to be the orthodox definition of the person of Jesus. It affirms that Jesus has "two natures, inconfusedly, unchangeably, indivisibly, inseparably; the distinction of natures being by no means taken away by the union, but rather the property of each nature being preserved, and concurring in one Person and one Subsistence, not parted or divided into two persons."[3] Put more simply, Jesus's human nature and divine nature are united in a single person; one is not part of the other, nor do they mix.

Second, when Rodriguez says "humanity was part of his godliness. And so is yours," he implies that we can be godly in the same way Jesus is godly. But Jesus isn't godly in the sense of being *like* God; He *is* God…and humans are not. While Rodriguez probably didn't write this tweet to explicitly make a statement about Jesus's identity, a lowered view of that identity is *embedded* in it (intentionally or not). This may sound like theological nitpicking, but it's actually quite important. If we downgrade either Jesus's humanity *or* His deity, we end up with a very different Jesus than the one we find in the Bible.

Theology-Lite Jesus

Jesus didn't have a theology, at least not in the way most Christians imagine he did or the kind they perceive for themselves...Jesus was far more relational than he was theological.[4]

—John Pavlovitz, progressive Christian author

Theology-Lite Jesus doesn't care much (if at all) about what people believe. He came to tell people *how to live*. As you might imagine from our discussion in chapter 5, this Jesus makes a frequent appearance in progressive Christian circles. After all, if Jesus was highly concerned with correct theology—a system of *beliefs*—it would challenge the common progressive idea that Christianity is primarily about behavior (and in particular, social justice).

The quote here from an article written by John Pavlovitz requires some additional context to more fully understand the claim he's making. Pavlovitz believes that Christians overrate the importance of theology because Jesus's own life (allegedly) didn't reflect a theological focus. He points out, for example, that "when Jesus gathers at the table with people, he doesn't burden them with doctrine or allow their beliefs or behavior to keep them at a distance." Pavlovitz also notes that people at the time of Jesus's earthly ministry didn't yet have the New Testament, so there was no developed Christian theology or commentary in place for them to learn from. They only had what they "saw, heard, and walked through together as a filter to understand [Jesus]." Pavlovitz concludes, "Maybe love really is all you need. Maybe that is the only theology that matters."

There are several reasons why this reasoning is problematic from a biblical perspective. First, theology is just a descriptive term for a set of beliefs. Even *if* Jesus claimed that correct beliefs are only minimally important relative to behavior, *that's a theology too*. The relevant question is *what* His theology was, not whether it was important. Second, just because Jesus didn't make people's beliefs or behavior a barrier to gathering with them doesn't imply doctrine wasn't an important part of what He taught. Part of Jesus's theology was that it was vital for all people to know—without barriers—that "whoever believes in him shall not perish but have eternal life" (John 3:16). In addition, as we saw in chapter 5, Jesus claimed to be God in many different ways and did miracles to authenticate those claims of deity. It was clearly important to Him that people would come to have correct *beliefs* about who He was, what He was going to do for them, and why it mattered. He certainly didn't see all this theology as a "burden" to people, as Pavlovitz says; Jesus said His truth would set them *free* (John 8:32).

Pavlovitz is right that the New Testament wasn't yet available for people to learn from, but they didn't need written documents *about* Jesus when they had Jesus Himself teaching and performing miracles (that said, it's worth noting that the Old Testament writings *were* available and taught in synagogues). In addition, the literacy rate was so low at the time that the vast majority of people gained *all* of their knowledge from unwritten sources. To suggest that without written texts ancient people couldn't have learned a deeper theology directly from Jesus than something akin to "just go be nice" is a bit of chronological snobbery.

Finally, when Pavlovitz says, "Maybe love really is all you need. Maybe that is the only theology that matters," he assumes everyone knows what love is. But once again, Jesus said the *greatest* commandment is to love God (Matthew 22:36-38), and a love for God defines what it means to love others (see chapter 5). Love, in the biblical sense, isn't whatever we make of it. It's rooted in *theological* truths about who God is, what He's done, and how we're to respond.

Non-Evangelizing Jesus

> Jesus does not tell us to convert the poor, the homeless, the imprisoned to Christ. He tells us the poor ARE Christ and that we must be converted to them.[5]
>
> —Nathan Davis Hunt, Twitter user

Non-Evangelizing Jesus is a cousin of Theology-Lite Jesus. Neither of them consider beliefs all that important; it's really just our behavior that matters. The subtle distinction between them is that Theology-Lite Jesus cared enough about what He had to say to go out and preach while on Earth, whereas Non-Evangelizing Jesus doesn't really care if His followers today tell others about Him at all—we just need to tend to people's earthly needs. (When tending to those needs takes on a secular social justice meaning—see chapter 10—this Jesus could also be called Social Justice Jesus.)

Loving others in the context of first loving God, however, means that we care for both their souls *and* earthly needs. That doesn't mean we always need to care for one *before* the other (that depends on the circumstance), but rather, that we can't care for the *whole* person while ignoring their most fundamental need for a relationship with God. Pastor and theologian Tim Keller says it this way:

> Evangelism has to be seen as the "leading edge" of a church's ministry in the world. It must be given a priority in the church's ministry. It stands to reason that, while saving a lost soul and feeding a hungry stomach are both acts of love, one has an infinitely greater effect than the other. In 2 Cor 4:16-18, Paul speaks of the importance of strengthening the "inner man" even as the outer, physical nature is aging and decaying. Evangelism is the most basic and radical ministry possible to a human being. This is true, not because the "spiritual" is more important than the physical (we must be careful not to fall into a Greek-style dualism!), but because the eternal is more important than the temporal (Matt 11:1-6; John 17:18; 1 John 3:17-18).[6]

When Nathan Davis Hunt tweets that Jesus didn't tell us to "convert" the poor, homeless, and imprisoned, that's simply untrue—assuming that by "convert," he means share the gospel in the hope that they would come to a saving knowledge of Jesus. Before Jesus ascended to heaven, He told His followers to make disciples of all nations, baptizing them in the name of the Father and of the Son and of the Holy Spirit, and teaching them to obey all He commanded (Matthew 28:16-20). Jesus wants us to share about Him with *everyone*, including but not limited to the poor, homeless, and imprisoned.

When Hunt goes on to say "the poor ARE Christ," he's presumably referencing what Jesus said about the sheep and goats in Matthew

25:31-46. There, Jesus describes the final judgment, when the sheep (those who are blessed) and the goats (those who are condemned) are separated for eternity. The King praises the sheep for having cared for Him when he was hungry, thirsty, and imprisoned. When the sheep ask when they had done that for the King, he replied, "Truly I tell you, whatever you did for one of the least of these brothers and sisters of mine, you did for me" (verse 40). This passage isn't suggesting that Jesus *literally* is the poor, but rather, that caring for the poor *flows out of* a love for God. We don't need to be "converted" to the poor, as Hunt says, but we do need to serve the poor as an outpouring of our conversion to *Jesus*.

Anti-Organized Religion Jesus

> While it seems popular to think Jesus came to build an army of sorts for God, and to then organize his followers to build him an empire on earth, I personally don't subscribe to such a concept...The thoughts and questions that God stirs my heart with—and the answers I find—are never going to be the same as everyone else, because my relationship with God is personal. Contrary to this is organized religion. Religion creates a corporate identity.[7]
>
> —Mick Mooney, blogger and author

One way people sometimes justify having a lowered view of the authority of the Bible or the importance of church is by claiming that Jesus Himself was opposed to so-called organized religion. Like the blogger quoted here, they believe that Jesus wants them to have an individualized faith untainted by the corruptions of alleged groupthink.

It's often Jesus's troubled relationship with the Pharisees that people have in mind when they think He was opposed to religion. For background context, the Pharisees were a Jewish sect that kept the law given to Moses and followed an elaborate system of additional rules to help them do so, often going far beyond the intent of the law (for example, specifying how many steps a person was allowed to take on the Sabbath). The Pharisees elevated such rules to the level of Scripture and prided themselves on how well they kept them. Jesus was often critical of the Pharisees, which led to ongoing conflict between Him and them. But Jesus wasn't critical of the Pharisees because they were *religious*. It was their self-righteous legalism, hypocrisy, and rejection of Himself that He condemned (see Luke 11:37-52; Matthew 23). Jesus said the Pharisees honored God externally, but their hearts were far from Him (Matthew 15:8).

With that in mind, Jesus's strained relationship with the Pharisees had nothing to do with his feelings about "organized religion." It's clear from Scripture that Jesus actively participated in and validated many aspects of the (organized) Jewish religion. He went to synagogue on the Sabbath (Luke 4:16), taught in the synagogue (Mark 6:2), considered what we now call the Old Testament to be God's Word (Matthew 15:3; Mark 7:13), and observed Jewish religious traditions such as Passover (John 2:13), the Festival of Tabernacles (John 7:2,10), and the Festival of Dedication (John 10:22). When Jesus prepared for the end of His earthly ministry, He also gave some very specific instructions for what His followers were to do *as an organized group* going forward— take communion, be baptized, make disciples, and more. There's no need to separate Jesus from organized religion that is true; it's false religion He was opposed to.

The irony in Mick Mooney's statement is that he's correct about Christianity leading to a "corporate identity" that's at odds with his personal conclusions. *Where he's mistaken is in assuming that his own answers are right and the corporate identity is wrong.* As Christians, our corporate identity is in Christ—"a chosen people, a royal priesthood, a holy nation, God's special possession" (1 Peter 2:9). When our personally derived answers don't line up with the corporate identity established in God's Word, it's not a problem with the Christian "religion"… it's a problem with us prioritizing the authority of the self.

Socialist Jesus

A popular meme shows a picture of Jesus before feeding the 5,000 (Matthew 14:13-21). The disciple with him says,

"B-b-but if you feed everyone, Jesus, that would be <gasp!> socialism!"

There are all kinds of ways people co-opt Jesus for political points, but one of the most common, given current cultural trends, is by suggesting that Jesus was or would be a socialist. Though socialism is a complex subject, we can quickly identify the basic problem with Socialist Jesus by looking at (1) what socialism is and (2) what the Bible says about helping the poor.

Well-meaning people sometimes think socialism simply means having society come together to provide for the needs of the less fortunate. But socialism isn't a loose term for people coming together in some way to alleviate poverty. *It refers very specifically to centrally planned economies that place power and resources in the hands of government leaders in order to forcibly redistribute wealth to a society.* So much more could be said, but that central idea alone is enough to demonstrate the problem.

Jesus *never* suggested that the government should undertake a massive economic redistribution program to provide for the poor. Was He opposed to people paying taxes? No. When the Pharisees asked Him if the people should pay the imperial tax, Jesus famously told them to "give back to Caesar what is Caesar's, and to God what is God's" (Matthew 22:21). But taxation is not equivalent to socialism, in which the government takes control of wealth generation and allocation. This is vastly different than people *voluntarily* using their own resources to help others out of a love for God. Paul said in 2 Corinthians 9:7, "Each of you should give what you have decided in your heart to give, not reluctantly or under compulsion, for God loves a cheerful giver."

People also sometimes suggest that because Jesus warned against the dangers of money, He would have wanted to create a socialist society in which everyone is of equal economic status. But this misses the point of Jesus's concern. He warned about money because it could become an *idol* in a person's life (Luke 12:14-21; 16:13). It's the *love* of money that's a problem, not money itself (1 Timothy 6:10). Jesus's concern about riches is not about rich people existing in society, but about where their hearts are in relation to Him. His solution wouldn't be to implement an economic system to eliminate their existence *because that's not the problem.*

Oh, and that meme I quoted? I hope you can quickly see the flawed thinking in it based on this discussion. For Jesus to feed everyone out of His private provision and miraculous act of multiplication has nothing to do with socialism. *Jesus* provided, *not* the government.

Universal-Christ Jesus

> What if Christ is a name for the transcendent within of every "thing" in the universe? What if Christ is a name for the immense spaciousness of all true Love? What if Christ refers to an infinite horizon that pulls us both from within and pulls us forward, too? What if Christ is another name for every thing—in its fullness?[8]
>
> —Richard Rohr, Franciscan priest and author

Richard Rohr is the founder of the Center for Action and Contemplation in Albuquerque, New Mexico. His book *The Universal Christ: How a Forgotten Reality Can Change Everything We See, Hope For, and Believe* is a highly influential *New York Times* bestseller—revered by the diverse likes of U2's Bono, Melinda Gates, Jen Hatmaker, and Oprah.

Rohr's central teaching is that the spirit of Christ is not the same as the person of Jesus. For Rohr, "Christ" is synonymous with God's love for the world, and Jesus was an exemplary *incarnation* of that universal spirit of love. This so-called Christ is in all things, from a sunset to a cup of coffee to the family pet. Absolutely everything in the universe is a manifestation of God. Rohr even dedicates the book to his dog, who he says was "Christ" for him.

You might assume that Rohr is just one more person throwing out a New Age idea for people who aren't interested in the Bible but want to embrace some spiritualized notion of love. Perhaps one of the reasons Rohr is influencing so many Christians, however, is that he points to select Bible verses to support his case, so to unsuspecting ears, he may sound biblically solid. I say "select" verses because the only way a person can come to the conclusion that the Bible teaches a Christ separate from Jesus is by taking specific verses out of context and ignoring nearly everything else in God's Word.

For example, Rohr points to Colossians 3:11 in support of his view: "Christ is all, and is in all."[9] But that's only part of the verse! Here's the rest of it: "Here there is no Gentile or Jew, circumcised or uncircumcised, barbarian, Scythian, slave or free, but Christ is all, and is in all." Paul was saying that all believers have *unity* in Christ, not that they are *the same as* Christ. It's also rather ironic that Rohr points to Colossians 3:11 as support for his case because just a few verses earlier, in Colossians 2:9-12, it couldn't be more clear that Paul saw Christ as a person—not an ethereal spirit of love—and that the person is Jesus:

> In Christ all the fullness of the Deity lives in bodily form, and in Christ you have been brought to fullness. He is the head over every power and authority. In him you were also circumcised with a circumcision not performed by human hands. Your whole self ruled by the flesh was put off when you were circumcised by Christ, having been buried with him in baptism, in which you were also raised with him through your faith in the working of God, who raised him from the dead.

Aside from ignoring the immediate context of individual verses, Rohr ignores the context of the whole Bible. The Old Testament contains many prophecies of a coming Savior known as the Messiah. The New Testament confirms these prophecies were fulfilled in Jesus. The Greek word translated "Messiah" is *Christos*, from which we get the word *Christ. When the New Testament refers to Jesus as Christ, it's specifically a reference to His messiahship. Christ* is a personal title with rich theological context, not a misunderstood word for universal love.

We've now looked at six false Jesuses in some depth, but as I mentioned at the beginning of this chapter, more than *200* people had a false Jesus to share about on my author Facebook page. So it's worth mentioning a few more that popped up repeatedly within those responses. I'll describe them very briefly and offer a "one line response" (OLR) to each.

> **Judge-Not Jesus** effectively said only one thing ever: "Do not judge, or you too will be judged" (Matthew 7:1). If ever a Christian suggests that something is morally wrong, there's a high probability that Judge-Not Jesus will be summoned to repeat the only statement He apparently ever made.
>
> *OLR: In its fuller context, Matthew 7 is a warning against hypocritical judgment, not all judgment (see also John 7:24, where Jesus explicitly says to judge—with right judgment).*

> **Prosperity Jesus** doesn't want anyone to ever be sick, poor, or have problems. If we only ask with enough faith, this Jesus will make sure we never suffer in any way.
>
> *OLR: People suffer for all kinds of reasons in this life (reasons that won't go away until the end of time), but God works through our suffering to produce endurance, character, and hope (Romans 5:3-4). See Costi Hinn's book in this chapter's "For Further Reading" section for a resource on the prosperity gospel in particular.*

> **Santa Claus Jesus** wants to give you everything you ask for. While Prosperity Jesus is interested in helping you avoid suffering, Santa Claus Jesus wants you to have everything else on your prayer wish list as well. Just ask and be nice all year.
>
> *OLR: God answers prayers according to what aligns with His perfect will—not according to what we might errantly think is best for ourselves or others (1 John 5:14).*

> **Therapist Jesus** came to give us good self-esteem. He doesn't want us to struggle, be sad, or feel there's anything

wrong with ourselves. He just wants us to be "authentic." As one of my blog readers jokingly described it, this Jesus is your "coach for a better life now, helping you to follow your dreams and destiny, and digs your hair highlights."

OLR: Jesus wants us to have a realistic understanding of our sinfulness and consequent need for Him as our Savior; He calls us to deny ourselves and take up our cross to follow Him (Matthew 16:24).

Activist Jesus was killed as an enemy of the state. His death was primarily an example of how we must fight to liberate the oppressed from evil societal structures.

OLR: Jesus's crucifixion was not a purely human event in which he was killed by people in power—His self-identified purpose for coming was to "give his life as a ransom for many" (Mark 10:45), and His death was "by God's deliberate plan and foreknowledge" (Acts 2:23).

Red-Letter Jesus wants us to primarily care about what He personally says or doesn't say, while downplaying or ignoring the rest of Scripture.

OLR: Jesus repeatedly validated the authority of Scripture in His own words, so even if we were to follow the Red-Letter Jesus approach, it would lead us to embrace all of Scripture (for example, Matthew 5:17-18; Luke 24:44-46; John 5:39).[10]

So far in this chapter, we've focused on personal discernment regarding the identity of Jesus. Now we'll conclude with three general principles to remember about the nature of helping *other* believers with discernment.

The Beauty of Discernment

When Christians speak up to clarify a biblical truth about something, their actions are often seen as being unloving, fear-based, or divisive. But the act of offering discernment is exactly the opposite: It's (1) loving, (2) truth-based, and (3) unifying. Let's see why.

1. Biblical discernment is loving.

All too often, when a Christian attempts to offer discernment in response to another Christian's statement, that person (or others observing) will perceive it as being unkind or unloving. Now, there *are* times when Christians deliver truth in unloving ways. That's a whole other conversation—one we'll have in chapter 11. But what I'm addressing here is the aversion Christians sometimes have to *any* sort of statement that suggests a person, group, or action is wrong from a biblical perspective. In many cases, those Christians even *agree* that the person, group, or action is wrong, but they think there's a negative tradeoff between drawing attention to our biblical disagreement and being loving. However, biblically speaking, it is not more loving for Christians to be a bunch of Pollyannas as they interact with secular culture. It's naïve.

As you've seen in this book, secularism is putting pressure on every aspect of our faith—what we believe, how we think, and how we live—and we are at varying stages of biblical understanding and spiritual maturity. When we see falsehoods being shared in the name of Christ and *don't* offer discernment, we're allowing those who may not yet have an accurate biblical understanding to be "tossed back and forth by the waves, and blown here and there by every wind of teaching" (Ephesians 4:11-15; see also 1 Timothy 4:16). Our love for our brothers and sisters in Christ should drive our willingness to offer discernment when needed.

Jesus didn't create the church to be an endless source of warm fuzzies to one another or to the world around us. That approach may draw *some* people to *some* version of Christianity, but it won't be a Christianity based on the teachings of Jesus Himself. Again, we're called to be salt and light in the world. Yet how can we preserve God's message when we refuse to guard the accuracy of His truth in the name of our own definition of love—one rooted in either comfortable silence or superficial niceties? That's not preserving God's message. It's preserving our ease. Discernment is loving because truth is loving, and discernment divides truth from error.[11]

2. Biblical discernment is truth-based, not fear-based.

In a sermon I heard recently, the pastor criticized Christians who engage in what he considered to be pointless quarrels with one another and with culture. While I agree that we shouldn't be engaging in pointless quarrels, it was clear from what the pastor said that he saw defending a biblical view on some important topics as a waste of energy when instead we could all just focus on doing good works. A core part of the rationale he gave was that when we spend time defending our beliefs, it gives the appearance that we feel threatened and are responding in order to somehow protect ourselves.

Underlying this pastor's comments was another common misunderstanding about discernment: that it's inherently fear-based. But when we attempt to clarify the line between biblical and unbiblical thinking, it's not because we're scared of or intimidated by what others believe. Rather, we're illuminating biblically significant distinctions because, as we just saw, *it's the loving and biblical thing to do*. Let's read Paul's words from 2 Timothy 4:2-4 one more time:

> Preach the word; be prepared in season and out of season; correct, rebuke and encourage—with great patience and careful instruction. For the time will come when people will not put up with sound doctrine. Instead, to suit their own desires, they will gather around them a great number of teachers to say what their itching ears want to hear. They will turn their ears away from the truth and turn aside to myths.

Paul wasn't telling Timothy to correct, rebuke, and encourage because he felt threatened. To the contrary, *because of his deep conviction that sound doctrine exists*, he wanted to be sure people would not turn away from that truth. Biblical discernment is truth-based, not fear-based.

3. Biblical discernment is unifying.

Another common misunderstanding about discernment is that it causes unnecessary division in the body of Christ. As the argument goes, Jesus prayed for unity, so we should seek unity rather than pointing out disagreement between believers. But take that thinking to the extreme: Should we align ourselves with Christians who think blowing up abortion clinics is "biblical"? Of course not. And I can't imagine that the same people who comment about our need for unity would say we should. *We all recognize that a line must be drawn at some point.*

As I said in chapter 5, unity without truth isn't even unity—it's pure individualism. True unity requires truth around which to unify. Ironically, then, given the common claim that discernment is divisive, discernment is actually unifying. It clarifies the truth around which believers should find unity.

Discernment Is a Stewardship to Be Treasured

In dispatching His twelve disciples, Jesus said, "I am sending you out like sheep among wolves. Therefore be as shrewd as snakes and as innocent as doves" (Matthew 10:16). Just as today, the world the disciples were about to enter was challenging. Jesus's command to them was to navigate what they would encounter by being *shrewd*—having "sharp powers of judgment," as the dictionary defines it. We, too, should be both shrewd and innocent, careful to guard God's truth for both our own hearts *and* those of others.

We should never lose sight of the fact that this is an incredible stewardship that God has entrusted us with—it's no small thing! We are carrying on Jesus's truth-teaching ministry and are responsible for proclaiming a right view of God, a right view of Jesus, and a right view of the Bible to the world. Yes, we can all feel hesitant sometimes to speak up when we know it can lead to uncomfortable disagreement, but when we recognize that's part of our God-given ministry, we should treasure our role in His plan.

FOR FURTHER READING

On Discernment

- There's no better way to become more discerning than by reading the Bible regularly. The more you read the Bible, the more you'll be in tune with what God has said and alert to what contradicts His Word.

- Marcia Montenegro's website *Christian Answers for the New Age* has many helpful resources related to discernment on New Age, Eastern religion, and occult ideas: http://www.christiananswersforthenewage.org/.

On the Identity of Jesus

INTRODUCTORY

- Costi W. Hinn, *God, Greed, and the (Prosperity) Gospel: How Truth Overwhelms a Life Built on Lies* (Grand Rapids, MI: Zondervan, 2019).

- Lee Strobel, *Case for Christ: A Journalist's Personal Investigation of the Evidence for Jesus* (Grand Rapids, MI: Zondervan, 2016).

IN-DEPTH

- Darrell L. Bock, *Who Is Jesus?: Linking the Historical Jesus with the Christ of Faith* (Brentwood, TN: Howard Books, 2012).

- Craig A. Evans, *Fabricating Jesus: How Modern Scholars Distort the Gospels* (Downers Grove, IL: InterVarsity, 2008).

- Larry W. Hurtado, *One God, One Lord: Early Christian Devotion and Ancient Jewish Monotheism* (Edinburgh, Scotland: T&T Clark, 2015).

QUESTIONS FOR DISCUSSION OR REFLECTION

1. Which of the false Jesuses in this chapter have you seen most often in culture? Why do you think that particular false Jesus is so commonly promoted?

2. What examples of false Jesuses have you seen that were *not* discussed in this chapter?

3. How would you explain to someone why helping fellow believers with biblical discernment is loving and unifying rather than argumentative and divisive?

4. What are some areas in which you think Christians need better discernment today? Where do *you* most need to grow in discernment?

PART 4:

FAITHFULLY DIFFERENT *LIVING*

CHAPTER 10

Revitalizing the Call to Biblical Justice

*Under the pressure of
secular social justice*

At the beginning of chapter 1, I shared how my article on Christians getting swept into secular views of social justice went viral during the unrest of 2020. Though it was liked and shared more than a quarter-million times, I also received plenty of scathing emails—from both secularists and Christians—because of the concerns I raised over the Black Lives Matter organization (not the phrase itself).

One of those scathing emails was from a Christian friend I had known for years. He told me that if I had read the book *White Fragility*, I'd understand how white people like me (and him) are contributing to the perpetuation of a society that is the "exact opposite of Jesus's vision of the kingdom of God." He said I should be the "opposite of proud" that my article had gone viral, warned me to not go "to the dark side," and labeled the readers who agreed with me "fearful people."

It's been a year since I received that email, and I still find it painful to reread his words today. Given the work I do, I've long been accustomed to criticism from nonbelievers, but the hostility I encountered from *Christians* over this subject—including a longtime friend—was, sadly, quite new.

Perhaps that's what makes social justice an especially difficult topic for Christians today. It's not just secularists and Christians in heated disagreement; it's Christians in heated disagreement with one another. And it's also not a subject we can simply push out of sight and mind in the interest of all getting along. Justice—as defined biblically—is one of our most important callings. God *commands* His people to do justice, and His heart for the oppressed is made clear throughout Scripture. While I'm guessing few, if any, readers need to be convinced that justice is indeed important to God, it's helpful to be reminded of some of what the Bible says in order to put us in the right mindset for this discussion:

- Proverbs 31:8-9: "Speak up for those who cannot speak for themselves, for the rights of all who are destitute. Speak up and judge fairly; defend the rights of the poor and needy."

- Isaiah 1:17: "Learn to do right; seek justice. Defend the oppressed. Take up the cause of the fatherless; plead the case of the widow."

- Jeremiah 22:3: "Do what is just and right. Rescue from the hand of the oppressor the one who has been robbed. Do no wrong or violence to the foreigner, the fatherless or the widow, and do not shed innocent blood in this place."

- Micah 6:8: "He has shown you, O mortal, what is good. And what does the LORD require of you? To act justly and to love mercy and to walk humbly with your God."

- Matthew 23:23: "'Woe to you, teachers of the law and Pharisees, you hypocrites! You give a tenth of your spices— mint, dill and cumin. But you have neglected the more important matters of the law—justice, mercy and faithfulness. You should have practiced the latter, without neglecting the former.'"

We can already note several preliminary principles from these verses. First, biblical justice is doing what's right *in God's eyes* for the marginalized; it goes hand in hand with walking humbly with God and being faithful. True justice cannot be separated from God because God's character *defines* what is just. Second, biblical justice assumes the inherent equality and dignity of all people, given that we're all image-bearers of God (see chapter 7). Everyone deserves justice, regardless of their nationality, class, race, gender, or other social status. Third, biblical justice is proactive. It requires us to speak up, defend, take up the cause, and rescue. We're called to *do* something about the injustices we see around us, not just avoid *causing* injustice.

Justice is part of where the rubber meets the road for our faith. As we saw in chapter 5, Christianity isn't only about what we believe or only about what we do, but rather, about having a relationship with Jesus that leads to a life generously poured out for others. It's important, however, that when we seek to serve others, we're doing so in a way that's consistent with a biblical worldview. In this chapter, we'll look at what that means, and why the dominant secular view of justice today is at great odds with what the Bible calls us to.

Why Is the Subject of Justice So Complex?

With limited space to address so vast a topic, it might seem I should dive straight into the details. But I think that's precisely what goes wrong in so many of these discussions. Christians often don't take the time to step back and look at the big picture of why this subject is so complex in the first place. We assume we should simply (1) rejoice that those with a secular worldview have a common concern for humanity, (2) lock arms, and (3) "do justice"! But in doing so, many Christians have locked arms with movements that are not only inconsistent with a biblical worldview but are *actively opposed to it*. It's only when we understand the nature of this subject's complexity, however, that we can fully appreciate how this is happening.

To begin, we should acknowledge that there are some basic points of agreement between those advocating for secular social justice and those advocating for biblical justice: Human lives matter, humans are equal, oppression is wrong, and the world isn't the way it should be. It's worth recalling that none of these beliefs have an objective basis in a secular worldview (see chapter 7), but for our current purpose, we'll set that point to the side. What we're interested in now is what secular social justice advocates *do* with their beliefs, not whether their beliefs are philosophically justified within their worldview.

Here's what makes all this so complex: While it's true that we do have some important beliefs in common, secular social justice advocates and biblical justice advocates disagree on the answers to three very important questions (we could actually identify several other relevant questions, but for simplicity, we'll focus on these):

1. Why are things the way they are? (We'll call this point A—the origin.)

2. How should things ultimately be? (We'll call this point B—the destination.)

3. What's the best way to get from point A to point B?

As we'll see in this chapter, secular social justice advocates and biblical justice advocates are working from both a different point A and point B, but people rarely take the time to identify and articulate those underlying assumptions. If we did, we'd see that those assumptions are so vastly different that there's no way our answers to question 3—what's the best way to get where we want to go—will be compatible.

To see why, we need to look at the answers to these three questions from both a secular social justice and biblical justice perspective.

Why Are Things the Way They Are? (Point A)

Recall that one of the points of commonality between those advocating for secular justice and those advocating for biblical justice is a belief that the world isn't the way it should be. Agreement on the state we're in, however, is quite different than agreement on the diagnosis of *why* we're in the state we're in. This *why* is the first critical point of divergence between secular and biblical justice.

From a biblical perspective, the world is broken because of sin. If you get *anywhere* in your "read through the Bible in a year" plan, you will get to this part of the biblical story—it's in Genesis chapter 3. God created humans with the ability to choose between right and wrong. When the first humans chose to be disobedient to God's commands, sin entered the world. We've been in a state of rebellion to God ever since, and this has affected multiple layers of creation—individuals, groups of individuals, entire societies, and nature itself. Our relationships with both God and fellow humans are broken. As the apostle Paul says, all of creation has been "groaning" until the present time (Romans 8:22). The entire storyline of Scripture is about how God offers us a rescue plan through Jesus. Sin isn't just a label for the bad things we do; it's the fundamental problem with the world.

From a secular perspective, there theoretically could be a lot of different answers as to why things aren't the way they should be. After all, with no agreed-upon authority outside of the self, there could be *millions* of different perspectives on the question. But that's not what we see today because there's a dominant social philosophy that drives nearly all secular social justice efforts. It's called *critical theory*.[1]

Critical theory grew out of the Marxism of the 1800s. Karl Marx taught that all of history has been one long economic class struggle between oppressed and oppressor groups, and that the only way for the oppressed to be liberated was for them to engage in violent revolution toward socialism. In the 1930s, intellectuals of the Frankfurt School in Germany broadened Marx's analysis to apply not only to economics but also to culture and mass media. In the decades that followed, this basic framework was extended to other areas: race, gender, sexuality, physical ability, and a host of other identity markers. Like the working class in Marx's analysis, people of color, women, and those in the LGBTQ community were identified as victims of *social structures* that empowered their oppressors and kept them marginalized.

From this perspective, all relationships between people are ultimately understood to be functions of group power dynamics. Those in power—the oppressors—want to keep their power, so they will work to maintain the oppressive societal structures that gave them their power to begin with. These structures include the "norms" of society, and those who are oppressed must work to be liberated from them. Meanwhile, oppressors who are enlightened enough to recognize their role in oppression must set aside their privilege to help free the oppressed. Note that in this view, oppression is more psychological than material; it's what happens when dominant groups impose their norms, values, and expectations on society as a whole.

From this very brief summary of critical theory, we can glean the basic answer to question 1 for secular social justice advocates: *People are oppressed because the structure of society has enabled and continues to enable oppressors.*

That's the critical (pun intended!) high-level takeaway for understanding a major assumption behind secular social justice in its various forms. But we need to dig into a further level of complexity to understand what those various forms are.

Saying that "people are oppressed because the structure of society has enabled and continues to enable oppressors" necessarily raises several important questions. What defines oppression and therefore identifies a group as oppressed? Once an oppressed group has been identified, what are the structures of society that oppress them? And what is the manner of oppression by oppressors through these structures of society?

Various critical social theories address these questions with respect to specific groups considered to be oppressed. For example:

- *Queer Theory* focuses on liberation from the oppression of gender and sexual norms.

- *Critical Race Theory* focuses on liberation from the oppression of systemic racism that perpetuates racial inequalities in society.

- *Feminist Theory* focuses on liberation from the oppression of the patriarchy (societal norms in which men hold primary power and privileges).

- *Postcolonial Theory* focuses on liberation from the oppression of the remaining effects of European colonialism.

Although each of these theories addresses the nuances of a specific type of oppression, the family resemblance within critical theory is clear: The problem with "the way things are" is that societal structures have produced norms within society that oppress certain groups (such as those listed here), and those groups must be liberated.

Adding further to the complexity of critical theory is the fact that most people are part of both oppressor and oppressed groups. A poor white heterosexual male, for example, is considered oppressed by class status but an oppressor by race, sexuality, and gender. A poor black transgender woman is considered oppressed by class, race, sexuality, *and* gender. If you've heard the popular term *intersectionality*, this is what it refers to—the unique experiences of oppression that people have when they belong to multiple oppressed groups.

With what we've now established regarding the secular social justice and biblical justice point A, we can already identify two important divergences between them. (Note that individual critical theories have different *types* of divergences from a biblical perspective, but my purpose in this chapter isn't to cover any one critical social theory in depth. Rather, I want to offer a broad perspective on critical theory overall so you can recognize and respond to its many manifestations in culture.)

1. Secular social justice and biblical justice advocates often differ on what constitutes oppression in the first place.

When the Bible speaks of oppression, it does so primarily in terms of orphans, widows, the poor, and the physically enslaved. Secular social justice advocates may share a concern for these groups, but they're also (and sometimes primarily) concerned with causes that, from a biblical perspective, are not necessarily legitimate examples of oppression. In some cases, these causes are even morally *wrong*.

Queer Theory, for example, views the very existence of gender- and sexuality-related categories to be oppressive because they're considered to be social constructs (a product of the way society talks about these subjects, not of any kind of biological realities). *In other words, simply speaking in terms of male and female or heterosexual and homosexual is considered to be a way that societies unjustly oppress people.* The Bible, however, clearly states that God created humans "male and female" (Genesis 1:27) and that there are God-given categories for human sexuality (Leviticus 18:22; 20:13; Romans 1:26-27; 1 Corinthians 6:9, 18; Hebrews 13:4). From a biblical perspective, therefore, gender- and sexuality-related categories aren't oppressive; they reflect the reality of God's design for humanity.

As another example, within the framework of Feminist Theory, many fight for reproductive justice—the idea that it's *unjust* for a woman to not have the choice to have an abortion. From a biblical perspective, however, every human life is made in the image of God and formed by Him in the womb (Psalm 139:13-16; Isaiah 44:24; Jeremiah 1:5). In a biblical worldview, the taking of an innocent human life is murder—a great injustice to the *preborn infant* who is killed. Secular social justice turns the biblical view upside down and makes justice about the mom having the right to do whatever she wants, rather than about the preborn infant having the right to life.

These are just a couple of examples of many that could be given if space allowed. But a key takeaway that underlies the issue of these and many other would-be examples is that secular social justice and biblical justice advocates disagree on what constitutes oppression because ultimately, they have a *different standard of justice.*

In a biblical worldview, the objective standard of justice is rooted in God's character, and oppression is defined in reference to that standard. In a secular worldview, there can be no objective moral standard (see chapter 7), so oppression is often defined in reference to the desires and feelings of individuals relative to the norms and expectations of society. For example, if someone doesn't want to identify as male or female, then they may feel oppressed by the perceived constraint society has foisted upon them by constantly speaking in those terms. If a woman doesn't want to have the baby she's pregnant with, then she may feel oppressed by society not allowing her to make the choice to end that pregnancy.

This is entirely consistent, of course, with the broader secular worldview tenets we've examined throughout this book: Feelings are the ultimate guide, happiness is the ultimate goal, judging is the ultimate sin, and God is the ultimate guess. Anything that systematically challenges the validity of one's feelings and imposes external constraints upon their happiness journey will be considered unjust and potentially oppressive.

2. Secular social justice and biblical justice advocates differ on the moral responsibility of individuals versus identity groups when analyzing why things are the way they are.

You may have noticed that in critical theories, everything is about what *identity groups* a person belongs to. The fact that I'm a white, middle-class, educated, cisgender, able-bodied heterosexual female, for example, tells a critical theorist what kind of oppressor I am and what kind of oppressions I face. In other words, as a white person, I'm an oppressor *by that fact of my identity*, regardless of my personal beliefs and behaviors. And as a female, I'm oppressed *by that fact of my identity*, regardless of whether I've personally experienced unjust treatment because of my gender. There's nothing I can do to transcend my group memberships. I can only learn how to view the world through the lens of my identity characteristics and deal with the hand I've been dealt—either by fighting for liberation for myself (where I'm oppressed) or by divesting myself of my "privilege" and fighting for the liberation of others (where I'm an oppressor).

From a biblical perspective, however, people are not guilty of oppression merely because of their identity characteristics. As 2 Corinthians 5:10 says, "We must all appear before the judgment seat of Christ, so that each of us may receive what is due us for the things done while in the body, whether good or bad." Groups can certainly be guilty of sin, but that remains a function of the collective sinfulness of the individuals involved (think of an organization like the Ku Klux Klan). And entire societies can be structured in ways that perpetuate sin, again due to the collective sinfulness of the individuals involved (think of

Jim Crow laws).² But that's very different than suggesting that entire groups of people are responsible for oppression based solely on identity characteristics. The idea that *all* white people, for example, are racist because they're guilty of contributing to racist societal structures in some way, shape, or form is a concept foreign to the Bible.

As you can see, these two differences at point A (why things are the way they are) are already highly significant, but even more differences will become evident as we look at the next two questions.

How Should Things Ultimately Be? (Point B)

It's far more difficult to explain the respective answers to why things are the way they are than it is to explain the answers to how things ultimately should be—good news if your head is spinning at this point. That's in large part because the point B for our two views is closely related to what we've already discussed.

From a biblical perspective, sin—the problem with the way things are—continually haunts humanity. The world is broken and is in the process of being redeemed, but it will not be fully redeemed *until the end of time*. Revelation 21:1-5 gives us a beautiful picture of what that will look like. God will create a new heaven and a new earth, and the current heaven and earth will pass away. He will dwell among His people and "wipe every tear from their eyes." Death and mourning will be no more! This is an incredible promise. But it should also be a reminder that things will *not* all be made right in our current universe. That doesn't mean we should turn a blind eye to injustices, of course. Christians are clearly called to do justice wherever we can, but the goal isn't to create an earthly utopia—that's impossible given the ongoing reality of sin. No reconfigured societal structure will ever fully end oppression this side of judgment day.

From a secular social justice perspective, point B can be a bit nebulous. In the simplest of terms, the answer to how things (at least theoretically) should be is that all oppressed people are liberated from their oppression. *In this view, liberation means complete group equality of outcome, status, power, and wealth.* That said, the goal of critical theory isn't only about a distant vision of perfect equality. It's also very much about the intermediate goal of people becoming "enlightened" enough to see the world in the way it prescribes. As one university course syllabus puts it, the aim of critical theories is to

> unmask the ideology falsely justifying some form of social or economic oppression—to reveal it as ideology—and, in so doing, to contribute to the task of ending that oppression. And so, a critical theory aims to provide a kind of enlightenment about social and economic life that is itself emancipatory: persons come to recognize the oppression they are suffering as oppression and are thereby partly freed from it.[3]

Point B, from a biblical perspective, is to right true injustices whenever possible while recognizing that things will not be made perfectly right until the end of time, whereas point B, from a secular social justice perspective, is to achieve perfect equality of outcome, status, power, and wealth in the here and now (and enlighten as many people as possible along the way). The reality of how great these differences are will become clear as we answer our third and final question.

What's the Best Way to Get from Point A to Point B?

For secular social justice advocates, the historical structure of society is presumed to be the fundamental reason why anyone is currently oppressed, so nothing less than an ideological revolution is needed to get from point A to point B—a complete overturning of everything considered to be normal for our society. How should that be accomplished? That's a far-reaching subject because there are so many norms that would need to be dismantled. Fundamentally transforming society is a lot of work! But I want to highlight four major strategies that underlie much of the secular social justice advocacy that we see today.

1. Dictate who has the authority to speak. An assertion commonly made by secular social justice advocates is that we must "elevate marginalized voices." At face value, that sounds great! If people have been marginalized, we should want to elevate their voices so they have equal opportunity to be heard. But this phrase sits at the top of a much deeper ideological iceberg of critical theory, and we need to understand its fuller meaning in that context.

From a secular social justice perspective, members of oppressed groups have unique access to truth because of their "lived experience" of oppression. *In other words, our ability to know what's true is conditioned by our social status—those in dominant groups are "blinded" by their privilege.* For example, in this view, only Hispanic women possess knowledge that relates to their combined oppression in both race and gender. Because no one else has access to that truth, Hispanic women are said to have unique authority to speak on issues pertinent to Hispanic women. To assert that truth can be fully known *independent* of power structures is seen as just one more way people use power to oppress others.

Therefore, when secular social justice advocates speak of elevating marginalized voices, they don't simply mean we need to make sure everyone's voice is heard. They mean that if oppression is going to be reversed, those in oppressed groups must be given the authority to speak on related topics, and those on the outside must be silent or nearly silent.[4] Any arguments that arise from oppressor groups are considered to be examples of fragility rather than factually defensible positions. And if a person belongs to a marginalized group but agrees with the views of oppressors, they're seen as *contributing* to the oppression and are often no longer welcome to participate in the conversation.

2. Control language. Recall from chapter 8 that activists are well aware of the power of language; if you want to facilitate a shift in public perceptions of morality, it starts with redefining terms (such as *equality*, *diversity*, and *tolerance*). The same applies in the context of critical theory.

We already saw one example of this with respect to Queer Theory, which posits that the mere use of male-female language causes unjust oppression. (If you've ever heard someone say we need to "break away from the gender binary," this is what they mean.[5])

Another example is the importance of pronouns to the transgender cause. Whereas names have always been subjective and can often apply to men *or* women (for example, *Chris* or *Alex*), the pronoun *he* has always referred to a biological male, and the pronoun *she* has always referred to a biological female. When someone refuses to use the pronoun matching a transgender person's (new) gender identity, it's seen as an act of hate because it's a refusal to affirm the *validity* of the chosen gender. And, as we learned in chapter 2, you can only be loving if you're affirming others' choices according to a secular worldview. Language matters to activists because it signals acceptance of the terms of the revolution.

3. *Reframe how everyone everywhere thinks about the nature of justice and oppression.* Part of reframing how everyone thinks involves my first two points, but consider this one a catch-all point for saying that everyone everywhere needs to get on board with the revolution in order for it to be successful (see point four regarding what to do about those who refuse). These kinds of conversations can't be kept to small corners of the internet. People need to be talking about oppression—from a critical theory perspective, of course—in schools, businesses, government, media, entertainment, organizations, and more. This is why we're seeing critical theory ideas *everywhere*—because activists seek ideological revolution, and revolution requires people to constantly care about the cause.

4. *Vilify those who don't align with critical theory views, especially if they're part of an oppressor group.* When you're seeking a revolution, there can be no tolerance for those who get in your ideological way; revolution in no way implies a calm dialogue between people with opposing views in order to facilitate better understanding. Remember, we're talking about emotionally heated terms like *oppression. When you're claiming to fight against oppressors on behalf of the oppressed, people who disagree with you are not simply intellectually wrong—they're morally evil.* This is a vitally important distinction because it provides the moral justification for the vilification of dissenters.

While there are multiple groups of people who fall into the (morally evil) "oppressor" camp, there's one I want to highlight here: *Christians*. Yes, Christians are considered to be an oppressor group. And it's important to understand why.

Given that the goal of secular social justice is to free people of any external constraints to being their authentic selves, it shouldn't be surprising that many activists see Christianity as oppressive by its very nature. They recognize that Christianity is based on the assumed authority of God, and with external authority come external constraints and claims to truth. But secular social justice advocates consider Christianity oppressive for a more specific reason as well: *It's been the religious "norm" in America for the last 400 years.*[6] As we've seen in this chapter, secular social justice advocates blame societal norms for present injustices, so Christianity is considered oppressive simply by virtue of the fact that it's long been the dominant religious influence in America. And because Christians have "oppressor" status, they aren't just seen as *wrong*—they're seen as *evil*.

Making matters worse, Christians believe that objective truth is knowable by all people, which bluntly challenges the secular social justice claim that authority can and should be based on lived experience. In a biblical worldview, no group has special access to knowing what's true merely because of its social location in a given society. Social pressure certainly exists and can influence our thinking, but this pressure can't be generalized and absolutized to the extent that one group's claims become unchallengeable. Christians, of course, should always want to actively listen to people's experiences and feelings so we can better understand one another, but those experiences and feelings don't dictate truth; truth is what corresponds to reality and truth can be known through reason, evidence, and Scripture. But that view is, once again, considered evil: Christians are seen as using objective truth as a *weapon* to deny the authority of people's lived experiences (with the alleged motivation of wanting to remain in societal power).

While much, much more could be said about the point A to point B route of secular social justice advocates, I'll point interested readers to my reading recommendations at the end of this chapter so we can now transition to looking at the nature of the point A to point B route for *biblical* justice advocates.

As a working definition, we might say that biblical justice is a justice (1) defined by the objective standard of God's character, (2) deserved by all humans given our inherent equality, and (3) lived out by God's people as a proactive, self-sacrificial, and generous care for the marginalized. Furthermore, this generosity is specifically rooted in the recognition that all we have belongs to God, and we are called to be wise stewards of it (1 Chronicles 29:14; 1 Corinthians 4:7).

Some perspective on what this has historically looked like for Christians is particularly helpful. A great book that contains highlights of how Christians have helped the marginalized throughout history (as well as highlights of the atrocities committed in the name of Christ) is *Bullies and Saints: An Honest Look at the Good and Evil of Christian History* by historian John Dickson.[7] Dickson points out:

> We take for granted today that charitable services are widely available. This was not the case in the ancient world. The notion that rich citizens had a moral obligation to care for the destitute was almost non-existent in Greece and Rome in this period...charity formed no part of the major moral discourses of the era.[8]

But everything changed after the birth of Christianity.

The earliest description of a church service after the New Testament era shows that collections were already being taken for "orphans and widows, and those who, through sickness or any other cause, are in want, and those who are in bonds."[9] By the year AD 250, the church in Rome was supporting more than 1,500 people in daily needs.[10] About the same time, a pandemic broke out and Christians were known for "visiting the sick without regard to the danger, diligently ministering to them, [and] tending to them in Christ; being infected with the disease from others, they...willingly [took] over their pains."[11] Dickson notes, "When [emperor Constantine] eventually freed churches from persecution [in the early fourth century] and then exempted them from taxation, he was setting loose the largest charitable movement the world would ever see."[12]

Being freed from persecution doesn't automatically mean a religious group will engage in sweeping charitable efforts, of course. *Those efforts happened because justice, rooted in a biblical worldview, was an integral part of the Christian calling.* As such, Christians have continuously served the poor and oppressed throughout history—often in ways that permanently changed the world as we know it.

One beautiful example is a man named Basil of Caesarea (AD 330–379), who oversaw the creation of history's first dedicated welfare center and public hospital. While the rich of the time could employ their own doctors, there was no such thing as medical care for those who couldn't afford it—and Basil wanted to change that. He created a health-care center that included six departments: one for the poor, one for the homeless, one for orphans, a separate section for lepers, rooms for the aged and infirm, and a hospital for the sick. Basil's efforts were deeply rooted in his Christian faith. He believed that if people had resources and withheld them from those in need, they were in some sense *stealing* from them. He once preached (based on Luke 12:13-21):

> The bread that you hold back belongs to the hungry. The coat that you guard in a chest belongs to the naked. The shoes that you have left wasting away belong to the shoeless. The silver that you have buried in the ground belongs to the needy. In these and other ways you have wronged all those you were able to provide for.[13]

Basil's steadfast commitment to justice for the poor inspired the creation of hospitals throughout the Eastern Roman Empire, leaving a lasting legacy.

Space doesn't permit me to catalog the vast number of similar examples of biblical justice throughout history, but I do want to highlight the modern-day example of my dear friend Katie. Katie and her husband have two biological children and didn't feel the *need* to have more kids, but they decided this year to become foster parents with the potential to adopt. When we were talking the other day about what led them to foster, she commented with her characteristic frankness:

I think some people think that those who foster are people who just *love* kids and can't get enough of them. And there are certainly some wonderful families like that. But that's not really how we feel. We would be fine without more kids! Honestly, we just wanted to do this out of obedience to the Lord because Christians are called to serve, and this is the need we saw.

I love that. How often do we only look for ways to do justice when it happens to be convenient, or when it fits with what we most enjoy doing? Katie's words were a convicting reminder to me that at the heart of biblical justice is a *self-sacrificial* obedience to loving others in need (with love defined by what it means to first love God). If more Christians loved others in this way—myself included!—perhaps we wouldn't get so caught up in secular ideas of justice. We would have our hearts and hands full with what God has already called us to do.

As a final note, I want to acknowledge that Christians who share a biblical view of justice—agreeing on points A and B—can disagree about the best *way* to get from point A to point B. The subject of immigration policy is a great example. Two Christians can share a biblical view of justice while disagreeing on how the government should best handle the flow of people wanting to enter the United States. We should graciously be mindful that one approach is not *necessarily* less "biblical" than another. That doesn't give us room to assert absolutely anything in the name of biblical justice, but we must be discerning and recognize when our disagreements are over point A and B questions, and when they're over how we can best get from an *agreed-upon* point A to an *agreed-upon* point B.

Revitalizing the Call to Biblical Justice

The subject of secular social justice, biblical justice, critical theory, and cultural manifestations of all the above is vast. This chapter only scratches the surface, but I want to conclude with three of the most important points I hope readers will take away from this overview.

1. We can't always take words at face value today.

As we've seen in this chapter, there are many words and phrases used by secular social justice advocates that *sound* consistent with a biblical worldview but have a loaded meaning that actually represents a view that's *antithetical* to Christianity. We need to be careful about the words we choose in conversations so as not to affirm what we should not be affirming. At the same time, when someone uses a word that *you* know has multiple layers of meaning, don't assume *they* know the same. Ask questions to understand what a person means by the terms they're using before engaging further in discussion.

2. Critical theory and its derivatives are not just analytical "tools."

Christians who want to find common ground with secular social justice advocates often defend critical theory as just being a helpful analytical tool and claim that we should be able to learn from it just like any other secular academic theory—a "take what's helpful and leave the rest behind" approach. This is problematic for three major reasons.

First, it doesn't help a person's case to say something is "just" an analytical tool because that, in and of itself, is neither positive nor negative. Anything can be an analytical tool. Some tools lead to an accurate analysis and some don't—it depends on the tool. As we saw in our discussion of point A, there are significant problems with critical theory *even as* an analytical tool for diagnosing the problems of the world, starting with the most important question of all: How do we define justice and oppression?

Second, it's very naïve to think that secular social justice advocates *only* want everyone to analyze the world in the same way. They do want that, but they also want to *use* that (problematic) analysis to *overturn society*. This is why we see the push for critical theory-based ideas throughout education, corporations, media, entertainment, and more. The aggressive push alone should tell us that advocates think of this as more than a helpful tool! It's the *only* permissible tool in their view, and it will be wielded against anyone who gets in the way of the revolution.

Third, just because there are some nonproblematic ideas *in* critical theory doesn't mean we need to somehow accommodate critical theory in our biblical views of justice. The concept that racism can be embedded in certain societal structures, for example, shouldn't be controversial (slavery is perhaps the most obvious example of this). But that doesn't mean we should be looking for ways to fold critical theory ideas into our biblical views on justice just because critical theory happens to agree with Scripture in some form and be popular right now! A broken clock is right twice a day, but that doesn't mean we need to find ways to use it.

3. The pervasive acceptance of secular social justice (even within the church) should not make us so skeptical that we're ready to jump every time the word justice comes up.

This, I think, has been one of the saddest outcomes of the recent focus on justice topics. When we as Christians rightly become concerned about critical theory, we sometimes become overly paranoid that when someone even *says* the word *justice*, they must be caught up in secular social justice ideas. That may or may not be the case for any given person. But we should recognize that justice, when *biblically defined*, is an incredibly important part of the Christian calling. Rather than recoil from justice discussions because the word has been co-opted for so many unbiblical views, the prevalence of the subject should remind us all of how important it is to God. Critique unbiblical notions of it, yes. But then ask yourself, What am *I* doing for *biblical* justice? If we can't readily answer that question, it's time to revitalize our calling.

Only the Bible Offers the Right Lens for Justice

When my friend reacted so negatively to my blog post warning Christians about the (Critical Race Theory-rooted) Black Lives Matter organization, he chastised me for using a "single lens through which to view the entire world." But the critical theory that underlay his own view is just as much a single lens. The reality is that we *all* have a lens through which we view the world. The question for us as Christians should be whether we're using the *right* lens—a biblical lens. As we've seen in this chapter, adding a critical theory lens to the biblical lens is not only unnecessary, but also results in a great distortion of the biblical view.

That said, it should never be enough for us as Christians to merely *see* justice in the right way. Once our vision is clear, we need to live up to our calling to *do* justice. As we talked about in this chapter, we must critique errant ideas, but our corrections should come with the credibility of living out our faith in the service of others. Our words and actions *together* give glory to God and are a witness to the world of how beautiful biblical justice is.

FOR FURTHER READING

Introductory

- Voddie T. Baucham Jr., *Fault Lines: The Social Justice Movement and Evangelicalism's Looming Catastrophe* (Washington, DC: Salem Books, 2021).

- Thaddeus J. Williams, *Confronting Injustice without Compromising Truth* (Grand Rapids, MI: Zondervan, 2020).

In-Depth

- James Lindsay and Helen Pluckrose, *Cynical Theories: How Activist Scholarship Made Everything about Race, Gender, and Identity—and Why This Harms Everybody* (Durham, NC: Pitchstone Publishing, 2020). Note that this book is not written from a Christian perspective. It's also not a light read, but the insights are incredibly valuable and well worth your time for understanding individual critical theories and their relationship in more depth.

Dr. Neil Shenvi also has a plethora of excellent, in-depth resources on critical theory from a Christian perspective on his website Shenvi Apologetics.com. They are indexed at https://shenviapologetics.com/critical-theory-all-content/.

Also, I highly recommend the resources provided by the Center for Biblical Unity (https://www.centerforbiblicalunity.com/), including their small-group curriculum, *Reconciled: A Biblical Approach to Racial Unity*.

QUESTIONS FOR DISCUSSION OR REFLECTION

1. How would you summarize the difference between the secular social justice and biblical justice views of point A—why things are the way they are? How about the difference between the two views of point B—how things should ultimately be?

2. What are some examples of social structures that secular social justice and biblical justice advocates would agree are oppressive (historically or today)? What are some examples on which they would disagree?

3. Given the discussion in this chapter, how would you say secular social justice approaches that are rooted in critical theory fail to do *true* justice (in a biblical sense)?

4. What are some ways in which you could do more for biblical justice?

CHAPTER 11

Recommitting to Speaking Truth

*Under the pressure of
secular cancel culture*

Imagine for a moment that you're casually scrolling through social media one day when you see that a secular-minded friend has posted a picture of the following sign that they had just proudly erected in their front yard (in case you haven't seen it, this is a real and popular yard sign):

> In this house, we believe:
> Black Lives Matter
> Women's rights are human rights
> No human is illegal
> Science is real
> Love is love
> Kindness is everything

Your head starts to swim as concepts from the last ten chapters wash over you in quick succession, and the following thoughts go through your mind:

Wow! This sign seems to be a secular polemic against views it's implicitly and greatly mischaracterizing.

"Black Lives Matter"? Of course black lives matter—virtually no one disagrees with that. But that doesn't mean everyone should necessarily support the Critical Race Theory-rooted organization of the same name or Critical Race Theory-based solutions for racism (chapter 10).

"Women's rights are human rights"? In this context, the phrase *women's rights* is a euphemism for so-called abortion rights, but (1) there's no objective basis for rights in a secular worldview, and (2) in a Christian worldview, abortion is the unjust taking of an innocent life—not a right (chapters 7 and 8).

"No human is illegal"? That just doesn't logically make sense. The word *illegal* has nothing to do with one's identity as a human—it refers to a human's status with respect to established laws in societies. I know this is a reference to wanting open borders, but should societies have no laws, or just no laws about immigration? Why assume the exception?

"Science is real"? Well, yeah, everyone agrees that science is real in the sense that the scientific method has produced many reliable insights about the way in which the natural world works. But that doesn't imply it's our only source of knowledge about reality (chapter 4).

"Love is love"? There's no objective basis for defining love in a secular worldview, so within that worldview it would be logically consistent that there could be a million valid understandings of love that are *not* equal to one another (chapter 7). But if "Love is love" is meant to appeal to an objective standard of morality—that all forms of love and sexuality are equally acceptable—where is that standard coming from, and does it include types of love that aren't morally popular, such as bestiality and pedophilia (chapter 8)?

"Kindness is everything"? That seems to be an objective statement about the nature of reality. But on what authority can a secularist claim that—how do *they* know kindness is everything if they have no objective source for information about the nature of the world (chapter 7)? Furthermore, if we're all here as the result of a blind, undirected process of evolution, why does kindness even matter (chapter 4)? Aren't we just a bunch of molecules? It sure sounds like this assertion is borrowing from the biblically based view that humans are inherently valuable (chapter 7). I wonder if they think the idea that "Kindness is everything" can be derived from science, given that they seem to champion science as their primary epistemology.

You sure have a lot of thoughts! Your heartbeat quickens, you arm yourself with your copy of *Faithfully Different*, and you prepare to respond in some way. But then the questions set in:

- Is this something a Christian should even say anything about?

- Do I know this person well enough that I should say something?

- If I say something, should I say it publicly on social media or reach out privately?

- Do I have the time right now to deal with the inevitable back-and-forth that will transpire on social media if I give a response?

- What if no matter how gracious I am, this person gets annoyed (or even angry) with me and this ends up hurting our relationship?

- Do I really need to correct every secular idea I see? And if not, when should I?

If you've grappled with questions like these before, you're not alone! Given the prevalence of secularism, Christians are *constantly* faced with opportunities to "speak truth." But even when we know it's important to speak truth, it can be extremely difficult to know when, where, how, and with whom to do that.

If you're hoping for some black-and-white answers in this chapter, I'm sorry to say you won't find them. We aren't bulldozers of truth that roll over everyone and everything regardless of the situation. There's much to consider at any given time. But in this chapter, we'll take a big-picture look at the pressures of cancel culture in particular, what it means to speak truth from a biblical perspective, and some important questions to ask yourself before speaking up.

Understanding the Pressure of Cancel Culture

I'm not an experienced boater, but I've been on enough small boats in my life to know that I get terrified when I see a bigger and faster watercraft of some kind headed my way. I hate the feeling of the impending loss of control when those large waves are about to rock my little-boat world. Now, if I wasn't paying attention to the larger water environment, I wouldn't understand the reason for the sudden change to my boat's stability; I would feel the *effects* of the waves produced by the bigger watercraft, but I wouldn't know their source. And if I didn't know their source, I wouldn't have any information with which to better navigate in the future.

In the same way, if all you understand about the difficulties Christians are encountering with speaking truth is that everyone seems to get more easily offended today than ever, you're missing the context of the giant watercraft that's been circling for a few years now. That giant watercraft is *cancel culture*.

Like the term *virtue signaling, cancel culture* means different things to different people. But in common usage, it typically refers to the mass withdrawal of support from public figures who have said or done something that isn't considered socially acceptable. That withdrawal of support can range from a torrent of social media outrage directed at an individual to a boycotting of their work or the demand for their termination from a job.

As one example, *Harry Potter* author J.K. Rowling experienced a massive public backlash from the transgender community after posting a series of tweets affirming that there are meaningful differences between biological women and transwomen.[1] After the initial wave of "rebuke," Rowling unapologetically doubled down on her view, drawing even more public ire. But even if she *had* tried to apologize to get back into people's good graces, the cancel culture wouldn't have cared. Repentance (whether warranted or not) is of no value—it's a "one strike and you're out" policy. Journalist Alexi McCammond experienced that when she was hired to be the editor-in-chief of *Teen Vogue* magazine. She was let go shortly after, when staffers discovered she had posted several racially insensitive tweets as a college freshman.[2] McCammond took full responsibility for what she had said, apologized, and emphasized her growth since that time, but the outrage outweighed her words and the publisher let her go.

Cancel culture can also direct its efforts toward businesses, organizations, and institutions. The Girl Scouts were overwhelmed by social wrath, for example, for tweeting, "Congratulations Amy Coney Barrett on becoming the 5th woman appointed to the Supreme Court since its inception in 1789."[3] Because of Barrett's pro life views, pro-choice advocates quickly took to social media to condemn the Girls Scouts for their statement. The organization promptly deleted the tweet and issued an apology.

We could go through hundreds of other examples, but you get the point. These kinds of incidents are in the news nearly every day.

It might be tempting to chalk all this up to mere social hysteria. But it's no coincidence that people are suddenly responding to opposing views in the way they are. *Cancel culture is deeply rooted in the secular social justice ideology we discussed in chapter 10.* With the rise in the influence of critical theory-based social justice ideas has come the rise in cancel culture.

A *Vox* article by writer Aja Romano offers a window into these roots:

> The idea of canceling began as a tool for marginalized communities to assert their values against public figures who retained power and authority even after committing wrongdoing…In similar ways, both "wokeness" and "canceling" are tied to collectivized demands for more accountability from social systems that have long failed marginalized people and communities…Taken in good faith, the concept of "canceling" a person is really about questions of accountability—about how to navigate a social and public sphere in which celebrities, politicians, and other public figures who say or do bad things continue to have significant platforms and influence. In fact, actor LeVar Burton recently suggested the entire idea should be recast as "consequence culture."[4]

There's quite a bit to note here about the nature of cancel-culture thinking.

First, I hope you picked up on a bunch of words we looked at in chapter 10—*marginalized communities, power,* and *social systems.* These are three key concepts from critical social theories. Within this framework, canceling is seen as a *tool of the oppressed* to deal with the *sins of the oppressors.* As professor Anne Charity Hudley says, "Canceling is a way to acknowledge that you don't have to have the power to change structural inequality…It's a collective way of saying…'I may have no power, but the power I have is to [ignore] you.'"[5] Given what we discussed in chapter 10, this helps to explain why so many people see no problem with cancel culture. Harsh actions are assumed to be *morally justified* because they're thought to be taken on behalf of the *oppressed.* When everything is implicitly framed in terms of a fight against evil oppression, a lot of leeway will be given to what's considered to be acceptable action.

Second, cancel culture is believed to facilitate accountability for "wrongdoing." This, of course, should lead us to ask how people define wrongdoing. Once again, what we learned in chapter 10 is highly relevant. Recall that from a biblical perspective, one of the biggest problems with secular social justice is that it lacks an objective standard for defining justice in the first place. As we saw, oppression is often defined with respect to how people *feel* about dominant groups imposing their norms, values, and expectations on society as a whole, and that doesn't necessarily correspond with what would be considered oppressive from a biblical perspective. As a result, people today are often being canceled for stating ideas that are wrong in the eyes of the world but not wrong in the eyes of God. When a person like Romano states that cancel culture is really just about accountability for when people "say or do bad things," that sounds reasonable on the surface, but it's actually a very dangerous idea. *It implies people are accountable to a mob that's ready to retaliate as soon as someone's words or actions stray from the mob's own standard of justice.*

Third, note the suggestion that cancel culture is really just about *consequences* and could be recast as "consequence culture." This is a bit of a word game—an appeal to redefine terms in order to create a more positive view of what's taking place. (Sound familiar? See chapter 8.) This is an effective strategy because most people believe there should be consequences for harmful behavior. For example, the #MeToo movement exposed ongoing sexual abuse by several celebrities and other public figures. When people are abusive, certain consequences (public and otherwise) are necessary in order to prevent more people from becoming victims.

But cancel culture goes far beyond suggesting that there must be consequences for those who have physically harmed others. Cancel culture punishes people merely for having *ideas* that are considered harmful. Once more, this is closely related to the critical theory-based ideology we explored in chapter 10. Oppression is often seen as more psychological than material, so the revolution requires *ideas* supporting the oppressive norms of society to be dealt with swiftly. In a very real sense, the mob becomes the thought police and feels morally justified in taking on that role because they believe there must be consequences for people who use their power to express so-called oppressive ideas.

Some readers may be wondering at this point, *But don't people care about free speech anymore?* That's a great question. And the answer is no. Many people do *not* value free speech. Honestly, this point took me a long time to grasp. I assumed that *everyone* valued free speech in America and that those promoting cancel culture just didn't realize the kinds of ruinous effects their actions could have on that freedom. Oh, my naiveté! I eventually came to understand that many people today believe free speech is a *bad* thing because it allows those in power to continue oppressing people through their words. From this perspective, the social cost of free speech to marginalized people is too high for it to be of positive value.

It's interesting to note, however, that many of the people who believe free speech is a bad thing don't advocate for its legal regulation. That's not because they don't think it *should* be regulated, but because they assume those in power will only regulate it in ways that will continue to benefit themselves rather than the marginalized.[6]

Now, chances are, you're not a famous figure who has to tiptoe around cultural sensibilities in order to avoid being publicly canceled. *But the same waves that are crashing on them are crashing on the rest of us in our everyday lives.* That's why I've taken the time here to explore the giant watercraft of cancel culture. This broader cultural mentality has significant explanatory power for why so many of us feel constrained today in what we can and can't say—whether on social media, at work, or anywhere else. If culture is the air we breathe, we've inhaled an expectation for self-censorship to appease man rather than to please God.

We may know we're supposed to "speak truth" as Christians, but the awareness of cancel culture's mentality has shaken our confidence and gutted our courage. It's time to get back to the Bible to see what it means to speak truth.

What Does It Mean to Speak Truth?

It's amazing how many angry, condescending, mocking, or outright vicious statements I've seen Christians make in the name of speaking truth. But from a biblical perspective, speaking truth is not merely a descriptive term for the process of verbalizing true statements. It's sharing truth out of our love for God and love for others. When we share from that right motivation, speaking truth is not just expressing words, it's an *act of love* (Ephesians 4:15).

This is the case whether we're talking about sharing truth with believers or nonbelievers. In the context of conversations with fellow believers, sharing truth is often related to helping one another with biblical discernment. If a Christian has an unbiblical understanding of who Jesus is, for example, that could significantly affect the nature of their faith and their relationship with the Lord. As we saw in chapter 9, the *loving* thing to do is to share truth with them about who the Bible says Jesus really is. Because we talked about the importance of discernment in chapter 9, I'm going to focus now on what it means to share truth specifically with nonbelievers (we'll focus on the truth about salvation in particular in chapter 12—here we're looking at truth about all things).

We have a wonderful model of that in the account of Paul's interactions with the Athenians in Acts 17:16-34. We're going to walk through the passage a few lines at a time to draw out some key takeaways about speaking truth that are relevant to us today. Keep in mind as you read this that Paul faced his own *physical* cancel culture everywhere he went. He was stoned, beaten, imprisoned, and ultimately martyred, but he kept on speaking God's truth because "to live is Christ and to die is gain" (Philippians 1:21). Having the right eternal perspective made all the difference for Paul, and it should for us as well.

> While Paul was waiting for them in Athens, he was greatly distressed to see that the city was full of idols. So he reasoned in the synagogue with both Jews and God-fearing Greeks, as well as in the marketplace day by day with those who happened to be there (verses 16-17).

The passage begins by saying that Paul was *distressed* by the idolatry he saw while waiting for Silas and Timothy to rejoin him in Athens. If you have a biblical view of the world, it's natural to feel this way by what surrounds you. But note that the passage doesn't say Paul was distressed and then went to chill out in a secluded place while waiting for his co-laborers to arrive. It says that *in response* to his distress over this idolatrous culture he went to reason with people about Jesus. He *did* something when he saw the opportunity. And he didn't wait for the opportunity to come to him; he sought opportunities in the marketplace with whomever "happened to be there."

> A group of Epicurean and Stoic philosophers began to debate with him. Some of them asked, "What is this babbler trying to say?" Others remarked, "He seems to be advocating foreign gods." They said this because Paul was preaching the good news about Jesus and the resurrection. Then they took him and brought him to a meeting of the Areopagus, where they said to him, "May we know what this new teaching is that you are presenting? You are bringing some strange ideas to our ears, and we would like to know what they mean." (All the Athenians and the foreigners who lived there spent their time doing nothing but talking about and listening to the latest ideas) (verses 18-21).

This passage actually makes me laugh. Wouldn't it be great to live in a culture where people are so interested in understanding varied ideas that they'll ask you to elaborate on teachings about Jesus because they *want* to know what they mean? While that may be foreign to us in our current cultural moment, there *is* something our culture has in common with the ancient Athenians—they lacked an understanding of Christianity. They didn't comprehend what Paul was saying, nor what he was "advocating." Christianity may not be new as an idea today, but our culture certainly lacks an accurate understanding of what the Bible teaches. Mischaracterizations abound, and a significant part of speaking truth is helping people to understand what God's Word actually says, in contrast to what they *think* it says.

Let's see how Paul handled the lack of understanding in his own day. He started preaching as follows:

> People of Athens! I see that in every way you are very religious. For as I walked around and looked carefully at your objects of worship, I even found an altar with this inscription: to an unknown god. So you are ignorant of the very

thing you worship—and this is what I am going to proclaim to you.

The God who made the world and everything in it is the Lord of heaven and earth and does not live in temples built by human hands. And he is not served by human hands, as if he needed anything. Rather, he himself gives everyone life and breath and everything else (verses 22-25).

Note that Paul started his sermon by acknowledging what he had "carefully" observed in their culture. He didn't just start speaking truth. He found a connection point with their altar to an unknown god in order to draw their interest. He also started with the most foundational question: What is the nature of God? Paul knew that it wasn't enough for his audience to simply acknowledge the existence of a generic unknown god (like the one so many today believe in), but that it was crucial for them to know *who God is*.

We, too, should recognize the importance of speaking truth not just about the fact that God exists, but about the specifics of what He has revealed in His Word. As we saw earlier, that's offensive to many people because it threatens the presumed authority of the self, but it's the loving thing to do regardless of their response. Out of our *love* for others, we should want them to come to a saving knowledge of the truth (1 Timothy 2:4).

In addition, note Paul's confidence here in preaching *the* truth, not *a* truth. He didn't try to reach his audience with some kind of false humility and say, "Hey guys, we all have some different beliefs, and they're all good. But let me tell you about *my* truth!" Rather, he proclaimed that what he was saying is true for *everyone*, and he didn't shy away from telling his audience that their current beliefs were wrong.

In the same way, when sharing the truth, we want to be clear that we're not merely sharing our faith as something that "works" for us, but as something that is objectively true for all people. Perhaps that seems obvious to you as a Christian, but we have to remember that the default secular perspective today is something quite opposite—that we're all on our own journey of discovering what feels right to each individual. Some people are quite aware of the difference, and that's why they're offended by the objective truth claims of Christianity. But others haven't deeply considered how truth might be about more than their own feelings.

Paul then went on to talk about who *man* is:

> From one man he made all the nations, that they should inhabit the whole earth; and he marked out their appointed times in history and the boundaries of their lands. God did this so that they would seek him and perhaps reach out for him and find him, though he is not far from any one of us. "For in him we live and move and have our being." As some of your own poets have said, "We are his offspring" (verses 26-28).

It might not sound like Paul was saying much about who man is here, but that's only because today we take our relationship to our Creator for granted. The Athenians who believed in gods saw them as temperamental, unpredictable, and greedy—not as a solo creator who made man for the purpose of seeking Him in relationship. This was a very different view for Paul's audience. Interestingly, Paul also once again showed a familiarity with their culture by quoting their own poets to draw their attention. He then moved on to how man must *respond* to God:

> Therefore since we are God's offspring, we should not think that the divine being is like gold or silver or stone—an image made by human design and skill. In the past God overlooked such ignorance, but now he commands all people everywhere to repent. For he has set a day when he will judge the world with justice by the man he has appointed. He has given proof of this to everyone by raising him from the dead (verses 29-31).

Paul didn't avoid preaching a message of needed repentance; he told his audience that judgment was coming. But he also told them that

God has given *proof* that this is true by raising Jesus from the dead. He didn't get into all the details at that point (at least, as far as we know), but he wanted his listeners to understand that there was objective evidence to back up what he was saying. Again, he was not just speaking *his* truth—he was speaking *the* truth. Having a good understanding of apologetics isn't important only for our own faith (see chapter 6), but for effectively engaging with others. If we're going to tell people something is true for everyone regardless of their feelings, we better be ready to offer some good reasons for accepting that.

> When they heard about the resurrection of the dead, some of them sneered, but others said, "We want to hear you again on this subject." At that, Paul left the Council. Some of the people became followers of Paul and believed (verses 32-33).

The response to Paul's words was mixed. Some mocked, and some eventually believed. But Paul spoke truth while knowing that not everyone would embrace what he had to say. And that is what we should do today.

This example is not exhaustive, but it's certainly instructive. In one short sermon, we can learn a lot from how Paul challenged the culture's beliefs and spoke truth about God, man, the need for repentance, and the coming judgment. *Speaking truth encompasses more than addressing a handful of culturally hot topics.* God's truth defines all of reality, and we should therefore seek opportunities all the time to share about that truth. But we all know how hard it can be to do that, given today's cancel culture mentality and our personal circumstances. So let's turn now to some practical considerations for what this can look like in everyday life.

Four Questions to Consider Before Speaking Truth

In offering these four questions to consider before speaking truth, I don't mean to imply that we need to belabor every decision to share

God's Word. But given that it's not feasible to respond at all times to all people, I hope the following questions will serve as a helpful grid as you consider when to engage with nonbelievers.

1. Is this something worth speaking up about?

This is a difficult question to answer because it involves so many factors, but it's an important one to start with. Some things really are worth speaking up about more than others. Identifying those things is going to be an individual judgment call without hard-and-fast rules, but here are a few considerations.

First, tread lightly on pointing out people's logical inconsistencies. Let's say, for example, that one day your atheist friend shares a cute bunny picture on social media that simply says, "Kindness matters." That's probably not the right occasion for publicly (or even privately) explaining the logical implications of an atheistic worldview and that kindness *doesn't* matter in any objective sense given your friend's fundamental assumptions about the world (see chapters 4 and 7).

That said, there *are* good times and places for helping people see when the values they already hold to are more consistent with a biblical worldview than with a secular one. Imagine that you're engaged in a personal conversation with that same friend, but this time, they say something like, "I don't need religion. I just focus on what's important. Kindness is what matters most." The fact that your friend said, "I don't need religion" gives you a natural reason to respond from your perspective as a religious person. Now you potentially have a great opportunity to get them thinking about how we would know that kindness matters, how we define kindness, how that differs between worldviews, and so on.

Second, when people are merely speaking from a place *consistent* with their worldview, it's often better to wait for an opportunity that more explicitly presents itself as a launch point for conversation. Say, for example, that your secular-minded friend shares a social media post celebrating LGBTQ Pride month. Casually dropping off a response like "I won't celebrate sinful choices" is not going to do much for conversation. The person's views on sexuality are a consistent working out of their *entire* worldview built on the presumed authority of the self, just as your views are a consistent working out of an entire worldview built on the presumed authority of God's Word. In other words, there's a lot more going on here than whether the two of you agree on celebrating Pride Month. I'm not saying that it's *wrong* to share your view in this way, but that it's likely not the most *effective* way of sharing truth. With such a response, all you've done is restate your worldview without giving them anything thoughtful to consider about yours *or* theirs.

The same would be true if you posted a Bible verse and an atheist friend responded, "I don't believe God exists." There's nothing in the response that would make you think, *Hmm, I need to reconsider things.* All the friend did was inform you of their own belief. The yard sign quoted at the beginning of this chapter likely falls in this category: It's just one big announcement that someone holds a secular worldview.

But remember how Paul saw an opportunity to use his observation of the altar to an unknown god as a launching point for conversation? We can look for similar opportunities to have more fruitful discussion. Let's say that on another occasion the same friend posts an article criticizing churches that refuse to perform same-sex marriages and comments on how Jesus would be shocked at how "hateful" Christians are today. Now you have a good opportunity and reason to graciously speak truth in response to a mischaracterization. Public mischaracterizations of Christianity are often some of the best opportunities to speak up because people at least understand why you feel the need to do so, even if they disagree with what you have to say.

Third, sometimes the consideration has more to do with the person than the issue. The issue itself may be something worth speaking up about, but if you already know the person is hostile to conversation or is just making comments to get a reaction, it may not be worth addressing the issue at a given time. That's not to say the *person* isn't worthwhile, but rather, that time may be necessary for their heart to soften enough to hear what you have to share. In the meantime, pray that God would work that person's heart toward that point.

Fourth, remember that speaking truth is proactive, not just responsive. Paul went out and preached to whomever "happened to be" in the marketplace. For all its problems, social media can give us some unique opportunities to share truth with many people we might not otherwise have the chance to engage with more personally. Far more people will see what you say than will respond, but they *will* see it. Like Paul, be someone who speaks to *all* of God's truth, not just the same couple of hot cultural topics all the time. As I mentioned in chapter 8, there's so much to share about what we as Christians are *for*—both on social media and in person.

2. What is my motivation for saying something?

Once you've identified an occasion on which you believe it's important to speak truth, don't say a word until you've asked yourself this: What is my motivation for speaking up right now? *At all times, our central motivation should be to bring glory to God.* Full stop. If our heart is in the wrong place in a given circumstance, the truth that needs to be spoken may well be delivered in a way that could ultimately do more harm than good. Sometimes, speaking truth in the wrong way is worse than not speaking truth at all! As I said in chapter 5, if people hate us as Jesus warned they would, we need to be sure they hate us for the right reason—because of the truth we share, not because of the way in which we share it.

What are some wrong motivations to watch out for? Consider these:

- to win an argument

- to look smart

- to look virtuous

- to make someone feel foolish

- to put someone who annoys us "in their place"

I have to admit that if I saw a list like this in a book that I was reading rather than writing, I would probably glance right past it, thinking those things don't apply to me. Perhaps you feel that way too—you know you aren't perfect, but most of the time you feel your heart is in the right place. Yet sometimes that's the most dangerous place to be. When a wrong motivation is front and center, it's easier to catch ourselves because it's so obvious. It's when we sincerely want to bring glory to God *but also want to show others how smart we are*, or we sincerely want to bring glory to God *but also want to make someone look just a wee bit foolish for that offensive thing they said* that we can end up responding in the worst ways.

None of this is to say that we need to be quiet unless our motivations are pure as the driven snow. If that were the case, none of us would probably ever say a thing. We're all flawed people who don't love God perfectly, nor do we love others perfectly. But acknowledging that should make us even more aware that when we *do* speak, we need to ask ourselves, "Am I doing this to bring glory to God?"

3. Should I say something privately or publicly?

A major consideration when sharing truth in response to someone publicly (either online or in person) is whether they will in some way be embarrassed by your comment. It should go without saying that the tone and content of your comment should not belittle them in any way, but we have to remember that if we're in some way saying that a person is wrong, they will likely find that embarrassing in and of itself— and we all have a tendency to get defensive in those kinds of situations. Say, for example, that a friend comments about how science and religion are opposed to one another. Even if you graciously and logically explain why that's not the case, there's a good chance that your public correction (either online or in front of others in person) won't be taken in the way you hoped—especially if the friend hasn't thought out their position well enough to be confident in responding.

In the case of social media, I understand that a person should expect comments in response to their posts, but this is where we have to remember that sharing truth should ultimately be an act of love. It's not about how someone should theoretically respond given that they've posted something for social consumption; it's about the purpose of why you're sharing what you are—to lovingly speak truth for the glory of God. With that in mind, you may find it best to send certain types of comments privately or have a conversation in person later, regardless of what you feel you *should* be able to do.

The bottom line is to remember that you usually have a choice between sharing truth publicly and privately. Consider wisely which is best for any given situation.

4. What is the best way to say what I'm going to say?

This is the million-dollar question. And I can't really tell you the best way to say what you're going to say without knowing the person, subject, context, and so on. But, again, here are several factors to consider:

- Identify common beliefs as a starting point, when possible. You might say, for example, "We share a concern for human rights, but where we differ is [fill in the blank]."

- Assume the best in people, especially when it comes to stances on moral issues. People usually hold the positions they do because they genuinely believe those positions are the most loving ones to have. Engage in conversation with them as fellow humans who want the best for others rather than as people who are out to angrily reject God. Even when they *are* out to angrily reject God, they may not be aware of it, so speaking to their more consciously felt position of having the loving view is much more effective and charitable.

- Preface your statements with, "From a biblical perspective…" In this way, you're articulating the source of authority for what you're saying, even if they disagree that your source is authoritative. That's helpful because it establishes that you don't see what you're sharing as just "your" truth—you look to an external source. That can open the door to explaining more about why the distinction of authority matters (see the next point).

- When possible, structure your response as a comparison between worldviews and their sources of authority. For example, in a conversation with someone who believes in God but says they are "spiritual, not religious," you might say, "Our difference in views comes down to what we see as the right source of authority for determining truth. From a biblical perspective, God exists and has revealed Himself in the Bible, so no matter what I think or feel sounds right, I'm going to abide by what the Bible says because I believe God Himself said it. From your perspective, God exists but hasn't given us any kind of scripture to know more about Him, so everyone is on equal footing to figure life out." You could draw out the implications from there for whatever issue you're discussing, and then ask if they would like to know more about why there is good reason to believe the Bible really *is* God's Word (get your apologetics ready!).

- Try asking questions rather than making statements. Most people enjoy talking about their views if you ask in a way that shows you're truly interested in hearing what they have to say. Some of your questions can then be oriented toward getting them to think about the basis for their beliefs and how they've arrived at their conclusions.

- Express yourself in a way that people will at least know *you* believe what you're saying is from a place of love. The reality is that people will often respond negatively to truth, no matter how you say it. They may think you're hateful, arrogant, narrow-minded, or any number of other things—and they will probably tell you as much. You simply can't judge how lovingly you spoke truth based on how a person responds.

The Truth Cannot Be Canceled

Given the nature of cancel culture, you can basically expect to offend people when you speak the truth—to the degree that they may cut you off completely. But we need to be okay with getting canceled if it's happening because of the truth we share. After all, *truth itself can never be canceled.* People who don't want to hear truth can put on proverbial earmuffs and try to shut out one person at a time, but there will always be more of God's people who will speak up. God cannot be stopped.

And don't be fooled into a false sense of ease by thinking that when you keep your beliefs to yourself no one will dislike you. Plenty of people today will dislike you for even *identifying* as a Christian—before you ever say a word. Remember, Christianity itself is seen as oppressive and therefore evil. Silence won't take you much further in culture than speaking truth will. But it *will* take you further away from what God has called you to.

FOR FURTHER READING

- Gregory Koukl, *Tactics, 10th Anniversary Edition: A Game Plan for Discussing Your Christian Convictions* (Grand Rapids, MI: Zondervan, 2019).

- Erwin W. Lutzer, *We Will Not Be Silenced: Responding Courageously to Our Culture's Assault on Christianity* (Eugene, OR: Harvest House, 2020). This book also deals with several of the social justice subjects discussed in chapter 10.

QUESTIONS FOR DISCUSSION OR REFLECTION

1. How have you seen the cancel culture mentality affect Christians?

2. Which aspects of Paul's sermon to the Athenians do you think are most relevant to Christians today?

3. Which types of subjects are easiest for you to speak truth about? Which are most difficult?

4. What fears do you have that prevent you from speaking up more often? What would help you overcome those fears?

CHAPTER 12

Reshaping Our Hearts for Sharing the Gospel

Under the pressure of secular relativism

I've shared quite a bit of research data in this book about Christian attitudes and beliefs. Much of it should be eye-opening if we really stop to think about it—for example, the giant statistical gap between those with a biblical worldview and those identifying as Christians. But I have one more research statistic to share with you that is perhaps the most shocking of all, at least to me personally: Almost half of *practicing Christian* millennials (47 percent) agree that it is "wrong to share one's personal beliefs with someone of a different faith in hopes that they will one day share the same faith."[1]

Read that again: They believe it's *wrong* to evangelize!

This finding is even more shocking in the context of the other (more positive) beliefs this group has about evangelism:

- 96 percent agree that part of their faith means being a witness about Jesus.

- 94 percent agree that the best thing that could ever happen to someone is for them to come to know Jesus.

- 86 percent agree that when someone raises questions about faith, they know how to respond.

- 73 percent agree that they're gifted at sharing their faith with other people.

On the surface, this collective picture doesn't seem to make much sense. For example, when you read that almost half of practicing Christian millennials think it's wrong to share their beliefs, you might think it's because they just don't understand that evangelism is part of the Christian faith. *But 96 percent said they know it is.* Or, you might think it's because they don't understand how important it is for a person to know Jesus. *But 94 percent said it's the best thing that could happen to someone.* Then you might think it's because they just don't feel equipped for evangelism. *But 86 percent said they know how to respond to questions, and 73 percent even said they're "gifted" at sharing their faith!*

So what is going on here?

The research report summarized the findings this way: Millennials are "ready—but not willing—to talk about faith."[2] I think that statement is right, but it merely restates the problem: They're unwilling because they think it's wrong. The question is *why* they think it's wrong given that they otherwise seem to be ready. And the answer lies in understanding secular pressures against evangelism that affect *all* generations.

You see, millennials aren't the only Christians who struggle with evangelism in a secular culture. But their attitude toward it is like a canary in a coal mine alerting us to how a rapidly encroaching secularism easily distorts a biblical view on the subject. That's because the millennial generation is much more aware of secular resistance to evangelism than Christians of older generations. *That awareness alone has altered their views.* As Barna Research points out:

> Younger Christians tend to be more personally aware of the cultural temperature around spiritual conversations. Among practicing Christians, Millennials report an average (median) of four close friends or family members

who practice a faith other than Christianity; most of their Boomer parents and grandparents, by comparison, have just one. Sharing the gospel today is made harder than at any time in recent memory by an overall cultural resistance to conversations that highlight people's differences. Society today also casts a negative light on proselytization that many older Christians do not fully appreciate.[3]

In other words, the belief among nearly half of millennials that evangelism is wrong is a result of their more significant and consistent exposure to secular views on the subject relative to older generations. From a biblical standpoint, sharing the gospel is not only not wrong, it's *commanded* by Jesus. We are explicitly told to go and make disciples of all nations (Matthew 28:19-20)! So how is secular culture causing cognitive dissonance for so many Christians—where they believe both that Jesus commands something *and* it's wrong? That's what we need to understand so we can reshape our hearts for sharing the gospel and help future generations withstand what are surely going to be continued secular pressures.

Four Secular Pressures Against Evangelism

As we near the end of this book, it's fitting that we should revisit the four pillars of secularism one last time. Say it with me now: Feelings are the ultimate guide, happiness is the ultimate goal, judging is the ultimate sin, and God is the ultimate guess. Through the lens of each of these pillars, we can better see why secularism inherently leads to a view that it's *wrong* for Christians (and those of other religions) to evangelize.

1. When feelings are the ultimate guide, evangelism is seen as arrogant.

When we share our faith, it's not just because we want others to know what *we* believe—it's because we know others need to have the same (biblical) beliefs about who Jesus is in order to (1) have the correct understanding of reality, and (2) put their trust in Him for eternal life (John 3:16; 14:6).

Given all we've learned about secularism and the authority of the self, we should immediately see why these Christian convictions would make many nonbelievers' heads explode with frustration. *Christians believe there's an objective reality that everyone's beliefs should conform to and that there are significant implications if they don't.* If that's true, then feelings *aren't* the ultimate guide! The assumption behind a Christian's desire to share the gospel—that there's an authority outside the self with whom we need to be reconciled—is an affront to the secularist's most basic paradigm.

If there really is an external authority who should be our guide for life (and not just our feelings), it's not arrogant to share that truth with others any more than it's arrogant to help someone understand that 10 plus 10 equals 20. But when people believe feelings are the ultimate guide, they often do see evangelism as arrogant. Why? Because they ironically make that evaluation from the assumption that their *relativistic* view is correct. You see, they don't view an evangelistic conversation as one between two people who both believe they're right, but rather, as a conversation between one person who believes they're right (you) and one person who believes *everyone* is right when they follow their feelings (them). From this perspective, they see you as arrogant because you're supposedly the only person in the conversation who thinks they're right. But there are two logical problems here, as you may have noticed: First, if they believe that everyone is right, that should mean you're right too! And second, if they believe they're right that everyone is right, they think they're right as much as you do (got all that?).

We can see these assumptions play out in a wikiHow article titled "How to Stop People From Trying to Convert You to Another Religion," in which Nicolette Tura gives advice on dealing with a loved one who wants to "convert" you. Tura says,

> Sometimes the problem with religious family members is
> that they have multiple attempts to try and show you the
> "right way"…When they tell you about how great their reli-
> gion is, say something like, "It sounds like you've found

something that really makes sense for you. I'm happy for you! I've also found a religion that really feels good for me."[4]

Notice how Tura puts "right way" in scare quotes. This is a subtle way of saying that religious people think there's one right way even though there's not. And then she goes on to imply that religion is about what "makes sense" or "feels good" for the individual. In her view, this is an effective way out of a conversation because it's now been established that both parties have found something that *feels* right, and that's all anyone needs to care about.

Similarly, in an opinion piece that speaks out against teachers talking with kids about faith in a public school setting, a writer for *Church & State Magazine* says,

> When public school teachers decide to preach to children, they are in effect saying that parents have made the wrong choice. These teachers are saying they know better than a child's own parents what is best for that child. They are substituting their own religious beliefs for the beliefs of the parents. This isn't just illegal, it's unethical and arrogant.[5]

Public school questions aside, this writer asserts that for anyone to believe they know what's best for another person is *arrogant*—unethical even! Once again, we see that the underlying assumption is that feelings are the ultimate guide, so no one can legitimately claim to know what's best for any other person. Of course, they too are claiming to know what's best for others (to keep faith out of schools), but they miss that irony. Apparently, it's only arrogant when it's a religious person claiming to know what's true.

2. When happiness is the ultimate goal, evangelism is seen as an imposition.

While the first point was about how people see *you*, this one is about how they think your evangelism affects *them*. Evangelism is seen as an imposition or burden.

When happiness is the ultimate goal, anything that gets in the way of what makes you happy is viewed as a bad thing. It's like you're running down the beautiful path of life chasing after the butterflies of your choosing, and then someone rudely stops you to say you're going the wrong way. How dare they! You don't *want* to go the other way! You're happy doing what you're doing, so why must they bother you? Why do they want to try to make you feel like you *have* to take their path or else there are consequences? Why are they so interested in *imposing* their beliefs on someone else? *Get out of my way and let me do my thing. You do you, I'll do me.*

One college student, for example, made the case in his collegiate paper that it's time to stop allowing religious groups to "proselytize" on campus because "the experience of being preached to can be insulting, since it suggests that one's beliefs are inferior to those of the preacher. An interaction could be interpreted as an imposition of beliefs on people who dissent from them."[6] It's fascinating that this student assumes his readers will all agree that an "imposition of beliefs" is inherently bad (God forbid that an interaction might be interpreted that way). But it's unsurprising as an extension of the belief that one's happiness is the ultimate goal.

There's another sense of the word *imposition* that's worth spending some time on here as well. An increasing number of people today are seeking to "decolonize" their faith—to undo the effects of the *historical* (and more literal) imposition of Christian beliefs onto their ancestors.

In the view of those decolonizing, colonization is thought of as "a violent process whereby colonialist settlers invade the land of native people in order to dispossess and plunder it through rape, genocide, and other egregious acts of violence against indigenous people."[7] My purpose here isn't to sort out how anyone should or shouldn't think about colonization, but rather, to explain the connection between this view of history and the view of Christian evangelism today. To that end, writer Deborah Jian Lee explains what decolonizing faith means for those, like her, who retain a Christian identity but reject "colonial Christianity":

Across the wide sweep of colonial history, the systematic demonization and erasure of local religion served as a key strategy to empire building. The consequences can still be seen today across the globe…For some, that means decolonizing their Christian faith from white patriarchy and capitalism. For others, that means connecting to ancestral faith practices, such as Yoruba, Buddhism, ancestor veneration or particular tribal traditions. For others, it's an amalgam, a synthesis of severed history, personal heritage and truths from other traditions.[8]

As you can see, when people who identify as Christians talk of decolonizing their faith, they aren't simply talking about letting go of purely cultural faith traditions like Western worship styles or dress. They're talking about letting go of the biblical worldview rooted in the inspiration and authority of Scripture because of its perceived *association* with the violence of colonization. In the process, they're adopting an "amalgam" of beliefs that reflect those of their precolonial ancestors (while continuing to identify as Christian). As Lee says, "Where Western Christianity has relied historically on doctrine and dogma aimed at the individual, many non-European spiritualities can lean toward prioritizing experience, context, and values that connect with the entire community."[9]

There's no doubt it's a historical tragedy that colonizers sometimes committed horrible acts in the name of Christ or attempted to force people to convert to Christianity (something the Bible *never* suggests should happen). But the errant use of the Bible as a weapon doesn't make it untrue. And the core biblical beliefs we've discussed in this book are not reflective of "Western Christianity"—they're reflective of the historical teachings of Jesus Himself (a Middle Eastern Jew). If we throw out Jesus's teachings, we're not throwing out Western culture; we're throwing out what God has revealed about truth for all humankind. People who decolonize faith in this way, then, are really a subset of the progressive Christian movement. They reject the Bible as an objective basis for their beliefs in favor of their own indigenous spirituality.

The reason this rapidly growing movement is so relevant to our main point is that it's a reminder of how deeply people can feel about the perceived problem of people "imposing" their beliefs on others in evangelistic efforts. For some, like the college student I quoted earlier, imposition is more of an insult and annoyance. But others see evangelism through the eyes of a hostile colonialism, when the attempted imposition of beliefs had a more tangible (and sometimes tragic) effect. I trust that you'll understand that this historical imposition is completely different than how the Bible calls us to share our faith with love and respect. But we need to be aware that many people see colonial imposition and a loving attempt to share the gospel through the same lens of anger and resentment, and that will inevitably shape the nature of some interactions.

3. When judging is the ultimate sin, evangelism is seen as condemnation.

The Bible uses the word *judging* in two very different ways. The first is in the sense of discernment—judging between right and wrong. This is the type of judging Christians *should* do. The second is in the sense of condemnation—passing a final sentence on a person's life. This is the type of judging Christians should *not* do because only God has the authority to make that decision (Psalm 7:11; 9:8; 50:6; Isaiah 33:22).

From a secular perspective, however, judging is nearly always assumed to be condemnation; that's why it's seen as the ultimate sin. If you tell someone there's something wrong with the life journey they're on, a secularist will essentially think you're trying to play "God" over them—who made *you* final judge over their life? And this view is even more pronounced when it comes to evangelism. Now you're not just "condemning" various choices, you're "condemning" their whole life if they don't believe what you do! Of course, in reality we're not claiming to know someone's final standing before God when we share what He's said about salvation, but that's how our message is often *perceived*.

We can see an example of this perception in an article written by Jewish author Remy Maisel. Maisel shared how she was approached by a group of Christians one day and recounted what she said to them in response:

> Look, I can't really believe in God...But I live the way you want me to anyway. I do the right thing, most times. I have a strong moral code. I've got tradition and community. If you want me to walk away from here tonight believing in God, that's not going to happen. But I am going to walk away and try to be a good person. Can't that be enough?

She went on to reflect on how the experience made her feel:

> Part of me was purely angry. For millenia [sic], Jews have starved, fought and died to avoid converting. Fought for the right not to be Christian. To practice openly. And here were these people, stopping me on my way home, basically implying that I was wrong and needed to be saved or fixed? How dare they?[10]

You can sense Maisel's indignation at the idea that anyone *dared* tell her she needed to be saved. After all, in her thinking, she does the "right thing" and tries to be a "good person." Because what a person believes doesn't figure into her equation of what might be important in the scope of eternity, Maisel sees evangelism as a personal condemnation *of how she lives her life.*

This is really important to remember: Christians share the gospel with the assumption that what a person believes matters, but most secularists *receive* the gospel with the assumption that *behavior* is all that matters. And when behavior is assumed to be all that matters, the gospel is seen as a very personal condemnation of how a person has been living their life.

4. When God is the ultimate guess, evangelism is seen as silly, weird, annoying, and/or a waste of time.

Recall from chapter 2 that the presupposition of secularism is that confidence in the truth of any specific religious worldview is unfounded, leading to the secular pillar of "God is the ultimate guess." We saw that for some people, this manifests itself in a belief that all religions are equally true. God is a guess in the sense that cosmic truth is perceived to be far beyond what we could ever understand, so all religions are equally valid attempts to explain the mysteries of reality. And we saw that for others, this manifests itself in a belief that all religions are equally false. God is a guess in the sense that there's no good reason to believe He exists, but if you want to take a blind leap of faith, go for it.

Given these assumptions of secularism, evangelism can be seen as silly, weird, annoying, and/or a waste of time, depending on the person. It's *silly* to those who believe all religions are equally false because there's no reason to believe God even exists. It's *weird* to those who believe that all religions are equally true because it makes no sense to try to convince others you're right when truth is beyond the grasp of us all. It's *annoying* to that same group because they just want to be left alone to pursue their own understanding of the world. And it's a *waste of time* to all secularists for all the above reasons!

With all of this said, we should see that there's a giant secular iceberg sitting under its tip that says almost half of millennials think evangelism is wrong. Secular culture says sharing one's faith is arrogant, imposing, condemning, silly, weird, annoying, or a waste of time. In other words, it's wrong...for *many* different reasons.

Breaking Down the Gospel Message

If you find it hard to share the gospel, take comfort in knowing you're not alone. We live in a tough culture! But there are three points you may find helpful.

First, simply understanding the secular perspectives we just discussed can help us shape our message more effectively. For example, if we know that people think we're "playing God" when we evangelize, we can be more careful to articulate that we're not claiming to personally know their final standing before God, but rather, we are sharing what we believe God has said about salvation in the Bible. Second, we need to feel confident that we understand the core gospel message and how to break it down for others. Oftentimes, we've internalized our faith so much that it's difficult to know where to start when we explain it to someone else! So that's what we're going to do now—break down the key parts of the gospel message. Then we'll conclude with the third point that you may find helpful: knowing the answers to three tough questions.

The Problem

When we talk about people needing to be saved, we're implying that they need to be saved *from* something. A conversation about salvation, then, should start with a conversation about the predicament we're in.

The Bible says that all people have God's moral law written on their hearts (Romans 2:14-15) and are guilty of breaking it (Isaiah 64:6; Romans 3:10, 23). When we sin, we rebel against God, and our sins relationally separate us from Him (Isaiah 59:2). This separation from our Creator and Sustainer is the most basic problem of human existence.

Two of God's attributes frame how He deals with this sin problem: His love (Psalms 86:15; 136:1; John 3:16; Romans 8:37-39) and His justice (Deuteronomy 32:4; Psalms 9:7-8; 33:5; Isaiah 61:8). Because God is just, He *must* act in judgment against sin, and He has set the penalty as death (Romans 6:23). Though people sometimes assume God wouldn't penalize humans for sin if He's loving, overlooking sin would actually make God *unjust* and therefore imperfect. Given His perfectly just character, God can't simply let people do whatever they want without consequences. We wouldn't expect an earthly judge to set guilty criminals free out of "love," so why would we expect that of a perfectly just God? Love without justice is not love at all.

This, then, is our grim situation: We are all guilty of sin and stand condemned before a just and holy God.

Our Inability to Save Ourselves

It's human nature to think that if we just work hard enough, we can do anything we set our minds to. But the Bible is clear that no amount of human effort is sufficient for earning our way out of paying the penalty for sin—*no one* can be good enough. Romans 3:10-12 says, "There is no one righteous, not even one; there is no one who understands; there is no one who seeks God. All have turned away, they have together become worthless; there is no one who does good, not even one." And Isaiah 64:6 says that "our righteous acts are like filthy rags."

Left to our own devices, we remain stuck in our state of condemnation.

God's Provision for Forgiveness

There's an important difference between God and an earthly judge who sets guilty criminals free. God is both the judge and the offended party. That means He is in the unique position to both set the penalty *and* absolve humans of their guilt as He sees fit within His just character. And here's the good news: In His perfect love, He decided to make provision for our forgiveness. Payment for sin was required by His justice, but He made that payment Himself through Jesus's death on the cross in our place.

God's Offer of Salvation

God made provision for the forgiveness of sin, but that doesn't mean everyone will automatically be reconciled to Him and inherit eternal life. We must respond. John 3:16-18 makes this clear:

> God so loved the world that he gave his one and only Son, that whoever believes in him shall not perish but have eternal life. For God did not send his Son into the world to condemn the world, but to save the world through him. Whoever believes in him is not condemned, but whoever does not believe stands condemned already because they have not believed in the name of God's one and only Son.

This, then, is God's offer of salvation: Those who believe in Jesus will have eternal life! No one has to remain condemned. By putting our trust in Jesus as our Savior, we are forgiven of our sins (1 John 1:9), made right with God (Romans 5:1), and able to live forevermore with Him (John 3:16). This offer is the product of God's grace alone; He didn't have to make it, and there's no alternative through our own initiative. As Paul says, "It is by grace you have been saved, through faith—and this is not from yourselves, it is the gift of God—not by works, so that no one can boast" (Ephesians 2:8-9).

Our Response

So how does a person accept God's offer of salvation? The Bible doesn't give us a checklist, but Romans 10:9-10 gives us the basic idea of where our heart and mind should be:

> If you declare with your mouth, "Jesus is Lord," and believe in your heart that God raised him from the dead, you will be saved. For it is with your heart that you believe and are justified, and it is with your mouth that you profess your faith and are saved.

It should also be said that salvation isn't just about what happens after we die. It's also about a transformed life now. When we're saved, our bodies become a temple of the Holy Spirit (1 Corinthians 6:19), and the Spirit produces fruit in our lives (Galatians 5:22-23). Our new identity in Christ necessarily changes how we think and live.

Overcoming Three Barriers to Evangelism

In spite of all we know about the importance of sharing the gospel, there are some difficult questions Christians often have that can create barriers for doing so. Sometimes these questions are so subconscious that we don't even realize they're causing hesitancy in some way. So let's bring them to the surface and tackle them head-on.

1. Is Jesus really the only way?

God could have chosen to leave us in our universal state of sinfulness and judge humankind accordingly. He didn't *have* to offer us a way out. But once God, in His love, determined to offer a way for humans to be justly forgiven of their sins, some kind of atonement was necessary. As we just saw, He chose to make payment for our sins *Himself* through Jesus's sacrifice on the cross. Theologians debate whether God could have chosen another kind of atonement, but the important thing for us to know is that the Bible says Jesus's sacrifice on the cross was, in fact, the *only* way He offered: "Salvation is found in no one else, for there is no other name under heaven given to mankind by which we must be saved" (Acts 4:12; see also John 14:5-6; Romans 3:25; 1 Corinthians 15:3; 2 Corinthians 5:21; 1 Timothy 2:5).

A view called Christian universalism teaches that Jesus's atonement was indeed the only way God offered salvation, but that *all* will be reconciled to God because of that sacrifice. They typically believe that hell exists, but that it's only a temporary punishment and ultimately, all people will be saved. While it's outside the scope of this chapter to fully examine and refute this view, the verse that most directly answers it is John 3:16: "God so loved the world that he gave his one and only Son, that whoever believes in him shall not perish but have eternal life." Jesus explicitly stated here that perishing is an alternative to eternal life. He also warned repeatedly that not everyone will be saved (Matthew 7:13-14; 25:34, 41, 46).

In short, the Bible affirms that Jesus is the only way to God in two senses: (1) His atonement makes reconciliation with God possible, and (2) only those who believe in Him will inherit the eternal life that atonement offers.

2. Will a loving God really send people to hell?

We've already seen in this chapter why, theologically speaking, a just God must punish sin and that there are eternal consequences for those who reject God's free gift of forgiveness. But if we're honest, many of us still feel uncomfortable with the idea of hell—both believing in it ourselves and talking about it as a reality with others. In fact, research has shown that more people believe in heaven than hell, though the Bible clearly speaks to the reality of both.[11] Jesus very directly said, for example:

When the Son of Man comes in his glory, and all the angels with him, he will sit on his glorious throne. All the nations will be gathered before him, and he will separate the people one from another as a shepherd separates the sheep from the goats...

Then the King will say to those on his right, "Come, you who are blessed by my Father; take your inheritance, the kingdom prepared for you since the creation of the world..."

Then he will say to those on his left, "Depart from me, you who are cursed, into the eternal fire prepared for the devil and his angels..."

Then they will go away to eternal punishment, but the righteous to eternal life (Matthew 25:31-32, 34, 41, 46).

Despite what the Bible clearly states in passages like these, Christians sometimes absorb the idea from culture that Christianity is inherently a fear-based religion because of its teaching on hell—and thus want to avoid the subject altogether. But let's get clear on this: People *should* fear the reality of hell if they're not in right relationship with God. That said, fear is not why people follow Jesus. Rather, Christians follow Jesus out of love for Him. We don't (or at least shouldn't) fear hell because there is "no condemnation for those who are in Christ Jesus" (Romans 8:1). We believe that God so *loved* the world that He provided a way for us to be reconciled to Him. Sin is a serious matter with serious consequences, but Christianity is ultimately a story of love.

3. What about those who have never heard about Jesus?

Many people think, *If God exists, He must be fair. And because not everyone will hear about Jesus, there must be multiple paths to salvation. Sending a person to hell because they didn't believe in someone they had never heard of would be unjust.*

But as we've already seen, the Bible is clear that there is only one path to salvation, and that's through Jesus. The fact there are some people who never hear about Jesus doesn't mean we should infer something that contradicts the rest of Scripture.

The reality is that the Bible doesn't explicitly tell us what happens to people who have never heard about Jesus. But there are multiple passages that indicate *all* humans are accountable for what can be known through general revelation—what God has revealed through nature. For example, Romans 1:19-20 says:

> What may be known about God is plain to them, because God has made it plain to them. For since the creation of the world God's invisible qualities—his eternal power and divine nature—have been clearly seen, being understood from what has been made, so that people are without excuse.

And Romans 2:14-15 describes what God has revealed of Himself through our moral conscience:

> When Gentiles, who do not have the law, do by nature things required by the law, they are a law for themselves, even though they do not have the law. They show that the requirements of the law are written on their hearts, their consciences also bearing witness, and their thoughts sometimes accusing them and at other times even defending them.

From these passages, we learn that there are no people who are ignorant of God's existence and moral requirements. So when we talk about those who have "never heard," it's important to understand that there's a sense in which everyone has at least "heard" of God, even if they don't have access to His special revelation in Scripture.

So where does that leave us with the answer to our question? Christians have different views. *Restrictivists* believe that before Jesus came, people were saved by trusting in the promise of a *future* Savior

(Hebrews 11), yet maintain that those who live after Jesus must hear and accept the gospel to be saved. They trust that the results will be just, given God's perfect character. *Inclusivists* believe that those who haven't heard about Jesus can be saved based on how they respond to God through His general revelation. They acknowledge that the only reason anyone can *ever* be saved is because of Jesus's sacrifice, but believe that His sacrifice can apply to those who don't know about it (just as it retroactively applied to those who lived in Old Testament times).

Note that inclusivism is *not* the same as pluralism. Pluralism is the idea that many paths can lead to salvation, and therefore a person can consciously reject Jesus and still be saved. This view contradicts biblical teachings. Inclusivists believe that those who hear about and reject Jesus will be lost, but that those who *never* hear may be saved based on their response to general revelation.

This is one of those questions to which we don't have all the answers we'd like. But that fact shouldn't detract from the truth we do know: God is perfectly just, so we can be confident He will do what's fair on judgment day.

The Gospel Is Still Good News

Given all these challenges to sharing the gospel, Christians sometimes think that the best thing we can do is just live good lives as an example to others. But as I hope I've shown in this book, secular culture doesn't even agree with God on what a "good" life would look like. And it's naïve and unbiblical to think that the more we look like culture—passively glossing over the worldview differences that should drive our thinking and living—the more people will seek Jesus. Why seek Jesus when who He is and what He taught apparently makes no tangible difference in the lives of Christians, other than that they (sometimes) go to church on Sundays and pray in the quiet of their homes? How does this challenge people to consider the radical claims that Jesus was God Himself, has authority over our lives, made reconciliation with our Creator possible through His sacrifice on the cross, was supernaturally raised from the dead, and is our only hope for eternal life?

It doesn't.

Our faithfully different lives matter.

And our words matter.

That's why we *must* share the gospel: "Faith comes from hearing the message, and the message is heard through the word about Christ" (Romans 10:17).

Be confident in this: No matter how secular culture sees it, the gospel is still good news. It's still the *best* news: God loves us, we matter, we can have a relationship with our Creator, and we can live for eternity in perfect harmony with Him and others.

It would sound like a fairy tale if it weren't true. Praise the Lord that it is.

FOR FURTHER READING

- Michael Sherrard, *Relational Apologetics: Defending the Christian Faith with Holiness, Respect, and Truth* (Grand Rapids, MI: Kregel, 2015).

- In addition to the above resource, see the several other apologetics books recommended at the end of chapters 4 and 5 for guidance on how to make a case for the truth of Christianity to nonbelievers.

QUESTIONS FOR DISCUSSION OR REFLECTION

1. Do you find evangelism difficult? Why or why not?

2. If a Christian friend said to you that they think it's wrong to share their faith in the hope that someone will convert to Christianity, how would you respond? What if they said that they think it's enough for our actions alone to "do the talking"?

3. If a non-Christian friend said to you that it bothers them when Christians share their faith because it's arrogant to think they know what's best for anyone else, how would you respond?

4. How would you explain to a non-Christian friend why a loving God still requires payment for sin and can't "just" forgive?

A Final Encouragement: Fruit Under Pressure

The fruit of the Spirit is love, joy,
peace, patience, kindness, goodness,
faithfulness, gentleness, self-control.

GALATIANS 5:22-23 ESV

You've probably heard the urban legend that if you put a frog directly into boiling water, it'll jump out, but if you put a frog in cool water and then *slowly* bring it to a boil, the frog won't notice the increased heat and will eventually cook to death. (That doesn't sound like a very encouraging way to start a conclusion titled *A Final Encouragement*, but stick with me.)

The frog in boiling water has long been used as a metaphor for how people often don't notice dangers that arise gradually rather than suddenly, yet gradually arising dangers often have the deadlier effect. There have undoubtedly been many people who have called themselves Christians but found that the gradually rising temperature of secular pressures cooked the life out of their faith. Those are the ones who end up in deconversion statistics. But a better metaphor for the challenges faced by those who still have a biblical worldview is *fruit under pressure.*

For those who don't cook much, a pressure cooker is a sealed chamber that traps the steam generated as food is heated. As the steam builds, the pressure increases, and that increased pressure raises the boiling point of the water. The food cooks much more quickly than with conventional methods due to the higher temperature and the pressure cooker's ability to force moisture into the food. Given this mechanism, pressure cookers rapidly turn fruit into mush. Previously solid and distinct pieces of fruit lose their shape; apples become applesauce and peaches become peach jam.

In the same way, the types of secular pressures we've explored in this book can be so strong that they seemingly force their way into our lives—into what we believe, how we think, and how we live out our faith. As a worldview minority, we're surrounded by those pressures on all sides. If we don't establish and maintain biblical clarity, we become like fruit in a pressure cooker, losing our distinctiveness from the culture around us and giving in to a collective softness in our faith.

But there's an important difference between real life and a pressure cooker. In a pressure cooker, the food is trapped on all sides. There's nothing the food can do but give in to the pressures to cook it. *In real life, we may be surrounded by secular pressures, but we don't have to have the lid on. We can choose to reach up and out to God.*

When we keep our eyes on the Lord through consistent prayer, Bible study, and fellowship with other believers, we're no longer trapped by worldly influences. We've taken the lid off. And the fruit of the *Spirit* maintain their God-given and distinctive shape rather than softening to an unrecognizable form.

> *Love* remains a godly love, rather than becoming one rooted in subjective feelings.

> *Joy* remains a godly joy, rather than becoming one equated with circumstantial happiness.

> *Peace* remains a godly peace, rather than becoming one stemming from worldly appeasement.

> *Patience* remains a godly patience, rather than becoming one that only bears with like-minded people and ideas.

Goodness remains a godly goodness, rather than becoming one defined by popular consensus.

Faithfulness remains a godly faithfulness, rather than becoming one tempered by the authority of the self.

Gentleness remains a godly gentleness, rather than becoming one that's indistinguishable from apathy.

And *self-control* remains a godly self-control, rather than becoming one that navigates according to a worldly compass of freedom and restraint.

So keep reaching up.

As you faithfully do so, the differences in your believing, thinking, and living will remain an intact and convicting witness for the Lord—even when it seems the world is powerfully against you.

And when in doubt, keep coming back to Paul's words in Romans 8:31-39:

> If God is for us, who can be against us? He who did not spare his own Son, but gave him up for us all—how will he not also, along with him, graciously give us all things? Who will bring any charge against those whom God has chosen? It is God who justifies. Who then is the one who condemns? No one. Christ Jesus who died—more than that, who was raised to life—is at the right hand of God and is also interceding for us. Who shall separate us from the love of Christ? Shall trouble or hardship or persecution or famine or nakedness or danger or sword? As it is written:
>
> "For your sake we face death all day long;
>   we are considered as sheep to be slaughtered."
>
> No, in all these things we are more than conquerors through him who loved us. For I am convinced that neither death nor life, neither angels nor demons, neither the

present nor the future, nor any powers, neither height nor depth, nor anything else in all creation, will be able to separate us from the love of God that is in Christ Jesus our Lord.

Amen.

Notes

Chapter 1: Welcome to Your Place in a Worldview Minority!

1. Natasha Crain, "5 Ways Christians are Getting Swept into a Secular Worldview in This Cultural Moment," *Natasha Crain*, June 9, 2020, https://natashacrain.com/5-ways-christians-are-getting-swept-into-a-secular-worldview-in-this-cultural-moment/.

2. My author Facebook page can be found at www.facebook.com/natashacrainauthor.

3. I've edited the original comments for grammar and readability.

4. A summary of findings can be found in the Pew Research Center article "In U.S., Decline of Christianity Continues at Rapid Pace," *Pew Research Center*, October 17, 2019, https://www.pewforum.org/2019/10/17/in-u-s-decline-of-christianity-continues-at-rapid-pace/. Detailed research findings are available at https://www.pewforum.org/wp-content/uploads/sites/7/2019/10/Detailed-Tables-v1-FOR-WEB.pdf.

5. Brandon Showalter, "Only 1 in 10 Americans Have Biblical Worldview, Just 4 Percent of Millennials: Barna," *The Christian Post*, February 28, 2017, https://www.christianpost.com/news/1-in-10-americans-have-biblical-worldview-just-4-percent-of-millennials-barna.html.

6. Cultural Research Center, "CRC Survey Shows Dangerously Low Percentage of Americans Hold Biblical Worldview," *Arizona Christian University*, March 24, 2020, https://www.arizonachristian.edu/wp-content/uploads/2020/03/CRC_AWVI2020_Report.pdf.

7. Barna Research, "Competing Worldviews Influence Today's Christians," *Barna*, May 9, 2017, https://www.barna.com/research/competing-worldviews-influence-todays-christians/.

8. Cultural Research Center, "CRC Survey Shows Dangerously Low Percentage of Americans Hold Biblical Worldview."

9. Cultural Research Center, "Millennials Have Radically Different Beliefs About Respect, Faith, and America," *Arizona Christian University*, September 22, 2020, https://www.arizonachristian.edu/wp-content/uploads/2020/10/CRC_AWVI2020_Release10_Digital_03_20200922.pdf.

10. Pew Research Center, "America's Changing Religious Landscape," *Pew Research Center*, May 12, 2015, https://www.pewforum.org/2015/05/12/chapter-1-the-changing-religious-composition-of-the-u-s/.

11. Theism refers to belief in a god who is in some way interactive with his creation. Judaism, Islam, and Christianity are examples of theistic religions.

12. Pew Research Center, "In U.S., Decline of Christianity Continues at Rapid Pace."

13. Francis A. Schaeffer, *The Great Evangelical Disaster* (Wheaton, IL: Crossway, 1984), 47.

14. Open Doors USA, "Christian Persecution," *OpenDoors*, https://www.opendoorsusa.org/christian-persecution/.

Chapter 2: Surrounded by Secularism

1. For an excellent and accessible overview of the historic relationship between church and state, see Hunter Baker's book *The End of Secularism* (Wheaton, IL: Crossway, 2009).

2. Peter Singer, *Practical Ethics*, 2d ed. (Cambridge: Cambridge University Press, 1993), 186.

3. Atheists sometimes reject the idea that atheism is a worldview because they have no central authority for answers to worldview questions. But if a person's foundational belief about reality is that no God exists, there are certain logical implications that flow from that belief that will determine their answers to key worldview questions. Saying that atheism is a worldview is not saying that every atheist will answer every question in the same way, but rather, that atheists share important assumptions about the nature of reality. We'll discuss this more in chapter 7.

4. Pew Research Center, "The Religious Typology: A new way to categorize Americans by religion," *Pew Research Center*, August 29, 2018, https://www.pewforum.org/2018/08/29/the-religious -typology/.

5. I'm not suggesting that everyone who accepts evolutionary theory has a secular view of man. Evolutionary creationists who accept the Bible's teachings on the nature of man—irrespective of how we physically came to be—would not be secular in their views of humankind. That said, Christians differ on whether evolutionary theory is compatible with an authoritative view of the Bible. For those interested in an objective comparison of the scriptural and scientific case for and against various views Christians have on the age of the earth and evolution, see part 5 of my book *Keeping Your Kids on God's Side* (Eugene, OR: Harvest House, 2016).

6. Secular Student Alliance homepage, https://secularstudents.org/.

7. The Satanic Temple homepage, https://thesatanictemple.com/.

8. The Satanic Temple, Informational Pamphlet, https://cdn.shopify.com/s/files/1/0428/0465/files/ Informational_Pamphlet.pdf?v=1607544027.

Chapter 3: Why Secularism Is Compelling—Even for Christians

1. Glennon Doyle, *Untamed* (New York: The Dial Press, 2020).

2. Author and blogger Alisa Childers has an excellent review of this book from a biblical perspective in her article "Untamed: The Gospel of Glennon Doyle," *Alisa Childers*, June 6, 2020, https:// www.alisachilders.com/blog/untamed-the-gospel-of-glennon-doyle.

3. Editorial reviews, *Untamed*, *Amazon*, https://www.amazon.com/Untamed-Glennon-Doyle -Melton/dp/1984801252.

4. Glennon Doyle, Media page, https://untamedbook.com/#media.

5. Harm Reduction International, "What is harm reduction?," *Harm Reduction International*, https://www.hri.global/what-is-harm-reduction.

6. Jason Rantz, "Seattle homeless shelter buys heroin pipes with city funds, teaches rectal injection method," *MyNorthwest*, February 22, 2021, https://mynorthwest.com/2593799/rantz-seattle -shelter-city-fund-heroin-pipes-injection/.

7. The People's Harm Reduction Alliance, Welcome page, http://phra.org/welcome#phra.

8. Statista, "Percentage of U.S. population who currently use any social media from 2008 to 2021," *Statista*, April 14, 2021, https://www.statista.com/statistics/273476/percentage-of-us-population -with-a-social-network-profile/.

9. Jimit Bagadiya, "367 Social Media Statistics You Must Know in 2021," *SocialPilot*, https://www .socialpilot.co/blog/social-media-statistics.

10. Simon Kemp, "WhatsApp is the World's Favorite Social Platform (And Other Facts)," *Hootsuite*, April 22, 2021, https://blog.hootsuite.com/simon-kemp-social-media/.

11. As one example, see AllSides Media Bias Chart, *AllSides*, https://www.allsides.com/media-bias/media-bias-chart. While this is based on political bias, there is often a correlation with worldview bias, particularly at the extreme ends (on both sides).

12. Bradford Richardson, "Media covered Women's March three times more than March for Life: Study," *The Washington Times*, January 30, 2017, https://www.washingtontimes.com/news/2017/jan/30/womens-march-three-times-more-coverage-march-life/.

13. George Yancey, "Anti-Christian Media Bias Is Real, But Not the Way You Think It Is," *The Stream*, December 8, 2018, https://stream.org/anti-christian-media-bias-real-not-way-think/.

14. WebFX Team, "The 6 Companies That Own (Almost) All Media [INFOGRAPHIC]," *WebFX*, https://www.webfx.com/blog/internet/the-6-companies-that-own-almost-all-media-info graphic/.

Chapter 4: Regaining a Supernatural Worldview

1. Ricky Gervais, "Why I'm an Atheist," *The Wall Street Journal*, December 19, 2010, https://www.wsj.com/articles/BL-SEB-56643.

2. Charles Taylor, *A Secular Age* (Cambridge, MA: Belknap Press, 2018).

3. Nearly all atheists hold to a naturalistic worldview, but it's worth noting that some distinguish themselves from naturalists.

4. As cited in J.P. Moreland, *Scientism and Secularism: Learning to Respond to a Dangerous Ideology* (Wheaton, IL: Crossway, 2018), 38.

5. Joe Rogan, podcast notes from *The Joe Rogan Experience* episode #1366, *PodcastNotes*, October 22, 2019, https://podcastnotes.org/joe-rogan-experience/richard-dawkins-god-religion/.

6. "What he wrote," *The Guardian*, May 13, 2008, https://www.theguardian.com/science/2008/may/13/peopleinscience.religion.

7. Zoltan Istvan, "Religion Is Harming Society And Lives," *The Huffington Post*, July 18, 2016 (updated December 6, 2017), https://www.huffpost.com/entry/atheist-presidential-cand_b_11005072.

8. Bill Maher, *I'm Swiss (and other Treasonous Statements)*, HBO special, 2005.

9. "Bill Maher On Islam: 'All Religions Are Not Alike,'" *Real Clear Politics*, September 23, 2012, https://www.realclearpolitics.com/video/2012/09/23/bill_maher_on_islam_all_religions_are_not_alike.html.

10. I share and expand upon these points in chapter 1 of *Talking with Your Kids about God* (Grand Rapids, MI: Baker Books, 2017). In addition, chapters 2 through 6 explain the evidence introduced in this chapter in significantly more detail.

11. Fazale Rana, "Fine-Tuning For Life On Earth (Updated June 2004)," *Reasons to Believe*, June 7, 2004, https://reasons.org/explore/publications/tnrtb/read/tnrtb/2004/06/07/fine-tuning-for-life-on-earth-updated-june-2004.

12. Hugh Ross, "Probability For Life On Earth," *Reasons to Believe*, April 1, 2004, https://reasons.org/explore/publications/tnrtb/read/tnrtb/2004/04/01/probability-for-life-on-earth.

13. See part 2 of *Talking with Your Kids about God*.

14. Crain, *Talking with Your Kids about God*, 104.

15. Thomas Nagel, *Mind and Cosmos: Why the Materialist Neo-Darwinian Conception of Nature Is Almost Certainly False* (New York: Oxford University Press, 2012), 26.

Chapter 5: Reestablishing What We (Should) Actually Believe

1. Ilona Fried, "'Should' is a Dirty Word," *À La Carte Spirit*, November 19, 2014, https://alacarte spirit.com/2014/11/19/should-is-a-dirty-word/.

2. Cultural Research Center, "Vast Majority of Americans Stitch Together Patchwork Worldview of Conflicting Beliefs, Making 'Syncretism' Top Worldview Among U.S. Adults," *Arizona Christian University*, April 13, 2021, https://www.arizonachristian.edu/wp-content/uploads/2021/04/CRC_AWVI2021_Release01_Digital_01_20210413.pdf.

3. Barna Research, "Competing Worldviews Influence Today's Christians," *Barna*, May 9, 2017, https://www.barna.com/research/competing-worldviews-influence-todays-christians/.

4. GracePointe Church, Facebook post, February 7, 2021, https://www.facebook.com/gracepointetn/photos/a.394837242014/10157495440607015/?type=3.

5. Nadia Bolz-Weber, *Shameless: A Case for Not Feeling Bad About Feeling Good (About Sex)* (Colorado Springs, CO: Convergent Books, 2020), 60.

6. I highly recommend Alisa Childers' book on progressive Christianity, appropriately titled *Another Gospel?: A Lifelong Christian Seeks Truth in Response to Progressive Christianity* (Carol Stream, IL: Tyndale Momentum, 2020).

7. John Pavlovitz, "Progressive Christianity—is Christianity," *John Pavlovitz*, October 5, 2016, https://johnpavlovitz.com/2016/10/05/explaining-progressive-christianity-otherwise-known-as-christianity/.

8. Robert M. Bowman, Jr. and J. Ed Komoszewski, *Putting Jesus in His Place: The Case for the Deity of Christ* (Grand Rapids, MI: Kregel, 2007).

9. Lifeway Research, "Few Protestant Churchgoers Read the Bible Daily," *Lifeway research*, July 2, 2019, https://lifewayresearch.com/2019/07/02/few-protestant-churchgoers-read-the-bible-daily/.

10. Brian McLaren, *A Generous Orthodoxy* (Grand Rapids, MI: Zondervan, 2004), 19-20.

Chapter 6: Reexamining Beliefs When Confronted with Doubt

1. As of this writing, Janet's site is no longer online.

2. Lecrae, Facebook post, April 24, 2021, https://www.facebook.com/permalink.php?story_fbid=10158007140460222&id=13895090221.

3. John Marriott, *The Anatomy of Deconversion: Keys to a Lifelong Faith in a Culture Abandoning Christianity* (Abilene, TX: Abilene University Press, 2020).

4. Exvangelical, Facebook post, April 12, 2021, https://www.facebook.com/exvangelicalpod/posts/1953790988095625.

5. Marriott, *The Anatomy of Deconversion*, 78.

6. Roxanne Stone, "Evolving Faith conference offers evangelical 'refugees' shelter," *Religion News Service*, October 7, 2019, https://religionnews.com/2019/10/07/evolving-faith-conference-offers-evangelical-refugees-shelter/.

7. Marriott, *The Anatomy of Deconversion*, 88.

8. *Fundamentalism* can mean different things to different people. Skeptics, for example, often label anyone who isn't progressive in their beliefs a fundamentalist. Marriott's use of the term is specific to characteristics like those listed here.

9. Marriott, *The Anatomy of Deconversion*, 100.

10. Leah MarieAnn Klett, "Hillsong writer: 'I'm genuinely losing my faith,'" *The Christian Post*, August 12, 2019, https://www.christianpost.com/news/hillsong-writer-reveals-hes-no-longer-a-christian-im-genuinely-losing-my-faith.html.

11. David Daniels, "Legendary UK Rapper Jahaziel Renounces Christian Faith," *Rapzilla*, December 23, 2015, https://rapzilla.com/2015-12-legendary-uk-rapper-jahaziel-renounces-christian-faith/.

12. Joshua Harris, Instagram post, July 26, 2019, https://www.instagram.com/p/B0ZBrNLH2sl/.

13. Colby Martin, About page, *Colby Martin Online*, https://www.colbymartinonline.com/about.

14. Sean McDowell's interview with Colby Martin offers an excellent window into a deconstruction story, and I highly recommend watching it: "Progressive vs. Evangelical: A Dialogue for Clarity," Sean McDowell channel on YouTube, April 15, 2021, https://www.youtube.com/watch?v=BXjWhFHpxP0.

15. Dan Barker, *Losing Faith in Faith* (Madison, WI: Freedom from Religion Foundation, 2006), 102.

16. Ian Harber, "'Progressive' Christianity: Even Shallower Than the Evangelical Faith I Left," *The Gospel Coalition*, March 7, 2020, https://www.thegospelcoalition.org/article/progressive-christianity-shallower-evangelical-faith-i-left/.

17. Harber, "'Progressive' Christianity."

Chapter 7: Reclaiming What Rightfully Belongs to the Biblical Worldview

1. As I mentioned in an earlier endnote, almost all atheists are naturalists, but a few do identify with other views. For the purposes of this chapter, I'll assume the atheists I reference have a naturalistic worldview.

2. Nancy Pearcey, *Finding Truth: 5 Principles for Unmasking Atheism, Secularism, and Other God Substitutes* (Colorado Springs, CO: David C. Cook, 2015).

3. Pearcey, *Finding Truth*, 46.

4. Pearcey, *Finding Truth*, 46.

5. Pearcey, *Finding Truth*, 47.

6. "Human rights," *FutureLearn*, https://www.futurelearn.com/info/courses/introducing-humanism/0/steps/37107.

7. Average Atheist, "The Psychology of Atheism: A Look at R.C. Sproul," *Atheist Letters*, October 22, 2012, https://atheistletters.wordpress.com/2012/10/22/the-psychology-of-atheism-a-look-at-r-c-sproul/.

8. Martin Buber, *Tales of the Hasidim (The Early Masters / The Later Masters)* (New York: Schocken, 1991). Edited lightly for readability.

9. "What are human rights?," *United Nations Human Rights Office of the High Commissioner*, https://www.ohchr.org/en/issues/pages/whatarehumanrights.aspx.

10. Jerry A. Coyne, "You Don't Have Free Will," *Chronicle of Higher Education*, March 18, 2012, https://www.chronicle.com/article/you-dont-have-free-will.

11. John Dickson, *Bullies and Saints: An Honest Look at the Good and Evil of Christian History* (Grand Rapids, MI: Zondervan, 2021), 160.

Chapter 8: Reaffirming Biblical Morality

1. James Bartholomew, "Easy Virtue," *The Spectator*, April 18, 2015, https://www.spectator.co.uk/article/easy-virtue.

2. "Virtue Signaling," *Lexico*, https://www.lexico.com/definition/virtue_signalling.

3. "Virtue Signaling," *Dictionary.com*, https://www.dictionary.com/browse/virtue-signaling.

4. Micah Bowers, "The Art of Virtue Signaling: Why so Many Brands Get It Wrong," *toptal.com*, https://www.toptal.com/designers/brand/virtue-signaling.

5. Pew Research Center, "Attitudes on Same-Sex Marriage," *Pew Research Center*, May 14, 2019, https://www.pewforum.org/fact-sheet/changing-attitudes-on-gay-marriage/.

6. Kate Lister, "Sex Workers or Prostitutes? Why Words Matter," *iNews*, October 5, 2017, https://inews.co.uk/opinion/columnists/sex-workers-prostitutes-words-matter-95447.

7. Nicole Brodeur, "How 'Shout Your Abortion' grew from a Seattle hashtag into a book," *The Seattle Times*, December 13, 2018, https://www.seattletimes.com/life/how-shout-your-abortion-grew-from-a-seattle-hashtag-into-a-book/.

8. Amelia Bonow, "My abortion made me happy," *Salon*, September 23, 2015, https://www.salon.com/2015/09/22/my_abortion_made_me_happy_the_story_that_started_the_shoutyourabortion_movement/.

9. Drag Queen Story Hour home page, https://www.dragqueenstoryhour.org/.

10. "Libraries Respond: Drag Queen Story Hour," *American Library Association*, http://www.ala.org/advocacy/libraries-respond-drag-queen-story-hour.

11. See this article as one example: Liam Stack, "Drag Queen Story Hour Continues Its Reign at Libraries, Despite Backlash," *The New York Times*, June 6, 2019, https://www.nytimes.com/2019/06/06/us/drag-queen-story-hour.html.

12. "Drag Queen Story Time at Trinity!," *Trinity Church, Swarthmore*, November 3, 2019, https://www.trinity-swarthmore.org/drag-queen-story-time.html.

13. Cultural Research Center, "Survey Finds America's Traditional Moral Pillars are Fading Away," *Arizona Christian University*, June 2, 2020, https://www.arizonachristian.edu/wp-content/uploads/2020/06/AWVI-2020-Release-06-Perceptions-of-Morality-Moral-Choices.pdf.

14. A.W. Tozer, *The Knowledge of the Holy* (New York: HarperOne, 1961).

Chapter 9: Reinvigorating the Spirit of Discernment

1. Sinclair Ferguson, "What Is Discernment?" *Ligonier Ministries*, May 8, 2020, https://www.ligonier.org/blog/discernment-thinking-gods-thoughts/.

2. Carlos A. Rodriguez, Twitter post, July 8, 2020, https://twitter.com/CarlosHappyNPO/status/1280877268617830400.

3. For the full Chalcedonian Definition and a more detailed discussion, see Wayne Grudem, *Systematic Theology* (Grand Rapids, MI: Zondervan, 1994), chapter 26.

4. John Pavlovitz, "Christian, Here's Why Your Theology is Overrated," *John Pavlovitz*, August 9, 2016, https://johnpavlovitz.com/2016/08/09/christian-heres-why-your-theology-is-overrated/comment-page-1/.

5. Nathan Davis Hunt, Twitter post, June 3, 2021, https://twitter.com/nathandavishunt/status/1400600781867335683.

6. Tim Keller, "The Gospel and the Poor," *The Gospel Coalition*, https://www.thegospelcoalition.org/themelios/article/the-gospel-and-the-poor/.

7. Mick Mooney, "Why I Choose to Live My Faith Outside of Organized Religion," *The Huffington Post*, February 16, 2015, https://www.huffpost.com/entry/why-i-choose-to-live-my-f_b_6339134.

8. Richard Rohr, "The Universal Christ," *Center for Action and Contemplation*, https://cac.org/another-name-for-every-thing-the-universal-christ/.

9. Richard Rohr, "Christ Is Everywhere," *Center for Action and Contemplation*, December 6, 2018, https://cac.org/christ-is-everywhere-2018-12-06/.

10. The name Red-Letter Jesus is a reference to the organization Red Letter Christians, which prioritizes Jesus's words in Scripture. See their website at https://www.redletterchristians.org/.

11. For more on the subject of how the world perceives truth, see my article "Christians Must Care Less about Our Cultural Reputation," *Natasha Crain*, March 4, 2021, https://natashacrain.com/christians-must-care-less-about-our-cultural-reputation/.

Chapter 10: Revitalizing the Call to Biblical Justice

1. I'm well aware of all the debates over which ideas today should or shouldn't be considered part of critical theory and how to best define it. While I don't have the space in this chapter to wade into those debate, suffice it to say that my objective here is to help readers understand key *themes* in secular social Justice advocacy that have emerged from critical theory, not to elaborate on distinctions between academic and popular manifestations of it.

2. A full treatment of the subject of collective guilt in the Bible is not possible here. For more on this, see Neil Shenvi and Pat Sawyer's article "Do Whites Need Corporate Repentance for Historical Racial Sins?" at https://shenviapologetics.com/do-whites-need-corporate-repentance-for-historical-sins.

3. Syllabus for "PHIL-366: Marx and Critical Theory," Amherst College, Spring 2014, https://www.amherst.edu/academiclife/departments/courses/1314S/PHIL/PHIL-366-1314S.

4. A good example of this can be found in Be the Bridge's "16 Bridge-Building Tips for White People," https://bethebridge.com/docs/16Tips.pdf (Be the Bridge is a faith-based racial reconciliation ministry). The organization denies that they use Critical Race Theory as their guiding framework but acknowledges that they use concepts from it that they consider to be helpful. (A full statement on this can be found at https://bethebridge.com/wp-content/uploads/2020/08/Full-Statement-Aug-7.pdf.) However, it's clear from examples like these and many others in their materials that the concepts they "borrow" are an integral part of their ministry. For a review explaining the theological problems with their book *Be the Bridge*, see Neil Shenvi, "A Short Review of Morrison's Be The Bridge," *Shenvi Apologetics*, https://shenviapologetics.com/a-short-review-of-morrisons-be-the-bridge/.

5. For example, see Samantha Riedel, "How to Break Away From the Gender Binary," *Teen Vogue*, October 26, 2018, https://www.teenvogue.com/story/how-to-break-away-from-the-gender-binary.

6. You can see an example of how Christianity is given "norm" status in this infographic from the Smithsonian's National Museum of History and Culture (it has since been taken down from its original location on the Smithsonian website): "Smithsonian Aspects of White Culture," *Newsweek*, https://www.newsweek.com/smithsonian-race-guidelines-rational-thinking-hard-work-are-white-values-1518333#slideshow/1610610.

7. John Dickson, *Bullies and Saints: An Honest Look at the Good and Evil of Christian History* (Grand Rapids, MI: Zondervan, 2021).

8. Dickson, *Bullies and Saints*, 78.

9. Dickson, *Bullies and Saints*, 82.

10. Dickson, *Bullies and Saints*, 82.

11. Dickson, *Bullies and Saints*, 83.

12. Dickson, *Bullies and Saints*, 84.

13. Dickson, *Bullies and Saints*, 108.

Chapter 11: Recommitting to Speaking Truth

1. For a detailed description of Rowling's tweets and responses, see Abby Gardner, "A Complete Breakdown of the J.K. Rowling Transgender-Comments Controversy," *Glamour*, May 23, 2021, https://www.glamour.com/story/a-complete-breakdown-of-the-jk-rowling-transgender-comments-controversy.

2. For more on this story, see Sarah Ellison, "Inside the Teen Vogue mess—which is really a Condé Nast mess," *The Washington Post*, April 4, 2021, https://www.washingtonpost.com/lifestyle/media/teen-vogue-conde-nast-wintour-mccammond/2021/04/03/dafd2804-9104-11eb-a74e-1f4cf89fd948_story.html.

3. David Crary, "Girl Scouts tweet, delete post congratulating Amy Coney Barrett for Supreme Court appointment," *USA Today*, October 30, 2020, https://www.usatoday.com/story/news/nation/2020/10/30/amy-coney-barrett-girl-scouts-tweet-delete-congratulations-post/6082801002/.

4. Aja Romano, "The second wave of 'cancel culture,'" *Vox*, May 5, 2021, https://www.vox.com/22384308/cancel-culture-free-speech-accountability-debate.

5. Aja Romano, "Why we can't stop fighting about cancel culture," *Vox*, August 25, 2020, https://www.vox.com/culture/2019/12/30/20879720/what-is-cancel-culture-explained-history-debate.

6. An excellent example of this can be seen in an interview with political philosopher Brian Leiter. See Sean Illing, "A philosopher makes the case against free speech," *Vox*, March 10, 2019, https://www.vox.com/2019/3/4/18197209/free-speech-philosophy-politics-brian-leiter.

Chapter 12: Reshaping Our Hearts for Sharing the Gospel

1. Barna Research, "Almost Half of Practicing Christian Millennials Say Evangelism Is Wrong," *Barna*, February 5, 2019, https://www.barna.com/research/millennials-oppose-evangelism/.

2. Barna Research, "Almost Half of Practicing Christian Millennials Say Evangelism Is Wrong."

3. Barna Research, "Almost Half of Practicing Christian Millennials Say Evangelism Is Wrong."

4. Nicolette Tura, "How to Stop People From Trying to Convert You to Another Religion," *wiki How*, April 15, 2021, https://www.wikihow.com/Stop-People-From-Trying-to-Convert-You-to-Another-Religion.

5. "No Proselytism Zone: Keep Our Public Schools Free Of Teacher/Preachers," *Americans United for Separation of Church and State*, May 2016, https://www.au.org/church-state/may-2016-church-state/editorial/no-proselytism-zone-keep-our-public-schools-free-of.

6. Gary Yang, "It's time to put a stop to religious proselytizing on campus," *Daily Trojan*, September 20, 2018, https://dailytrojan.com/2018/09/20/opinion-its-time-to-put-a-stop-to-religious-proselytizing-on-campus/.

7. Ekemini Uwan, "Decolonized Discipleship," *Sistamatic Theology*, February 8, 2018, https://www.sistamatictheology.com/blog/2018/2/6/decolonized-discipleship.

8. Deborah Jian Lee, "Christians of color are rejecting 'Colonial Christianity' and Reclaiming Ancestral Spiritualities," *Religion Dispatches*, January 10, 2018, https://religiondispatches.org/christians-of-color-are-rejecting-colonial-christianity-and-reclaiming-ancestral-spiritualities/.

9. Lee, "Christians of color are rejecting 'Colonial Christianity' and Reclaiming Ancestral Spiritualities."

10. Remy Maisel, "Please Stop Trying to Convert Me," *The Huffington Post*, January 8, 2013, https://www.huffpost.com/entry/please-stop-trying-to-convert-me_b_2031389.

11. Caryle Murphy, "Most Americans believe in heaven…and hell," *Pew Research Center*, November 10, 2015, https://www.pewresearch.org/fact-tank/2015/11/10/most-americans-believe-in-heaven-and-hell/.

Other Books
by Natasha Crain

Keeping Your Kids on God's Side

Keeping Your Kids on God's Side introduces parents to 40 of the most important faith challenges facing kids today. It's an easy-to-understand "apologetics 101," covering the subject areas of God, truth and worldviews, Jesus, the Bible, and science.

Talking with Your Kids about God

Talking with Your Kids about God equips parents to have 30 must-have conversations with kids about God given the increasingly atheistic culture in which they're growing up. Sections include (1) the existence of God, (2) science and God, (3) the nature of God, (4) believing in God, and (5) the difference God makes.

Talking with Your Kids about Jesus

Talking with Your Kids about Jesus equips parents to have 30 must-have conversations with kids about Jesus given the challenges they'll encounter to Christianity. Sections include (1) the identity of Jesus, (2) the teachings of Jesus, (3) the death of Jesus, (4) the resurrection of Jesus, and (5) the difference Jesus makes.

A six-session small-group curriculum is also available for *Talking with Your Kids about Jesus*, including a Participant's Guide and DVD. In addition, videos for the curriculum are available through RightNow Media.

Connect with Natasha

Want more content like *Faithfully Different*? Natasha writes articles at www.natashacrain.com and hosts *The Natasha Crain Podcast*, available on your favorite podcast player and at:

www.natashacrain.com/podcast

You can also connect with Natasha on social media:

@natashacrainauthor

@natasharcrain

To learn more about Harvest House books and
to read sample chapters, visit our website:

www.HarvestHousePublishers.com

HARVEST HOUSE PUBLISHERS
EUGENE, OREGON